Gilles,

The Wine Lover's Guide to Auctions

May this book give
you a leg-up on
any of your auction
activities. Cheers!

Ursula

The Wine Lover's Guide to Auctions

The Art & Science of Buying and Selling Wines

Ursula Hermacinski

Foreword by Michael Broadbent, MW

SQUAREONE
PUBLISHERS

A NOTE ON GENDER USAGE: As you attend wine auctions, you will find that there are women in every position, from specialist to seller to auctioneer. To avoid long and awkward phrasing, however, the publisher has chosen to use male pronouns throughout this book. This decision in no way diminishes the skills and contributions of the many fine female professionals working in this field or the many female participants who attend these events.

COVER DESIGNER: Jeannie Tudor • COVER PHOTO: Getty Images, Inc.
TYPESETTER: Gary A. Rosenberg • EDITOR: Ariel Colletti

PHOTO CREDITS: The photos on pages 6, 21, 35, 37, 54, 55, 60, 62, 72, 88, 94, 109, 128, 148, 170, 184, and 198 are reprinted courtesy of Zachys Wine & Liquor, Inc.
The photo on page 15 is reprinted courtesy of Sotheby's.
The photo on page 65 is reprinted courtesy of Hart Davis Hart Wine Co.
The photo on page 105 is reprinted courtesy of Davis and Company.

Square One Publishers
115 Herricks Road • Garden City Park, NY 11040
(516) 535-2010 • (877) 900-BOOK
www.squareonepublishers.com

Library of Congress Cataloging-in-Publication Data

Hermacinski, Ursula.
  The wine lover's guide to auctions : the art & science of buying and selling wines / Ursula Hermacinski.
    p. cm.
  Includes index.
  ISBN-13: 978-0-7570-0275-5 (pbk.)
  ISBN-10: 0-7570-0275-7 (pbk.)
  1. Wine auctions. I. Title.

TP548.5.A93H47 2007
641.2'2075--dc22

                                        2006037310

Printed in the United States of America

10   9   8   7   6   5   4   3   2   1

Contents

To my mother
who suggested that I study art history,
and to my father
who asked what I'd do with my degree.

Acknowledgments

In the wine auction business, who can say whether it's hard work or good luck which makes the thing successful? A simple truth: enjoying great wine with great people made my thing successful.

I cannot imagine a more generous professional environment. After all, the first thing you do after making sure the wine is good is to pour a glass for somebody else. I'd experienced this great generosity right from the start of my adventure. First, with the two Michaels: Broadbent and Davis, who at Christie's let a girl (who didn't yet know anything about wine) join in the fun of this country's pioneering wine-auction efforts. That part was sheer luck—Michael Broadbent showed me how to taste wine, and Michael Davis taught me how to stop cracking up and losing it on the podium. Kevin Swersey taught me how to sell wine. Kevin offered his experience, expertise, support, and patience when he and I joined forces, on behalf of Christie's and Zachys, to introduce wine auctions to New York. I have no greater supporter, and he no greater fan. My wine-auction experience is so much richer for the ability to work with David Elswood, Don Zacharia, and Fritz Hatton. I've learned so much from each of these gentlemen, who have both been extremely generous to me in countless ways.

And so as not to perpetuate the notion of the wine world being a men's club, I have to spotlight some of the elegant ladies in this world. Thanks to Ann Colgin, who gave me my very first break, hiring me as a secretary at Christie's way back when. Jackie Quillen, America's first lady of wine auctions, and internationally respected Serena Sutcliffe provided most of the material relating to Christie's and Sotheby's early wine-auction days. Thanks to the great ladies of the Napa Valley Vintners, and the ladies with whom I worked on the many charity wine auctions—too numerous to mention—across the country. And a special thanks to Martine Saunier who has so generously taught me how to eat and drink Burgundy.

Thanks to each and every consignor who trusted me to sell his wine, and to each and every bidder who trusted me to take his money. And thanks to the vintners with whom I've shared a glass of wine over the years. Thanks to Rudy Shur at Square One Publishers who made it easy for me to start this process and to Ariel Colletti without whom I could not have completed this book. My Steamboat Springs friend, a very talented ex-English professor, Tripp Hartigan, spent many cold nights correcting my spelling and grammar, and many cold days on the mountain asking me important auction questions. I thank Tripp for keeping this project on schedule. If there is little in the way of a bibliography to *The Wine Lover's Guide to Auctions*, it is because after Michael Broadbent set the foundation. The rest of us were simply making it up as we went along. It's been a lot of fun.

Foreword

by Michael Broadbent, Master of Wine

I must preface my remarks by saying that I have long been a huge admirer of Ursula Hermacinski. We were colleagues in the early, happy, and successful years when Christie's in the United States dominated the wine auction market; and I soon came to regard her as the most outstanding auctioneer I had ever worked with in nearly 40 years in this very specialised business.

Before commenting on her book I think it is worth mentioning, particularly for the benefit of those (few?) who have never attended a wine auction, what makes her such a supremely successful auctioneer. It is an unique combination of facets, personality, and talents. First of all she has presence: the minute she steps up to the rostrum she commands respect and anticipation. Her manner is firm and authoritative without being lecturing, overwhelming, or egocentric. She has a perfect, clear, and seemingly effortless command of the auction process, and the voice and manner to convert technical mastery into an art form. Most obvious of all is an unforced persuasive charm. At commercial wine auctions she is firm and fair, constantly aware of the fine dividing line between seller and buyer, whilst, at the same time, using her warm personality to gently and patiently squeeze an extra dollar step from out of a hesitant bidder! At charity auctions, her charm and fluent, stylish gavel wielding moves up several notches. Not for nothing is she known as the Queen of the charity wine auctioneer circuit. Charity organisers know the value of Ursula's expertise, which is why she is continuously in demand.

From the above it will be obvious that she "knows her stuff" and the text that follows makes this abundantly clear.

I have read her book carefully and can say without hestitation that her descriptions of the auction process are immaculately detailed; they clearly explain every stage, from what the vendor needs to know and how to set about selling his precious wine, to the potential buyer, whether the latter attends the sale in person, leaves bids in advance, or takes advantage of direct telephone bidding. As something of a pioneer in this field, I personally regret the latter for it removes some of the life from the auction room and, frankly, slows the auction. I much preferred the early pioneering days, for my career as an auctioneer began at Christie's in London in 1967, and from 1969 in America with the hugely successful annual Heublein auctions which I advised on and conducted for twelve years. Then a similar role with the first charity wine auction in the United States with the now famous Napa Wine Auction in 1981, which Ursula later made her own inimitable province.

So here we have a wine success story allied to an unique insight into the workings of wine auctions—and, believe me, there is a great deal of work behind the scenes. The detail Ursula goes into is astonishing. I cannot think of anything to do with the auction process that she does not cover with accurate, and helpful, detail. She has managed, thanks to her intellect, knowledge, and understanding, to unravel the mysteries of wine auctions. Ursula clearly enjoys the wine auction scene; she makes everything not only helpful but fascinating.

Read on.

Michael Broadbent, MW
Christie's, London

The Wine Lover's Guide to Auctions

Introduction

You may have seen me, gavel in hand, step up to a podium. If you have, you know that I genuinely enjoy each quick-quipped, split-second auction transaction. And if you have ever seen me, corkscrew in hand, step into a wine cellar, you know that I am also fascinated by the fruits (juices) of my labor. I truly believe in the wine-auction process.

I've been an auctioneer for over twenty years. Most of that time was spent with the world-renowned auction house Christie's, in its offices in London, New York, San Francisco, and Los Angeles. Concurrent to the Christie's years, I presided over most of the nation's most successful charity auctions, including the granddaddy of them all, the Napa Valley Wine Auction. I have pounded the gavel in famous wineries and four-star restaurants, on the stages of great opera and theater companies, at world-class resorts, and in missions, museums, and zoos. At the apex of the dot.com era, I enjoyed an adventurous stint in cyberspace when I was brought onto the executive team of winebid.com. Each auction has been an opportunity to learn. This book shares my experience and knowledge so that you will be as comfortable at a wine auction as you are drinking a great bottle of wine at home. By the end of this book, you'll know everything that I know about wine auctions.

The traditional image of a dusty, oak-paneled room cushioned by the hushed tones of an equally dusty, but always elegant, bespectacled auctioneer is gone. The auctions of today are dynamic events filled with movement and momentum. They have also become more popular, particularly with the rise of Ebay and regional charity events. Yet despite this gain in profile, the wine-auction community is thought of as a secret society, with its own language and rules. Is this because wine itself is such a mysterious obsession? Probably not, as I have been surprised by collectors with sophisticated palates, boundless wine knowledge, and great collections, who consistently avoid the auction process. Regardless of the reason, sidestepping auctions means missing the opportunity for deeper immersion into the captivating world of wine.

The Wine Lover's Guide to Auctions provides a clear understanding of the auction process, from start to finish. After two decades of performing at the podium, I relinquish hints and insights that will give you an edge in the auction game. Whether you are attending auctions for entertainment, buying or selling at a commercial auction, or organizing your own charity event, *The Wine Lover's Guide to Auctions* will assist you by revealing every aspect of the process. My goal is to provide you with great confidence every time you enter the auction arena.

Once you are comfortable with the process because you have studied the rules and have a handle on the game, the excitement of auctions will have you hooked. There are great treasures to be found and fortunes to be won. I see the thrill in the audience each time I announce, "Starting now with lot number one!"

I have been on both sides of the podium, having also bought and sold my own wine at auction. I have enjoyed great successes and, believe it or not, been humbled. I want you to experience the success and minimize the mistakes. I want you to win.

The Wine Lover's Guide to Auctions is divided into four parts. We will begin, appropriately, with "Part 1: Getting Started," which elaborates on both the history and details of the auction process, as well as the fundamentals of wine basics. Only after we take a look at the wine-auction process as a whole can we get into the specifics that will set you apart as a cunning bidder and clever seller.

Chapter 1 provides an overview of the history of wine auctions. As you will see, the first wine auctions were similar to those of today in that they were about bringing wine to the people. At the beginning, though, these auctions sold wine in earthenware crocks or wooden cask and solely as a potable commodity. Centuries later, thanks to cork closures, glass bottles, and the benefits of aging, the idea of collecting this beverage began to take form, and the modern day wine auction was born.

To make the most out of your wine-auction experience, you should be familiar with various types of wine. Chapter 2 will break this huge topic down to its fundamentals, from production to identification. It will also describe and explain various bottle sizes and shapes. Then, you will read about storing and serving different types of wine. This background will serve you well when you choose, bid for, and win your first bottles.

The essential facts to know about auctions are discussed in Chapter 3. Whether new information for the novice or a review for the experienced collector, these facts are imperative to anyone interested in participating in an auction. I cannot tell you how often wine collectors ask me, "What is a lot?" I find it surprising that I am never asked what an auction is—because how many people really know how auctions work? In this chapter, I will explain different types of auctions, from cattle call to cyberspace. And, of course, I will tell you what a lot is. We will take a look at which wines are sold at auction and why. Auction houses only sell certain bottles and types of wine, and once you know this, you can tailor your consignment or hone your purchases to your best advantage.

In Chapter 4, you will be introduced to the auction workers and attendees. This knowledge will allow you to participate with the greatest of ease. There is an entire team of professionals responsible for putting these events together. From the warehouse workers to the world famous wine critics, they all make tremendous contributions to the auction process. You will be able to take concerns or questions to the correct worker once you are aware of the responsibilities of each player.

"Part 2: The Art of Bidding" is where your true auction work will begin. This section will prepare you to put down this book, pick up a catalogue, and head to an auction. You will be ready to raise a paddle and buy some wine. Bidding is often considered the most intimidating aspect of the entire wine auction scene. But as a potential bidder, you must realize that every other bidder in the room had a first time as well—and none of them had the advantage of having first read this book. You, on the other hand, will walk in knowing what a wine auction looks and sounds like. You will be aware of the paperwork you need to complete to obtain a bidding paddle. You will even be armed with bidding strategies to help you win the lots you want. You will bid confidently at your very first auction.

In Chapter 5, you will learn how to read a wine-auction catalogue, from its front cover to its index. There is so much code-like information crammed into each lot description that unless you take the time to decipher it, you may overlook important features of any given bottle of wine. You will be better educated to choose among the lots after this chapter because you will be able to thoroughly read the auction book.

Once you can navigate your way through the catalogue, you will continue to prepare for the auction. Chapter 6 will teach you to set bidding limits, review and mark the catalogue, and pre-register for the event. Then, we will explore your bidding options as you decide whether to bid in person or by absentee bid, and the advantages of each choice.

It is time for the auction! Chapter 7 is divided into two sections: Live Bidding and Absentee Bidding. The first half explores every aspect of what you need to know about attending an auction, including when to arrive, what to bring, and where to sit. Most importantly, it explains how to bid and offers helpful tips to put you in the best position to win the wine you want. The chapter's second half details how to successfully buy wine at an auction even if you can't attend. You will never miss an opportunity to bid at an auction again. After reading Chapter 7, you will be ready for the bidding battle.

Winning your first auction lot is quite an accomplishment and will feel great, but you need to be prepared for the post-auction work. Chapter 8 explains what to expect. From checking the accuracy of the invoice to thoroughly inspecting the bottles when they arrive, the after-auction steps are crucial towards determining that the wine you receive is the wine you were expecting.

Part 3 of *The Wine Lover's Guide to Auctions* is "The Science of Selling." Experienced sellers can tell you that there are advantageous ways to approach the situation, and then there are the mistakes that are frequently made. This eye-opening section will steer you in the right direction towards consigning your collection, or fill in the holes if you are a buyer just curious about the other side of the coin. You will read through each step of a standard consignment, from the first thought of selling wine at auction to receiving the nice, large check.

The first step towards selling wine at auction is choosing the auction house that is right for you. With so many truly excellent choices, how will you decide among them? Chapter 9 introduces "The Four P's"—guidelines by which to compare houses—to help you make this decision. You will learn how to contact the auction houses and speak their language, while seeing through the big smiles and chummy slaps on the back to the actual offer. You will also read about producing an inventory list that will best promote your bottles. This methodical look at getting your wine out of the cellar and into the glossy catalogue will lend ease to the nerve-racking process of determining which auction house shares a passion similar to your own.

Chapter 10 explains the charges associated with selling wine at auction, and may save consignors some money. Between staffing, temperature-controlled warehousing, and catalogue production, the companies' operational costs increase every year. As a result, these for-profit ventures are left trying to squeeze dollars out of narrowing margins. Regardless, auction houses are often willing to work out compromises in the various consignment fees. This chapter will educate you on where to ask for special discounted consideration when you are offering a terrific collection.

You will be inundated with paperwork throughout the process. The most important of these may be the contract, but it is necessary to to be aware of and review the accuracy of everything sent your way. Chapter 11 thoroughly explains the importance of each document. I know what to expect once the process begins and the flood of papers arrives, and I will help you stay in control of the game from beginning to end.

When you are up to Part 4 of *The Wine Lover's Guide to Auctions*, you will be ready to buy and sell at auction. As you probably know, though, there are other important aspects of wine auctions and wine appreciation. "The Fruits of Your Labor" will round out your wine knowledge by offering education on several related topics.

Chapter 12 includes a shopping list that will help you decide which bottles to purchase. There are some wines that, in my opinion, should be in every collection, and there are trophy bottles and prizes that simply cannot be resisted. With your newly acquired bidding skills, you will have a greater shot at adding these treasures to your collection. You will also read suggestions on what the cost will be to accomplish your goals. This is the fun (or fantasy) part.

We will then explore the big money world of charity wine auctions in Chapter 13. Due in part to both the unprecedented popularity of wine and the generosity of the wine industry, almost every city in America hosts some type of fundraising wine event. Today, almost $50 million is raised annually for various US charities. It is all for a good cause and in good fun, and fantastic prices are paid. Nonetheless, there are sometimes bargains to be found and I will tell you where to find them, as well as offer suggestions on hosting your own event.

Finally, Chapter 14 of *The Wine Lover's Guide to Auctions* looks at a variety of ways to enhance the pleasures of the wine-collecting experience. The best part of opening a good bottle of wine is sharing it with others. I review the most enjoyable ways to taste, drink, and talk about wine. There is no better way to learn about the grape.

Some readers may choose to head straight for the Resource section before settling into any of the earlier chapters. I welcome you to do so. This section offers valuable lists of important names and addresses, including the largest and most reputable auction companies, as well as a helpful glossary of wine-auction terms. I also recommend books for beginners and books that need to be within an arm's reach of any cellar.

Now it is time for the best part. Pour yourself a glass of wine and start your journey along the road of discovery. It is all here for you. No longer will any aspect of the auction process confuse you. You will never have to be uncomfortable or sit on the sidelines because wine auctions seem too complicated. It's fun—and it's easier than you think. *The Wine Lover's Guide to Auctions* is not a "dumbing down" of a complicated process. It is, instead, a thorough explanation of the game's rules. Beginners will suddenly find auction procedures within reach, while experts will discover informative facts and tips on every page. With *The Wine Lover's Guide to Auctions*, you will be able to experience the adventure of a wine auction, while avoiding mistakes and confidently playing the game to its fullest advantage. Discover what it is like to see the auctioneer point at you and say, "It's yours!"

Cheers.

PART ONE

Getting Started

1

A History of
Wine Auctions

The practice of selling a product or service to the highest bidder has been around for much of recorded history. The earliest auctions were for items that included land, animals, and agricultural products, and paved the way for the auctions of today. In this chapter, I will trace the history of early auctions through those of modern times, including such offshoots as Internet auctions.

THE FIRST AUCTIONEER WORE A TOGA

The word *auction* is derived from the Latin word *auctio*, which refers to "a gradual increasing." The first recorded auction occurred in Babylonia around 500 BC. The sale, which became an annual event, offered marriageable girls to the highest bidder. The Greek historian Herodotus described how the prettiest girls fetched the largest sums and how the proposed amount decreased when the less attractive girls were put up for sale. In fact, bidders would actually *receive* money in exchange for accepting the homeliest girls.

Early auctions such as these were backed by financial investors who arranged the venue, organized the goods sold, and covered expenses. Once an auction was established, a promoter would advertise the sale and serve as its auctioneer. Buyers and sellers were clearly delineated groups and specific taxes were imposed on each.

Romans made much use of the auction block, on which they sold the plunder of their imperialism. These pillaged goods included jewelry, artwork, and wine. Healthy and thriving vineyards existed throughout the Roman Empire, especially around the favorable climate of the Mediterranean, and there was a surplus of wine. The excess was exported in large wooden barrels to less topographically blessed areas of the great empire, where it would be auctioned off.

FROM COMMODITY TO COLLECTIBLE

The introduction of hand-blown glass bottles revolutionized wine drinking as well as collecting and trading. Their widespread use began in early seventeenth-century England. The short and squat bottles were sealed with glass stoppers that were fixed to the neck with twine or thread, and their bulbous bases prevented the bottles from lying on their sides. The techniques in glass production at that time produced bottles that were naturally dark—usually green—and this protected the contents from damaging light. Although coincidental, this was notably beneficial to wine storage and aging, a concept that had not yet been developed.

Wine was stored and shipped by the producer in *cask*—a term that describes both the quantity of wine in a cylindrical, barrel-like container, and the container itself. Once the wine was sold, the purchasers had to provide their own glass bottles. Often these purchasers, whether individuals, tavern owners, or innkeepers, would deliver their glass bottles, marked with a personal seal or engraved identifier, to the wine merchant to be filled. Other times, the purchasers would take delivery of the cask and fill the bottles themselves.

During the seventeenth century, the English gradually replaced the expensive and less effective glass stoppers with ones made of cork that came from trees in Spain and Portugal. The cork provided a more stable closure. The glass bottle and cork were the two crucial technological advances that would enable the proliferation of both drinking and appreciating wine.

Bottles evolved into a uniform cylindrical shape, similar to the wine bottle we know today, by the end of the eighteenth century. As a result of the new shape, the bottles could be stacked horizontally. This meant they were safer to ship and store, and also enabled long-term aging, a practice discovered accidentally. Once bottles were able to lay on their sides, wine lovers could accumulate larger quantities with less fear of spoilage. Connoisseurs began to notice that certain wines, particularly red Bordeaux (called Claret at the time) and Port, tasted significantly better when left in the cellar for long periods of time.

Meanwhile, in France, glass-blowing facilities did not develop until the end of the eighteenth century. In 1790, five bottle producers were recorded in Bordeaux, a town in southwestern France. The area surrounding Bordeaux was and is home to thousands of *châteaux*—estates with their own vineyards. As a result of the local glass blowing, some châteaux were able to begin bottling the wine themselves, freeing up barrels for the next *vintage*—the yield from a vineyard over one season. When purchased, the bottles would be packed in quantities of fifty or more and shipped in wicker baskets and hampers. These wicker baskets were eventually replaced by purpose-constructed wooden cases. The wood cases provided even better protection for both the glass and wine of the prepackaged bottles, as the cases could be easily stacked. The wine trade's unit of measurement was adjusted from "cask" to "case" to accommodate the change.

Cases of bottled wine were able to be shipped and stored for longer periods than those in cask had been. As a result, wine drinkers had greater opportunities to sample wines from different areas and different vintages. They began discussing vintages and vineyards, along with relative market values of various wines. For the first time, a particular wine could be considered special, more expensive, and therefore collectible.

WINE AUCTIONS IN ENGLAND

Wine was a popular drink among many wealthy English during the eighteenth century. It began to be stored in personal cellars, which encouraged collecting. Wines such as Port, Sherry, and Madeira were particularly prized beverages because of their *fortification*—the process of adding brandy during the wine-making process. This provided these wines with a stabilizing influence and an ability to age, which allowed them to survive the rigors of transportation to London with less spoilage than wines from other regions. Sweet wines from Germany and Hungary also traveled well and were popular drinks.

London auctions were already stylish events at this time. Collectible books and paintings would be auctioned off at fashionable coffee houses. Many of these auctions were accompanied by a printed catalogue that included specific conditions of the sale. They contained enticing descriptions of the goods being sold by the *consignor*—the person offering the item for sale. For the first time, auctioneers were required to be licensed and bonded, lending legitimacy to the events. By the middle of the 1700s, when wine bottles started to take on modern form, there were at least fifty registered auctioneers in London. The rising popularity of wine collecting coincided with the growth of successful auction houses such as Christie's and Sotheby's, ensuring the eventual development of the wine auctions we see today.

Christie's Auction House

In 1766, James Christie ventured out from his position as an auctioneer's assistant to form his own auction house, which he would call Christie's. Part businessman and part grand showman, Christie, along with his auctions, soon became a staple of the London social scene. Members of the aristocracy began to consign works of art to the young auctioneer. Cunning, social, and above all fiscally astute, Christie knew how to promote an auction. For a 1784 sale of a famous French transvestite spy's household furniture and decorations, Christie described the property as belonging to "a lady of fashion and an officer of Dragoons." Christie could throw a positive spin on any catalogue description.

Christie's very first 1766 auction was held on Pall Mall, a street of gentlemen's clubs where the auction house remained until 1823. Then Christie's moved a short

Why are there twelve bottles per case? Perhaps twelve was a logical amount of bottles by which the weight was both evenly distributed and able to be carried by any one man.

Although Christie's first wine-only auction was in 1769, it wasn't until 1788 that its catalogue first named the vineyards from which any of its wines' originated. The two vineyards named were Lafete [sic] and Château Margeaux [sic].

distance to King's Street, where the auction house's London headquarters are still located today. In addition to two chamber pots, a pair of sheets, two pillowcases, and four irons, the first of Christie's auctions sold a *lot*—items sold as a unit—that included wine. The auction's catalogue described this wine as "a large quantity of Madeira and high Flavour'd Claret, late the Property of Nobelman (Decease'd)." Christie's first auction to be devoted entirely to wine was held three years later. That 1769 auction would pave the way for many more specialized auctions over the next two hundred years.

Auctions reflect the general health of art and commodity markets, and over the next two hundred years, Christie's business had both good times and bad. Business was particularly poor during the great wars and their aftermath. Christie's King Street headquarters was actually burnt down by fire bombs during World War II.

Christie's salesrooms were rebuilt to the same plan and reopened in 1953. Yet much of the auction company's business was put on hold and their wine business was suspended, because of newly created post-war restrictions. According to these new rules, only members of the licensed wine-and-spirits trade could sell or buy at auction. These restrictions were eventually lifted in the late 1950s.

By 1966, Christie's was ready to sell wine again. No one could have predicted the international impact that Christie's hire for its new wine department would affect. No individual has done more to organize, systemize, glamorize, and popularize the art of selling fine wine at auction than Mr. J. Michael Broadbent.

Michael Broadbent Triggers a New Era in Wine Auctioning

Michael Broadbent did not grow up dreaming of great wines from Portugal and Bordeaux. His academic training was in architecture, a discipline that he never practiced. In 1952, at the age of twenty-five, Broadbent applied for and secured a trainee position at the London wine retailer Tommy Layton. He grabbed a broom, moved boxes, took orders, and made deliveries for a year, while developing and nurturing a keen interest in wine.

Broadbent joined Harvey's of Bristol's London office in 1955. The wine list there was stellar. Working under the great gentleman wine merchant Harry Waugh, Broadbent was set apart by his rapidly building wine knowledge, practical business sense, and precise attention to the taste of wine. Broadbent secured his Master of Wine certificate in 1960, adding the prestigious initials to the end of his name: J. Michael Broadbent, MW. He was soon promoted to Sales Director of Harvey's United Kingdom sales. This senior position allowed him contact with the entire network of the United Kingdom wine trade.

Broadbent was prime for a change from Harvey's just as Christie's was considering getting back into wine. After some personal correspondence with the Chairman of Christie's, Broadbent joined the auction house on July 1, 1966, enthusiastically ready to revitalize their wine department.

Broadbent's first step was to ally himself with Alan Taylor-Restell. Prior to this merge, Taylor-Restell's firm, W & T Restell, was the only wine-auction business in London. Christie's purchased this firm in order to jump-start its new department. Christie's first specialty wine auction was in London on October 11, 1966, and the new team was a success. Taylor-Restell's auction experience and Broadbent's fresh eye and maverick approach blended well as the business was reconstructed. Together they paved the way for a new, efficient, and effective way to sell wine at auction.

They developed many of the processes and procedures internationally utilized by today's auction companies. For example, Broadbent conceived and drew the original Ullage Chart, which appears in almost every auction catalogue. Its purpose is to describe the level of wine in the bottle of each lot. (The Ullage Chart is discussed in detail in Chapter 5.) Broadbent also created the practice of having a collector's wines accompanied by a descriptive inventory as the bottles enter the auction house, so that the information can be used in the auction's catalogue.

Broadbent's attention to accuracy of description is legendary among wine collectors. Throughout his career, he meticulously recorded every wine he tasted in a breast-pocket notebook. (You will learn how to write your own tasting note in Chapter 14.) Whether at a trade tasting, a lavish fancy dress dinner, or a friend's home, Broadbent made a thoughtful tasting note on each wine as it came his way. As a result, he has over 90,000 (a number that is constantly growing) notes. They are all entered neatly and accurately in hundreds of small notebooks that line the walls of the cellar staircase in his country home. Each of these notes, born from great discipline and unbound curiosity, was recorded in a specific and precise manner. For example, Broadbent uses a five-star rating system for wine. Five stars denotes an outstanding wine; no star indicates a lesser wine.

After over fifty years of tasting the world's finest and rarest wines, no one has greater wine-tasting experience than Michael Broadbent. Therefore, it was of great value to the entire world trade when Broadbent's tasting notes were organized and published in 1980. *The Great Vintage Wine Book* is a compilation of his notes. It was the first book of its kind and the precursor to today's various wine critics' newsletters and websites. Ten years and many thousands of tasting notes later, Broadbent released *The Great Vintage Wine Book II* in 1991. The first edition, with its dark green dust jacket, and the second edition, dressed in royal purple, stand out on every serious collector's library shelf. A third volume of his exceptional notes, *Vintage Wine: 50 Years of Tasting Three Centuries of Wine*, came out in 2002. Broadbent depicted a palate as sharp and uncompromising as ever.

Broadbent's tireless efforts and world-renowned successes during his thirty-two

The Institute of Masters of Wine started in 1953. Applicants enter a rigorous two-year program followed by extensive examinations, which test the candidate's ability to critically taste wine as well as answer advanced questions on the topic of wine. The exclusive title Master of Wine currently belongs to 250 wine experts worldwide.

Broadbent shared his
secrets on tasting and the
importance of making a
written note on each
tasting experience in his
first book, *Wine Tasting,*
originally published in
1968. *Wine Tasting* is still
in print and considered an
essential book for every
wine collector's library.

years at Christie's make him a legend of the modern wine-auction era. He headed the
first auction department devoted exclusively to wine, but it was not long before his
success encouraged competitors. Nearby Sotheby's would quickly become Christie's
biggest rival in the area of wine auctions.

Sotheby's Auction House

Home to the world's largest fine art auctions, Sotheby's began in late eighteenth-
century London as booksellers. The company's originator, Samuel Baker, held his
first book auction in 1744. Upon his death in 1778, the book-auction business was
taken over by his partner and nephew, John Sotheby. Business at Sotheby's gradually
grew into other areas, such as prints, maps, medals, and coins. With their continued
success came even further expansion of sales categories. A century of auction sales
later, Sotheby's growth necessitated larger premises, and in 1917 the company moved
into the Bond Street location that they have occupied ever since.

Sotheby's originally offered wine along with general sales only on rare occasion.
Then in 1970, four years after the development of Christie's specialized department
and in response to Broadbent's tremendous success in the wine-auction business,
Sotheby's opened its own wine-auction department. Throughout the 1970s and
1980s, Sotheby's wine sales achieved some successes, but Christie's was still the dominant force in the wine-auction world. The 1991 appointment of Serena Sutcliffe,
MW to head the Sotheby's London wine department would change this. Tall, strik-
ing, and fiercely intelligent, Sutcliffe proved a formidable challenge to Christie's sin-
gular foothold in London's wine-auction trade.

Serena Sutcliffe Joins the Trade

Serena Sutcliffe had been working as a translator in France when she developed an
interest in wine. In 1971, Sutcliffe returned to the United Kingdom and entered the
London wine trade. Serena found herself the only woman at many trade tastings.
The members of London's tight-knit, male-dominated wine trade did not make an
easy way for her. Undaunted and determined, Sutcliffe applied to the Masters of
Wine program. In 1976 she became the second woman ever to be awarded the prestigious title, and the members began to take Sutcliffe seriously.

Sutcliffe began a prolific writing career, many of her works considered definitive
source material on the subject she tackles. Two of Sutcliffe's earliest works, *Great
Vineyards and Winemakers* (1981) and *The Wine Drinker's Handbook* (1987), are found
in all thorough wine book collections. In 1986, Sutcliffe's *A Guide to the Wines of Burgundy* won *Decanter Magazine's* award for book of the year and the Silver Medal of the
German Gastronomic Academy. *Decanter Magazine* also chose her *Celebration of*

Champagne as its book of the year in 1988. That same year, the French government recognized Sutcliffe for her writing on the wines of France, naming her Chevalier dans l'Ordre des Arts et des Lettres.

By the time Sutcliffe was approached by Sotheby's to take charge of their wine business, she was well known and respected in the wine trade. The decision to join Sotheby's was riddled with concerns of jeopardizing her autonomy as a writer. True to form, however, Sutcliffe did not shy from the new challenge. Neither did Michael Broadbent, who now had very serious competition.

From the 1991 start when Sutcliffe accepted the position, the two locked horns in battle for the best consignments. The two politely, politically, and accurately describe their professional relationship and long-standing rivalry as "friendly competition." No doubt, Broadbent and Sutcliffe have tremendous respect for each other's many strengths. With one at the helm of each great auction house, the wine world has seen exciting competition of great auction sales.

Sotheby's holds the record for the most lucrative wine sale to date: the "Millennium Wine Cellar," sold in New York in November 1999. Consigned by a single private Norwegian collector, the auction consisted of over 3,000 lots, whose value commanded $14.4 million. Another notable auction under Sutcliffe's direction was the 1999 sale of Andrew Lloyd Webber's wine collection, which

Sotheby's in London.

sold for $6 million. Christie's, of course, responded with its own "Millennium Sale"— not as large, but a success nonetheless. The competition between the two houses never allows either to relish in its own success for too long before moving on to the next big consignment.

WINE AUCTIONING IN THE NEW WORLD

Broadbent began to extend Christie's wine auctions to include sales across the world. In 1969, the American wine and spirits company Heublein, Inc. nudged open the door to wine auctions in the United States.

Heublein Begins a Tradition

Encouraged by wine-auction activity in the United Kingdom, some in the wine trade saw great opportunity in America. Executives of Heublein, Inc. were the first to act on the potential of a US wine-auction market. Without a worry about competition or exclusivity, Heublein contacted Michael Broadbent to act as both consultant and auctioneer at the sales.

The first Heublein auction was held at the Continental Plaza Hotel in Chicago. The auction offered both European and Californian wines, sold for a total of $55,632—a grand sum in 1969. The Heublein auctions became an annual event, with Broadbent always at the podium. Consignments came from private cellars, wineries, and famous restaurants, both in the United States and England. Great, rare wine was suddenly more accessible to the then small group of passionate American collectors. Broadbent met and developed relationships with these collectors, whose bottles would later form the cornerstone consignments of the American wine-auction business's next generation. The well-heeled, suit- and tie-clad crowd included famous American collectors such as Lloyd Flatt, Marvin Overton, Tawfiq Khoury, and Frank Komorowsky.

A *star lot* is one that is very rare or very expensive. Usually an item seldom seen at auction and therefore able to attract attention, a star lot can be used to advertise an auction.

Many of the wines tasted and purchased at a Heublein auction became star lots at future sales. The Heublein auction venue changed each year, reaching and creating fine wine collectors from coast to coast. In its fifth year, the auction took in $273,500 from the sale of some 30,000 bottles. Heublein continued its successful annual auctions until 1983.

The wine-auction business in the United States was somewhat associated with the city of Chicago, where two of the first five Heublein auctions had been held. The spirit of competition awoke when Philip H. Tenenbaum, founder of the Chicago Wine Company, decided to hold his own auctions. The first, in 1977, realized $150,000 by selling around 500 lots. The Chicago Wine Company continues today with monthly sales and a loyal clientele.

During this time, the vast majority of lots in all US wine auctions were comprised of red Bordeaux. Classic vintage Port was also traded with great demand at the early auctions. Witnessing the strong results from the Bordeaux-centric Heublein auctions and solid prices from the relatively unknown up-start wine auctioneers in Chicago, Michael Broadbent was more convinced than ever that there was a place for "real" wine auctions—Christie's wine auctions—in America.

Christie's Leads the American Charge

Broadbent, not content with coming to the United States solely to conduct the Heublein auctions, was convinced that the American group of collectors was large enough to warrant a Christie's New York office. By 1977, he was pushing for the expansion to New York.

Unfortunately, when the Twenty-First Amendment of 1933 repealed prohibition, it also gave each state the right to enact its own separate legislation regarding the sale and storage of alcohol. New York State, for one, had no specific laws regarding the auction of wine, so wine was included in the "fair-trade" law of the time. This meant that wine, like liquor and beer, was to be sold at a fixed price and therefore not at auction. Broadbent was frustrated. Surely wine, the most civilized of beverages, could not be treated as just any alcohol! Broadbent would not let the matter die. He plotted and schemed on long trans-Atlantic flights and spoke endlessly on how to make Christie's US wine auctions a reality.

Then, during the course of the 1978 Heublein auctions, Broadbent met Jackie Quillen, a young and vivacious owner of a store called The Wine and Cheese Company. Broadbent and Quillen hit it off immediately and spent many hours talking about wine, food, travel, and archaic American wine laws. When Broadbent told Quillen about his desire to build a Christie's US wine department, Quillen warned that the largest expense involved—by many multiples—would be attorneys' fees. Nonetheless, Broadbent had found an ally, and started a crusade that would soon involve several states.

New York

In 1978, after successful conversations with Christie's and the New York State Liquor Authority, Broadbent predicted that wine auctions would be possible in the very near future. He was so confident in the auctions to come that he offered Quillen an immediate position to start collecting wine from consignors for the New York Christie's office.

Broadbent and Quillen's well-laid plans, however, were met with opposition at every turn. New York's largest retailers, Sherry-Lehman, Morrell & Company, and Zachys Wine & Liquor, Inc. did not want to see competition from wine auctions. Allegedly, these retailers had their own secondary market in buying back wine from collectors to whom they had originally sold the bottles. In the case of death or divorce, for example, retailers enjoyed a profit by buying back appreciated wine at the original purchase price. These retailers had a strong voice in New York City and, more importantly, in the law-making capital of Albany. Quillen, following Broadbent's lead, soldiered on.

The New York State Liquor Authority eventually granted Christie's a permit to conduct a wine auction and consignors eagerly agreed to participate in the historic inaugural auction. It was scheduled to be held in Christie's salesroom on December 6, 1980. Plenty of lead-time was required, less for cataloguing and organizing the wine than for filling out the forms required by the Bureau of Alcohol, Tobacco and Firearms (BATF). Quillen struggled with the endless conversion of *magnums, jeroboams,* and *imperials*—respectively, a term for 1.5 liter bottles, a term for 4.5 liter bottles, and a term for 6 liter bottles—into the required liquor terminology of gallons and quarts.

While Quillen was busy at her desk and in the warehouse, a small group of New York retailers filed a temporary restraining order against the State Liquor Authority, claiming that it was not in the Liquor Authority's power to grant an auction license.

The wine to be auctioned was in the warehouse, the catalogue was back from the printer, and the auction date was two weeks away, but the permit was withdrawn and the New York sale was cancelled. Unbelievably, this was not Broadbent and Quillen's only headache.

First, the intrepid duo used a temperature-controlled space with a full license for alcoholic beverage storage on the Lower East Side, a less-than-pleasant area at that time. Eventually, they were able to move the wine to Morgan Manhattan, a storage facility in Mount Clair, New Jersey, where Christie's and many of Christie's clients stored their fine and decorative art. The facility was much better than the previous warehouse, but Quillen and Broadbent had failed to realize that Morgan Manhattan did not have a permit to store alcohol. Broadbent flew across the Atlantic for a pre-auction meeting with Quillen without a hint of suspicion that there may be a problem.

New Jersey

Quillen was called to New Jersey with the news that Morgan Manhattan was surrounded by six squad cars. She arrived and was told by the police officers that in accordance with the mandates of the state's Liquor Control Board, the heel of every bottle of wine in the facility would have to be broken. Quillen turned green, thinking especially of the magnum bottles of 1870 Glamis Castle Lafite.

Quillen made several phone calls to buy some time, all the while aware that Broadbent was waiting for her to pick him up at Newark Airport. Quillen convinced the arresting officer, a reasonable gentleman of Alsatian descent with an interest in wine, to accompany her to Newark to collect Broadbent. Coincidentally, the office of the New Jersey Division of Alcoholic Beverage Control was at the same airport where Broadbent was waiting to be picked up. The police officer mistakenly thought that Broadbent had flown to the states to attend to this Morgan Manhattan issue, and was impressed with the seriousness that Christie's afforded the ordeal. Quillen did not let on that Broadbent just needed a ride into town. The officer assured Quillen that the wines would not be destroyed. However, Quillen was fingerprinted and booked for the storage of alcohol without a license—a felony.

Because Quillen had filled out and filed all the BATF forms, she was considered the party responsible for Christie's actions. A $200,000 bond was required for her release. Christie's merchant bank, Brown Brothers Harriman, raised the bond money. Another $25,000 was paid out to obtain the proper permit for Morgan Manhattan. Quillen's earlier prophecy about the huge legal fees was realized, more dramatically than anticipated. Thankfully, the bottles were now safe and laid down in a correctly licensed warehouse. But the temporary restraining order of the New York Liquor

Authority, brought about by the agitated New York retailers, was still in place. There was no way to hold a wine auction at Christie's in New York.

Disappointed, frustrated, and exhausted, both Broadbent and Quillen thought they had hit the end of the road. But Christie's still had a warehouse, now fully permitted and filled with fantastic wine; a printed catalogue; and a great story, almost reminiscent of prohibition days of running liquor.

Washington, DC

On completely separate Christie's business in 1980, Brian Cole, President of Christie's East (where less valuable items were sold), had been talking with Marshall Coyne, owner of the luxurious Madison Hotel in Washington, DC. Coyne had a collection of porcelain figures that he wished to sell. During their discussions, Coyne mentioned that he had heard about Christie's wine department's difficulties in New York, and asked Cole if he might consider holding the auction at his DC hotel. Christie's lawyers gave the go ahead, and Broadbent believed Washington, DC was enough of a draw to attract major collectors to the maiden sale. For the pre-sale tasting, Quillen and Broadbent gathered bottles of 1966 Great Growths, representing those in the actual sale, and held a tasting of six First and Second Growth 1966s at the Madison Hotel the evening before the auction. The charge was a hefty $30 per person. Broadbent was to lead the tasting, and there was a rush to get tickets.

The auction was a great success. Alas, when they hoped for a repeat DC performance six months later, several wholesalers blocked the second sale. Again discouraged but optimistic that another venue would present itself, Quillen kept gathering wine, and sure enough, luck was once again on Christie's side.

Illinois and Beyond

Unexpectedly, in 1981, an executive from Chicago's famous Marshall Field's department store inquired with Quillen about the possibility of joining forces in the wine-auction business. The laws in Illinois were amenable to wine auctions, and the team at Marshall Field's had seen firsthand the success of both the annual Heublein auctions and the new Chicago Wine Company auction events. The call could not have been better timed. Neither Broadbent nor Quillen had ever considered Chicago as a possible venue, but they had an entire sale ready to go and no other immediate options, so they gladly accepted the offer. The first auction was a great success to both consignors and bidders, and a great relief to Quillen and Broadbent. Christie's negotiated storage and licensing through Shafer's, a local retailer, and sent Michael Davis, a young, enthusiastic man from New York's customer service department, to oversee the new Christie's American wine-auction business.

After years of struggle, Broadbent's dream of expanding Christie's wine-auction empire came true. The Christie's Chicago auctions resumed the quality of the earlier Heublein sales. Sales were held at the grand Drake Hotel, then the smaller, more elegant Casino Club, and finally the oak-paneled rooms of the University Club. All three were wonderful Chicago landmarks and dignified environments for the serious business of wine auctions. Quillen and Broadbent were soon able to relinquish all responsibilities to Michael Davis's very capable team. For many years, the Christie's Chicago wine department was the sole leader in United States auctions of fine and rare wine.

Now it was Michael Davis's turn to expand his wine-auction empire. Noting the increasing amount of sophisticated collectors in southern California, Davis considered a wine-auction business in Los Angeles. With enthusiastic support from Michael Broadbent, Davis researched and reported back to London that the laws in California were equally favorable for wine auctions. In the fall of 1989, Davis mounted a road show and held his first wine auction at the classy Bel Age Hotel. The Los Angeles sales were extremely well received by local collectors. Once again, Christie's proved that the demand for fine and rare wine had expanded.

Christie's carried on as the uncontested American wine-auction leader until 1993. At that time, the climate in New York and the overall American economy forced some large cutbacks and layoffs in many businesses, and Christie's was not spared. The entire Chicago wine-auction department was closed down. After all of Broadbent's, Quillen's, and Davis's hard work, the bottle ran dry. It was the end of an era: the great days of Christie's US wine auctions came to an abrupt, two-year halt.

Broadbent stayed active as ever in the London auction scene and maintained his relentless international travel schedule. Quillen started a wine importing company with Frederick S. Wildman. Michael Davis and his team kept to the Christie's originally planned fall 1993 sale schedule that was in place. Now, however, the front of the catalogue read, "Davis and Company." Davis continued the great success he had built and enjoyed under the Christie's banner; only now, it was his own company. Davis and Company was so successful in dominating the midwest auction market that they were acquired by Sotheby's in 1998.

A NEW GENERATION OF AUCTIONEERING

New York State continued to ban the sale of wine at auction until approached by several retailers. In discussions beginning most seriously in 1992, a few top retailers considered the possibility of selling off stagnant inventory by offering the wine at auction. Informal conversations among these retailers and state legislators began. The possibilities became more concrete and, as time progressed, the shape and form of New York wine auctions emerged.

Legislators agreed to allow wine auctions. However, the nature of the property sold would be limited to wine already held by private collectors. This way, the state would be able to collect appropriate taxes at the point of the original sale to the collector. Then, after the wine was auctioned off, the state would once again be eligible to collect taxes on most of the wine sold: a double tax.

Another important restriction was set in place. The auctions could be held only by those who had held a New York retail license for at least ten years and who purchased an additional auction license. The retailers themselves no doubt pushed for this limitation, as the number of retailers eligible under this provision was a known entity and allowed them a certain level of control. Regardless of the stipulations, laws were in place to allow the sale of wine at auction in New York State by 1993.

New York City's top two family-owned fine wine retailers, Morrell & Company and Sherry-Lehman, entered the auction business. At the same time, Westchester County behemoth Zachys laid the tracks for its own entrance. Although not required by the new state laws, both Sherry-Lehman and Zachys decided to partner with one of the two big international auction houses. This provided the auction houses with a way around the laws that didn't allow them to hold their own sales.

Sherry-Lehman joined forces with Sotheby's and Zachys worked with Christie's. In April of 1994, Peter Morrell's team

Zachys in New York.

at Morrell & Company held the first NY wine auction, followed in November by the Sotheby's/Sherry-Lehman team. Zachys-Christie's launched their venture the following spring. The experience of the London auction houses along with the high-end clients of the New York retailing giants created an instant formula for success. The first Zachys-Christie's sale totaled just over $1.8 million, which was, at the time, the highest sale total by far for an American wine auction. The American wine auction was reborn.

Since 1999, the infant New York wine auctions have outsold the venerable London sales each year, with New York becoming the center of wine-auction action. Times were good in the mid- to late 1990's, and wine auctions, now covered extensively by *Wine Spectator* magazine, reaped the benefits of a new base of collectors with knowledge, enthusiasm, and money.

The Sotheby's/Sherry-Lehman partnership lasted one five-year contract cycle, during which time the partners enjoyed a lucrative and press-worthy relationship. At this point, Sherry-Lehman chose to concentrate on its vast retail focus and Sotheby's had no problem finding another retail partner. In the spring of 2000,

To this day, New York holds the record for the largest grossing wine auction. This was Acker Merrall & Condit's October 2006 sale, which grossed $24.7 million. All the wine belonged to one collector.

Sotheby's continued its sales with Aulden Cellars, to great, ongoing success. The Zachys-Christie's partnership also worked to great auction heights. The two companies finally parted ways in 2001 when Zachys decided to try the business on its own. In the meantime, Morrell & Company's auctions continued with loyal support from both buyers and sellers. Still another retailer, Acker Merrall & Condit, started to hold wine auctions in New York City. Acker Merrall & Condit first teamed with auction house partners William Doyle Galleries and then Tepper Galleries, before venturing out on its own.

The players of today's New York wine-auction market compete to offer the best consignments and work diligently to attract deep-pocketed bidders. In order to win particularly appealing consignments, the different auction companies will offer lower commissions and other creative financial incentives. Spirited bidding is ensured by luring buyers into the salesroom with pre-auction tastings and fancy lunches. Yet New York is by no means unique in these ways. Wine auctions have expanded beyond Europe and North America, and the nature of the sales is similar wherever one can find an auctioneer trying to sell a bottle of wine.

WINE AUCTIONS AROUND THE WORLD

Today, Christie's and Sotheby's wine-auction empires each stretch to many countries around the globe, and have tremendous impact on international wine-auction activity. Held in grand hotels and other lavish locations, these international auctions help keep Sotheby's and Christie's names fresh in the minds of the local affluent crowd. Yet it wasn't until the 1970s that the wine auctions of these companies began to spread beyond England and the United States.

Broadbent was the first to look overseas for expansion opportunities. He urged Christie's to seek oversees venues to accommodate the demand for classic collector wines. He began by organizing wine auctions in different venues across Europe. By the late 1970s, Broadbent had established Christie's wine auctions in Australia, and was selling wine in Japan ten years later. As a result of his work, Christie's currently holds regular specialty wine sales and maintains departments in London, Amsterdam, Paris, Los Angeles, and New York. The local staff in each city organizes the consignments from local sellers, catalogues the sales, and manages the bidders' purchases. Christie's London expert staff will frequently travel to these areas to hold special tastings for its top clients.

Sotheby's, too, realized the demand from international collectors. Since the inception of its wine department in 1970, Sotheby's has sold wine in Europe: Amsterdam, Dublin, Florence, London, Geneva, Regensburg, Germany, Verona, and Zurich; in Asia: Hong Kong and Tokyo; and in South Africa: Capetown and Johannesburg.

Australian Auctions

There are very few auction companies in other countries that can compete with Christie's and Sotheby's international business prestige and volume of wine sold. One of the largest foreign wine-auction companies is Australia's Langton's Wine Auctions & Exchange. Founded in 1988 by Stewart Langton, with partner Andrew Caillard, MW joining the following year, Langton's auction business initiated the development of Australia's fine wine market, with early auctions that catered almost exclusively to Australian collectors. In 1990 Langton's and Christie's formed a business alliance that is still enjoyed today, and the Langton auctions are no longer exclusive to the sale of Australian wine. Local bidders can purchase classic Bordeaux and Burgundy, as well as other top European and New World wines.

Yet Langton and Caillard's most important contribution to the Australian wine world was not their successful company. At the time of Langton's inception, the wine-collecting world at large did not yet have an appreciation of the great wines of Australia, and the only Australian wine seen on the secondary market abroad was Penfold's Grange Hermitage. In an effort to show the world the quality of indigenous wines other than Penfold's, Langton and Caillard embarked upon the huge task of classifying the nation's wine.

Langton's released its Classification of Australian Wine in 1991, with two subsequent re-classifications. Thanks to Langton's endeavor, Australian wine could now be qualified and quantified, and credibility was better established for the country's production. In the same year, the two Australian wine experts published the now-definitive *Langton's Australian Fine Wine Buying and Investment Guide*, a price guide to Australian wines traded on the secondary market. The *Guide* is now in its fifth publication. Since 2002, Langton's has also published *Langton's Fine Wine Index*, using prices from its auctions. The *Index* is invaluable to the wine collector-investor to monitor the price gains and losses of the Australian portion of his collection.

German Auctions

Enthusiasts of German wines enjoy a commercial auction season each September, when four major wine auctions are held. Each is devoted entirely to the sale of German wines from the area that is hosting the event. Two auctions are conducted in the Mosel, one in the Rheingau, and one in the Nahe combined with the Ahr. The sales showcase the efforts of the winegrowers' current vintage to determine the quality of that vintage. Winemakers submit their most special wines of the vintage, as opposed to their production that will be made available to the marketplace in the normal course of the year's business.

Any private collector can attend the auctions with the purchase of a ticket,

For schedule and ticket sale information, contact the publishers of the *Riesling Report* or visit their website at www.rieslingreport.com.

but bidding must be done through an official commissioner of the event. German wine fanatics from around the world attend the auctions whether or not they intend to bid because the wines available at the auction are poured at pre-sale tasting events. Most of the winemakers are present, and open to meeting and speaking with their fans.

At the end of the day, every company in each area of the world owns only its reputation, and customer service is the name of the game. But sales are the endpoint of the business, and sales are now frequently being found outside the actual auction houses. The gradual acceptance of the Internet into people's daily lives has opened up a new avenue for wine auctions.

ONLINE WINE AUCTIONS

The late 1990s saw technology mainstreaming into nearly all aspects of everyday life. The Internet, in particular, had far-reaching effects. Very few workplaces functioned without a computer on the desk of each employee. Anyone with access to a computer could now go online to buy books, music, and groceries. It was more convenient, faster, and often cheaper than before.

For the first time, auctions became a household way to trade any type of item. The fledgling company Ebay provided at-home auctions on nearly any type of item. Christie's and Sotheby's well-to-do crowds no longer had the only access to the excitement of auction. At the same time, wine was becoming more accessible and popular than ever. Circulation of *Wine Spectator* magazine increased wildly. California's wine country, the Napa Valley, was a frequent vacation spot. Three of the decade's buzzwords were Internet, auction, and wine. It was merely a matter of time before entrepreneurial wine aficionados looked at the many opportunities for wine on the World Wide Web.

Some of the first wine sites belonged to the traditional wine retailers, who used the Internet for advertising. With the development of shopping cart technology, many wine retailers added web-based sales to their existing business. Soon, exclusively web-based wine retailing was created with great support from venture capitalists, and sophisticated websites like www.wine.com offered an online marketplace for all types of wine. The first great sites were like the traditional retailers, in that they offered a tremendous number of different labels. These early wine websites enjoyed great success.

Wine websites even have certain advantages over retailers. They can add educational content on each wine that goes far beyond the traditional in-store shelf-talker, which cannot include much information beyond a bottle's numerical score. Also, Internet wine retailers do not need to incur the tremendous expense of either the real estate required to set up shop or the production of expensive auction catalogues.

The online auctioneers move wine in and out of their systems faster than a traditional company that is bound by the wait of the printed catalogue. In addition to the time a printer needs to produce the beautifully illustrated wine-auction catalogue, prospective buyers need time to study the wines offered and formulate their bidding strategies. This entire process takes at least a month. The reduction of this time is a big perk of online auctions. The wines come to auction much quicker and the consignor in turn receives his money in a shorter amount of time.

Wine auctions have adapted easily to cyberspace. A potential seller's wines are first appraised and estimated by specialists, just like at the traditional auctions. If the interested seller is content with the pre-sale estimates and reserves, he ships his wine to the online auction company. Next, the wine is photographed and catalogued by a specialist, and the information is uploaded on the auction website. Online auctions usually last one to two weeks. Registered buyers bid on the wines of their choice, and are automatically notified if they are outbid by another bidder. The original bidder can then keep bidding until he wins, or choose to drop out of the action. Finally, when successful, the winning bidder sends his payment to the company, and in return the wine is shipped. There is now basic auction software that can be further customized to fit the needs and desires of each online auction house. Except for the electronic nature of the transaction and the absence of the auctioneer and his gavel, the process is nearly identical to the traditional live auction.

Bidders often enjoy the convenience of online auctions, as they can bid any time from the start of the auction until it closes. With a weeklong auction, a bidder can research the wine or its price and perhaps bid more confidently. Some companies, such as WineBid.com, require consignors to send in their wine prior to the auction so they can attest to the condition of the bottle, further allaying fears of bidders.

Technology enables the cyber-bidder to take his desired amount of bottles out of a consignor's case—just like walking through the aisle at a wine shop. It is a very compelling aspect of the online auctions that bidders can buy wine in single-bottle quantities. Similarly, consignors can offer wines in small-lot quantities, something that the traditional live auction houses are less inclined to allow.

Other wine-auction sites such as www.winecommune.com allow a seller to list his wine and send it directly to the winning bidder after payment has been collected. This peer-to-peer auction model lowers fees to the seller and is popular with those vendors who have time to do the work themselves. Many fine bottles are bought and sold through this process. Its greatest feature is that the wine is moved only once, from seller to successful buyer.

Ebay functions similarly, in that the product is sent directly from seller to buyer. Ebay's policy on the sale of wine has changed several times. In 1999, wine auctions were banned because Ebay was concerned with the legal complexities of selling wine, particularly with issues involving the sale of alcohol to a minor. Now, however, although Ebay still generally prohibits the sale of wine on its site, there is a small group of licensed retailers, vetted by Ebay, who do offer wine each auction cycle. Ebay moniters that these sellers ship wine to the successful bidder in full compliance with each state's regulations.

Many of the traditional wine-auction houses augment their live action with some form of Internet activity. Langton's of Australia, for example, now offers an online wine exchange for direct purchases of fine wine in full-case quantities. Its website bridges the many miles between its live auction attendees and its international buyers. As the demand for Australian wine builds among collectors worldwide, Langton's online wine-auction business provides an auction arena built upon great expertise and credibility to people throughout the world.

> Online wine-auction activity contributes around $20 million to the total amount of wine sold annually at auction in the United States.

Many online wine-auction sites of the early, frenzied cyber-space land grab have come and gone. The online wine-auction businesses today are professionally run, serious entities. Most offer a good deal of personalized attention to both buyer and seller. From the acceptance of live-auction absentee bids via email to entirely separate Internet auctions, Internet technology is used by each established auction house to enhance the success of its traditional business model.

CONCLUSION

From ancient Rome to various points around the world today, wine auctions have claimed a considerable part of the wine trade. Auction sales in the United States alone total approximately $75 million every year. Through new vintages, new fashions, and new technologies, the auction process has essentially remained the same: an auctioneer attempts to extract as high a price as he can for each bottle of wine.

Today there are quite a few auction houses between which a potential seller or buyer can choose. Thanks to the competition between rivaling houses, auction prices are kept to very high standards, and the process has never been a more successful sales tool.

This chapter has explained where wine auctions came from and how they developed into where they are today. Before moving on to the details of these auctions, you will take a close look at wine. After inspecting different grapes and what happens to them before they arrive on the auction block as bottled wines, you will then read about wine collecting, serving, and drinking.

2

Essential Wine Basics

Wine auctions are dramatic events. From the catalogue's glossy pages to the auctioneer's excited inflection, the romance of wine auctions is seductive. However, success at these events relies on more than understanding the process. It also relies on knowledge of wine. Wine is a complex subject stemming from the simple idea that wine is the fermented juice of grapes. Understanding the basics of wine production will allow you to truly appreciate the bottles you see at auction. Before you step onto the auction floor, you should also be familiar with a variety of different wines and the different bottles in which they will be offered.

When the wine has been won, the best is still yet to come. We will discuss how to store wine in a cellar and whether the wine needs to age, as well as tips on sharing your new treasures with family and friends.

The more wine you purchase and the more auctions you attend, of course, the more polished your education will be. With a little study, you will better understand why certain wines are not only collectible, but are often traded at astronomical prices. This chapter is a great place to start building your wine proficiency.

WINE PRODUCTION

The key to making wine is in the growing and fermenting of grapes. These processes are handled, respectively, by *wine growers*—the vineyard workers, or farmers—and winemakers. Wines from the same type of grape and neighboring vineyards can be quite different, for two main reasons. First, the soil, which affects growing grapes, can be different even within the same vineyard. Secondly, the workers at each step of the process have a major impact on the resulting product.

Growing the Grapes

There are many different types of grapes in the world. The largest species of wine grapes is named *Vitis vinifera. Vitis vinifera* accounts for over 90 percent of the world's

A Brief History of Wine
Old World Traditions and New World Innovations

Europe's long wine-producing tradition stems from the temperate climate of the surrounding Mediterranean, which has facilitated grape planting and winemaking for centuries. The prolific planting of grape vines provided an abundance of wine. Then, as wine found its place in daily life and religious ceremonies, more and more vineyards were planted to satisfy the demand. Vineyards began to be further developed in northern and eastern Europe, where the colder weather varietals found success.

France's long wine-related history sets the standard for winemaking and wine drinking. Traditionally, French wines from Burgundy and Bordeaux commanded more respect and higher prices than bottles from other countries. Wines from Italy, Spain, and Portugal, although benefiting from the same temperate advantages, were not exported to the same extent as French wine during the seventeenth century. Bordeaux, located along the Gironde River, was already established as a great trading center. Merchants visiting the area for other business would enjoy the French wines and send bottles home, encouraging the start of the export wine industry.

The eighteenth- and nineteenth-century consumer demand from non-wine producing countries, particularly Great Britain, did much to affect the wine trade and, in turn, wine production. With ever-changing fashions and tastes from the wine-drinking public, wines from areas other than Bordeaux began to make an appearance at the well-laid table. The wines of Germany, Portugal, and Hungary were soon enjoyed and evaluated like the wines of France. Wine is a deep-rooted European tradition, and the wines from these areas are referred to as Old World.

Winemaking came to America from the Old World along with its immigrants. Grape vines were planted all over the new continent for both secular consumption and religious ceremony. The plants fared particularly well in the warm climates of the West Coast, coinciding with great demand from the large number of Spanish missionaries traveling northward from Mexico and a population of European immigrant farmers (particularly those from Italy) who brought their taste for wine. The onslaught of European immigration to Aus-

wine production. (The remaining 10 percent is comprised of wine made from fruit other than grapes.) These Old World varieties are now found throughout North America, South America, Africa, and Australia. There are several thousand different varieties, a handful of which are particularly important to wine lovers. Other grapes—*table grapes*—are grown to be eaten. (See the inset on page 30 for differences between wine grape vines and table grape vines.)

The health of a vine and the ripening quality of its grapes are affected by *terroir* (tehr-wahr), roughly translated from French as "earth" or "soil." It refers to the somewhat mystical combination of soil, sun, water, wind, and vineyard location, and the effect they together have on the final wine product. Each individual vineyard has its own *terroir*; one large vineyard may have several different *terroirs*. Because each *ter-*

tralia in the early twentieth century had similar effects.

Americans and Australians were able to experiment and develop wines from a blank canvas. Innovations in wine growing and winemaking led to wines of increasingly better quality, to the point where some Old World producers began to look behind the cellar doors of these New World wineries. Those in the Old World who were willing to share and receive this information found that they were able to adopt some New World practices.

The wines of South Africa, South America, and New Zealand are also included under the New World-wines umbrella. They do not have long histories of quality wine growing and made relatively new appearances at local wine stores in the 1980s. I often wonder about the wines of China and what they will be called when China eventually introduces its own quality production into the international marketplace.

In a general sense, New World wines are considered bigger, bolder, richer, fruitier, and higher in alcohol than their Old World cousins. The Old World wines, on the other hand, are considered more *restrained*—having flavors that are less forthcoming until full maturity. These differences are due to the environmental differences in which the Old World and New World grapes are grown. The New World wines are planted in and thrive in climates that are much warmer than most Old World vineyards. The warmer the climate conditions, the riper the fruit, the higher the sugars, and the higher the alcohol. New World winemakers rival their Old World counterparts in extracting the highest-quality wine from the highest-quality grapes grown, but the soil is different. A Cabernet Sauvignon grown on the valley floor in Napa County, California, will never taste the same as a Cabernet Sauvignon grown along the banks of the Gironde River in Bordeaux.

roir is unique, the same variety of grape grown in two different places can produce two very different wines.

The quality of the soil and its drainage is directly responsible for the amount of water that each plant receives. Soil can be dense (like clay) and drain poorly, or loose (like gravel or sandy dirt) with excellent drainage. Weather also plays a role in hydrating each vine. An exceptionally dry year may produce fruit that is very concentrated and high in sugars, resulting in wine that is bigger, bolder, and perhaps more alcoholic. Too much rain in one year can be detrimental, as each berry runs the risk of bloating and diluting itself. Then, the health of each vine depends on sunshine and the warmth it provides. It is up to the vineyard's team of workers to maintain the health of each plant by seeing that it gets what it needs.

Comparing Wine Grape Vines and Table Grape Vines

Wine-yielding grape vines differ from table grape vines in the following ways:

■ Wine-yielding vines produce smaller berries on thicker, more vigorous shoots.

■ The leaves of a wine-growing vine are circular with deep indentations while the leaves on table grape vines are angular.

■ The wine vine is a fruitful *hermaphrodite*—a self-pollinating plant—as opposed to the table grape vine, which is a mixture of fruitless male and irregular female plants.

Good soil, luck with the weather, healthy vines, and year-round vigilance afford grapes the best chance of turning into high-quality wine. Once the vines have matured and the grapes are ready for harvest, the science and art of the winemaker come into play.

Fermenting the Juice

The best way to learn about winemaking is to visit wineries after having read a bit on the subject. Winemaking will come alive when you are walking through a winery with a knowledgeable guide. Many wineries offering guided tours will be happy to provide a more in-depth visit upon request. I recommend you call ahead with such a request.

The vineyard manager oversees and augments the effect nature has on the vines; similarly, the winemaker oversees and augments the effect nature has on the grapes. After the grapes are harvested and brought to the winery, the winemaker watches the freshly picked grapes as they are dumped out of the pickers' bins into the winery's crusher. He thinks about the type of wine that will come from the grapes. He decides how to best usher the grapes through the fermentation and aging processes so that they may realize their destiny. Experienced winemakers, like great sailors, change their course often through the race, anticipating and reacting to variable conditions. The wine is worked on until it is bottled and in the marketplace—at which point it continues to evolve. Wine is a living, breathing juice that continues to age and change until it is drunk.

Each individual grape, also called a *berry*, acts as its own little winery, and can illustrate the winemaker's art. As a grape bunch ripens, millions of yeast cells settle on each berry. If the berry splits open for any reason, the sugar from the grape's juice reacts upon contact with the yeast on its skin, and turns into alcohol and carbon dioxide. This reaction is called *fermentation*. At the winery, this process is conducted at the hands of the winemaker. Many wine characteristics are born out of decisions made during fermentation.

WINE IDENTIFICATION

There are several ways to identify wine. The first identifying factor is by color: red, white, or rosé. Wines can then be identified by the variety of grape used in their production. This has become increasingly common as New World wines, which name the grape on their labels, gain in popularity. A third way to differentiate between wines is by place of origin: first by country, and then by region within the country. We will explore different wine characteristics by looking at wines in these three ways.

Identifying by Type

The type of wine is determined by both the color of the grape and the method of its fermentation. *Red wines* are made from red grapes, the color of the wine coming from the fruit's skin. The skins of red grapes stay with the juice during the fermentation process. The duration of the fermentation process varies according to the variety of grape and the desires of the winemaker. Many red wines contain a high amount of *tannins*—components from the seeds and skins of grapes that give wine a dry taste and the ability to age. When a red wine is particularly harsh and bitter at a young age, it is due to the presence of tannins, and the taste should become more palatable when the wine is allowed to mature.

White wines come from white grapes. Their skins are removed prior to fermentation. White wines range in color from nearly clear to golden brown. They can be fermented sweet, semi-sweet, or dry. *Sweet white wines* are made from grapes whose sugars are not completely turned into alcohol during fermentation. *Semi-sweet white wines* are low in alcohol and contain some residual sugar (or sugars not converted into alcohol during fermentation). When all the sugar ferments into alcohol, the wine is described as *dry*.

Pink wines, or *rosés*, are usually made from red grapes whose skins are removed from the process as soon as the wine has reached the desired pinkish color. The exception to this is some pink Champagne. *Champagne* refers to the sparkling wine from the French province of the same name. Certain Champagne wines have a rosy glow because they are made by blending a small amount of red grape juice with a larger amount of white grape juice.

Other countries also produce *sparkling wines* to great success. They are only called Champagne if actually from this province, although other sparkling wines are commonly—and mistakenly—called Champagne. Whether from France, America, or Australia, sparkling wines undergo a second fer-

It is generally accepted that a *young wine* is a wine less than five years old. A wine with more years in the bottle may be described as an *older wine*. However, a well-made older wine that is kept in proper storage can taste fresh and young, while a young wine not kept at its ideal temperature will lose its youthful character, and taste old and tired.

Medieval winemaker inspecting wine.

mentation while under pressure in the bottle. During standard fermentation, carbon dioxide escapes; during this second fermentation, the pressure keeps the gas inside the bottle, resulting in captured bubbles.

Identifying by Grape Variety

Identifying and understanding the different grapes described here will provide you with a basic understanding of the world's wine production. The term *varietal* describes the dominant grape used in a particular wine. Wines from New World regions, especially California or Australia, are referred to by the grape from which they were produced. We will first examine some of the most important and frequently used varietals. Many of the wines you will find at auction are made from these grapes. Then we will look at some other varietals that are quickly gaining in popularity.

The Noble Grapes

Learning about the six noble grapes will provide you with a solid foundation on which to build your wine knowledge.

It used to be taught that certain grapes were more important, or *noble*, than others. Cabernet Sauvignon, Pinot Noir, and Syrah are recognized as noble red varieties. Chardonnay, Sauvignon Blanc, and Riesling are the noble whites. All six noble varieties have "Old World" roots.

Cabernet Sauvignon is often considered the greatest of the red grapes. It is the backbone of many of the high-quality red wines from both Bordeaux and California. Harvested in almost every significant wine-producing region in the world, Cabernet Sauvignon is also a very easy grape to grow. In Tuscany, this grape is added to Sangiovese, the traditional red grape of Chianti, to make a new generation of Italian wines called Super Tuscan. In Australia, fermenting Cabernet Sauvignon and Shiraz together has created some of the continent's most exciting new wines. Lusty, bold, dark, and tannic when young, Cabernet Sauvignon is almost always blended with other red grapes to soften its edges and allow its dark fruit aromas to shine through. Its flavors consist of blackcurrant, cedar, cigar box, mint, and rich leather. (Turn to Chapter 14 for a discussion on wine flavors.)

Pinot Noir is the noble seductress. Rarely blended, as any other grape would obscure its subtlety, Pinot Noir produces the elusive red wines of Burgundy. Pinot Noir has been called the "Heartbreak Grape" because it is one of the most difficult grapes to grow. Its thin skin and tight, pine cone-shaped cluster make it susceptible to both rot and the beating sun. At its best, Pinot Noir delights with aromas and flavors that are incredibly complex and elusive. Flavor characteristics of Pinot Noir range from bright cherries and strawberries to plums and licorice.

Syrah is a wonderfully noble red grape. Not as widely planted as its two noble red cousins, Syrah's world-class achievements are found in wines from France's northern Rhône Valley as well as wines from Australia (where it is called Shiraz). Big and bold like Cabernet Sauvignon, Syrah has an incredibly deep black-fruit character, yet softens almost coyly on the finish. (Turn to page 204 for a discussion on the importance of a wine's finish.) Its flavors are black pepper, clove, blackberry, raspberry, and dark plum. Many describe a chocolaty finish to a fine Syrah. The greatest Syrah is Hermitage of the northern Rhône Valley. This wine is so desirable that almost every wine-growing region around the world plants Syrah vines, trying to produce its own version of this beautiful wine.

Chardonnay is the most famous of all white grapes. Chardonnay is grown easily and to great success all over the world. Sampled from the vine, Chardonnay is one of the blander-tasting grapes. The flavors in a glass of Chardonnay can range from the flinty, mineral quality of colder climate vineyards in Chablis to the lush and rich tropical-fruit tastes from Australia or California's Central Coast. It is the winemakers' choices that can coax the very best out of this noble grape. These choices can result in a wine that tastes either of citrus fruit, tropical fruit, green apple, or butter, or of cream, vanilla, or nuts.

Sauvignon Blanc is another versatile, noble white grape, but it is not as easily grown as Chardonnay. It has flavors of rich nuts, gooseberries, freshly cut grass, honey, clovers, and flowers. Sauvignon Blanc is widely known for its Californian varieties because the grapes used in these wines are advertised on the labels. In France, Sauvignon Blanc is often blended with Semillon, another white grape. Depending on the region, this makes either a dry white Bordeaux or the widely-known and completely noble sweet wine of Sauternes.

Riesling is a noble white grape that truly stands apart. It is known as the great white grape of Germany and has a highly desirable "fruity-acid" character. Within the juice of each grape are acids. When kept in balance with the sugars, tannins, and overall weight of a mouthful of wine, acidity is a welcome component. It acts as a preservative and is the key to longevity in a bottle of wine. As a result, Riseling has superb aging potential. It is made into both sweet and dry wines. Given the grape's great resistance to low temperatures, it can remain on the vine for a long time and develop a high level of sugars, which will produce a sweet wine. Alternately, when the grape's components—sugars, acids, and other proteins—are all in balance at harvest time, the winemaker can choose to pick the fruit earlier in the season, before the levels of sugar become very high. This would result in a dry wine with a lower alcohol content. Riesling recently fell out of favor when the wine-drinking population turned to heavyweight Chardonnay as its white wine of choice. Regardless, German Rieslings, with their flavors of minerals, petrol, raisin, cheese, honey, and tropical fruit, offer great pleasure as a wine drinker's palate becomes more sophisticated.

The Grape Big Picture: Other Important Grapes

While the above six grapes are considered the most popular, there are other wonderful grapes that also make many of the world's great wines. These grapes and the regions where they are most successfully *vinified*—converted into wine by fermentation—should be familiar to every serious wine drinker.

Red Grapes

❑ *Merlot:* A great grape of Bordeaux, Merlot is often blended to add soft, luscious juiciness to Cabernet Sauvignon. Château Pétrus, a highly prized wine from the Pomerol region of Bordeaux, is made primarily of Merlot.

❑ *Cabernet Franc:* Another great red grape of Bordeaux, this is the predominant grape of the great Château Cheval Blanc from the St. Emilion region of Bordeaux.

❑ *Petit Verdot and Malbec:* These are the other two blending grapes used to make the great red wines of Bordeaux. Red Bordeaux is made by blending any of the five varieties: Cabernet Sauvignon, Merlot, Cabernet Franc, Petit Verdot, and Malbec.

❑ *Nebbiolo:* Barolo and Barbaresco, the greatest wines from the northwest of Italy, are made of Nebbiolo. It has flavors of chocolate, cherries, and violets.

❑ *Sangiovese:* The single grape in Chianti, Italy's classic red wine from Tuscany. It has a primarily fruity taste of plums or cherries.

❑ *Tempranillo:* Spain's highest-quality red grape, Tempranillo has a distinct flavor of red berries. It is used in each of its most famous wine-producing regions.

❑ *Zinfandel:* This grape is most closely associated with big red wines from California. Although not native to the west coast of the United States, Zinfandel thrives as a varietal there. Many are delighted by its raspberry and cherry character.

White Grapes

❑ *Viognier:* A white grape native to the Rhône Valley, Viognier is now grown to popular demand in California and Australia. The best examples offer a perfume-like quality, often with an exotic fruit flavoring.

❑ *Gewürztraminer:* This is a spicy, flavorful grape from Alsace and Germany. It can be fermented to be dry or sweet. The sweet wines, Vendange Tardive and Sélection de Grains Nobles, are particularly famous.

❑ *Semillon:* It is usually mixed with Sauvignon Blanc to make the sweet wines of Sauternes and the dry white wines of Bordeaux. Semillon is also used for blending elsewhere.

❑ *Chenin Blanc:* At its best in the Loire Valley of France, Chenin Blanc's balance of fruit and acid makes a good bottle age indefinitely. With a huge range of seductive and pure flavors, Chenin Blanc can be made sweet, dry, and even sparkling to great success.

Identifying by Region

Wine is often identified by the place it was grown and produced. For example, a glass of sparkling wine can be only be called Champagne if it has been made in the Champagne region of France. A glass of Bordeaux is grown and made only in Bordeaux, France. Red Burgundy is a glass of Pinot Noir produced in Burgundy, France—and must not be confused with E. & J. Gallo's Hearty Burgundy, which is made in Modesto, California and contains no Pinot Noir. Let's look at several popular winemaking regions.

The Wines of France

The red wines of Bordeaux, France are considered to be among the finest red wines in the world. The large amount of fine red Bordeaux produced, its availability to collectors, and its longevity in bottle have made it the cornerstone of wine collecting and wine trading. In fact, from the auctions held in nineteenth-century London coffee houses to glamorous sales at modern-day New York's finest restaurants, red Bordeaux has made up the majority of wine bought and sold at auction. Red Bordeaux is made from a blend of grapes. The *blend*—the amount of each of the grapes—can change from vintage to vintage, but only these five grapes may be used: Cabernet Sauvignon, Merlot, Cabernet Franc, Petit Verdot, and Malbec. Bottles from Old World regions do not indicate the proportion of the blend. Instead, they name the wine-producing estate where the wine was made. In Bordeaux, these wine-producing estates are called *châteaux*.

Winemakers from the Old World must adhere to strict regulations when designing their labels. These two labels are from Bordeaux.

The Bordeaux winemaking region is divided into different geographical areas called *appellations*. Of these areas, it is most important to be familiar with St. Estephe, Pauillac, Margaux, St. Julien, Graves, and Sauternes. There are also other notable wineries in the regions of St. Emilion and Pomerol, which are located on the right side of the Dordogne River. These wineries are referred to as the *right bank châteaux*.

The red wines of Bordeaux are further identified by a ranking system that was developed in 1855, and is still used today. The *Classification of 1855* was introduced by Bordeaux wine brokers in an effort to equate quality to market price. The Classification of 1855 organizes wines into *growths*—five different levels of quality. The *first growths*—bottles from Châteaux Lafite, Latour, Mouton, Margaux, and Haut Brion—are among the world's most expensive and highly prized wines. Auction prices decrease as the wines appear further down the Classification of 1855. A *third* or *fourth growth*, for example, will be less expensive than a *first* or *second growth*.

Burgundy is the other most important wine-producing area in France. Its wines, however, have not appeared at auction in the same numbers as those of Bordeaux. The old, arguable theory is that the wines from this area are made of grapes—Pinot Noir and Chardonnay—that are not as long lived in the bottle as the five grapes of Bordeaux. Because a wine's condition is a bidder's primary concern, few traditional collectors would take the chance of buying Burgundy at auction. However, this is changing and some of Burgundy's finest wines now command top dollar. Wine drinkers, upon experiencing the magic of great Burgundy, have little choice but to turn to auction to collect rare Burgundian treasures.

The Rhône Valley is located to the south of Burgundy, and is increasing in importance as its wines grow in popularity as well as in value. The winemaking area of the Rhône is a long stretch, some 140 miles, and the red wines from the northern Rhône are vastly different from those produced in the south. Syrah is the strong and sturdy red grape of the northern Rhône, while Grenache, a softer, sweeter red grape, dominates the blends in the southern Rhône.

The Wines of Italy

Venturing beyond the many incredible wines of France's different regions, most wine lovers head straight to Italy, the wines of which continue to gain in popularity. The traditional red wine of Tuscany is Chianti, made from Sangiovese grapes, while the newer, exciting Super Tuscans are made from blending Sangiovese with Cabernet Sauvignon or other Bordeaux grapes. Barolo and Barbaresco from the Piedmont region in northwest Italy are the new darlings of wine auctions. They are each made from the Nebbiolo grape. These wines have been around for a long time. The renewed interest stems from the grape's rich blend of blackberry, prune, rose, chocolate, and tobacco qualities.

It is unnecessary to memorize the Classification of 1855 Bordeaux wines because auction catalogues are always provided in advance of the auction. You can reference the chart when you are researching the wines to be auctioned, and will discover that it will become increasingly familiar every time you use it.

The Wines of Portugal

"Port" refers to the northern Portuguese town of Oporto, which has important access to both the Atlantic Ocean and the Douro river. Port wines are made through the process of fortification. (Chapter 1 explained that fortification is the process of adding doses of brandy during fermentation.) This slug of alcohol kills off remaining yeasts, leaving the sugar to remain without converting further into alcohol and resulting in a sweet wine. Port has always enjoyed an important presence at wine auctions. It has an incredibly long life, so it is often possible to obtain very old vintages.

The Wines of the New World

Among the New World regions most important to the auction arena are the winemaking areas in California and Australia. Each of these New World wine countries are known for great success with a particular varietal: Cabernet Sauvignon in California, and Shiraz (or Syrah) in Australia. However, each of these countries also has tremendous success with other varietals, both red and white. It can be difficult to distinguish between an Australian Chardonnay and a California Chardonnay. Concentrate on tasting for and identifying the specific winery from which each glass is from and you may find it easier to pinpoint the wine's country of origin.

WINE BOTTLES

Blown-glass bottles became the standard container for wine by the end of the seventeenth century. There have been variations in shape and size, but the glass bottle and stopper have not been improved upon for the transportation, storage, and aging of fine wines. The internationally accepted standard wine bottle holds 750 milliliters. Its shape can vary depending on the wine and the region it is from, but the shape does not affect the wine and differs mainly because of tradition. A bottle of a different size, on the other hand, will have a direct effect on its contents and should be understood by each auction bidder.

Unlike wine labels from Old World regions, New World labels include the grape varietal used to make the wine.

Bottle Shape

Bottle shapes have evolved over time, but the three shapes seen most often today have been around since the beginning of the nineteenth century. They provide visual association with a particular wine-producing region. Today, some producers have digressed from these classic shapes and come up with their own. These three, however, are the ones most likely to appear at auction in great numbers.

The most common bottle shapes are the Bordeaux bottle *(left)*, the Burgundy bottle *(middle)*, and the Hoch bottle *(right)*.

The *Bordeaux bottle* is tall and cylindrical with strong, squarish shoulders. Cabernet, Merlot, and Sauvignon Blanc—grape varieties used with great frequency in the wines of Bordeaux—are usually found in these bottles.

The *Burgundy bottle* has gentle, sloping shoulders. It bottles both major Burgundian varietals, Chardonnay and Pinot Noir, even when produced in California or elsewhere around the world. Syrah is also sold in this shaped bottle. *Champagne bottles* are shaped like the Burgundy bottle, but made of much thicker glass to accommodate the pressure from the carbon dioxide gas during the second fermentation. The indentation on the bottom of almost all bottles—the *punt*—is present today largely due to tradition. On Champagne bottles, however, the punt serves to decrease the pressure on the bottle's bottom, without which the bottle might explode.

High-quality German white wines, particularly Riesling, are bottled in taller, more slender bottles. These are called *Rhine* or *Hoch bottles*.

These bottle shapes are used for most of the world's wines, so any brand creativity is usually found on the label. The difference in the shape and design of any bottle is dictated by both tradition and innovation, and has nothing to do with the quality of wine inside.

Bottle Size

The size of each bottle is important to the wine drinker and collector because of the effect it has on aging. The smaller the bottle, the quicker the wine inside will age. It is an ironic fact that oxygen is vital to life yet can also be an enemy to that which it sustains, such as wine or cheese. The oxygen trapped in the neck of every bottle brings about a wine's aging. The smaller the volume of wine inside a bottle, the greater the effect this oxygen will have on its different constituents, hastening maturity. This is why Bordeaux collectors, who store wine in their cellars for long periods of time, traditionally favor large-format bottles. The wine ages more slowly and can supply future generations with great drinking pleasure.

The current standard bottle size, as regulated by country law, is internationally accepted as 750 milliliters. There are a variety of different bottle sizes, both larger and smaller than this standard size, that are also utilized today. (See Table 2.1 for the names and sizes of different bottles.) In some cases, two different names are used for the same volume of wine; other times, the same name can refer to two different-sized bottles, depending on region of origin.

The names of the larger bottles originate from the Bible. Jeroboam was a king of Israel. Rehoboam was a son of King Solomon. Methuselah was the oldest man in the Bible. Salmanazar was a king of Assyria. Balthazar and Melchior were two of the three kings of the Magi. Nebuchadnezzar was a King of Babylon, best known for his Hanging Gardens, one of the seven wonders of the ancient world.

TABLE 2.1. NAMES AND VOLUMES OF DIFFERENT WINE BOTTLE SIZES		
Name (and region of origin, where necessary)	**Volume in Liters**	**Standard Bottle (750 ml) Equivalence**
Split	187.5 ml	One-quarter
Half Bottle	375 ml	Half
Bottle	750 ml	One
Magnum	1.5 l	Two
Marie-Jeanne (Burgundy)	2.25 l	Three
Double Magnum	3.0 l	Four
Jeroboam (Champagne and Burgundy)	3.0 l	Four
Jeroboam (Bordeaux)	4.5 l	Six
Rehoboam (Champagne and Burgundy)	4.5 l	Six
Imperial (Bordeaux)	6 l	Eight
Methuselah (Champagne and Burgundy)	6 l	Eight
Salmanazar	9 l	Twelve
Balthazar	12 l	Sixteen
Nebuchadnezzar	15 l	Twenty
Melchior	18 l	Twenty-four

Corks

Expensive wine bottles must always be stored on their sides to ensure that the corks are kept moist. If a cork dries out, it runs the risk of shrinking, which could lead to *wine seepage*—loss of product from the bottle.

Until recently, all wine bottle stoppers were made of natural cork. Harvested from trees in Spain and Portugal, cork stoppers came into use in the first half of the seventeenth century, soon after the introduction of glass wine bottles. Under ideal conditions, corks are produced free of bacteria and inserted into bottles kept at proper temperature and humidity.

Given the tendency of natural corks to shrink, their susceptibility to harbor wine-spoiling bacteria, and their ever-increasing production cost, alternatives were inevitable. Synthetic (plastic) corks, screw tops, and *crown caps*—fastenings found on beer bottles—have all been introduced to provide more reliable closure. Although nobody debates the effectiveness of corkless stoppers, traditionalists protest their use. A good, thorough closure on the bottle, however, is particularly important if the bottles are to be preserved in storage.

Starting a Wine Collection

With a little forethought and planning, the leap from wine drinker to wine collector can be an easy one. The most important feature of a brand-new wine collection is the provision of proper storage conditions (see page 41), but there are many considerations before this step.

The initial stages of wine collecting can take place in an armchair, accompanied by a delicious glass of wine. As a thoughtful collector, you need to identify your collecting goals. Some people collect entirely for drinking while others collect entirely for investment; some collectors do both. This decision needs to be made before any other issues can be addressed. For the pleasure-based consumer, a well-planned collection means there will always be a "just-right" bottle to open. For the investor, there will always be wine coming in to store and wine going out to sell. In both scenarios, though, every bottle added to your collection should reflect your objective.

Once your mission is defined, you must think about the budget and size of the collection. Establishing a budget and sticking to it reduces the chance of impulse purchases with costly results. Budgets can, of course, be revised after you gain experience and confidence in your wine-collecting abilities. The collection's projected size is extremely important for determining the proper storage environment. Can you use a *VinoTemp* or *EuroCave*—free standing temperature- and humidity-controlled units for home use—to stock your wine? Do you plan on building a walk-in cellar? Will the wine be kept at an outside, professional storage facility? These questions need to be addressed before cases of expensive wine start showing up at your front door. Projecting the size of the collection from the beginning will keep your focus intact until your tastes change.

During the initial stages of a wine collection, you should be reading, talking, and tasting. There are countless basic wine books to help the collector become more knowledgeable about this immense field. Publications such as Robert Parker's *The Wine Advocate* and *Wine Spectator* magazine are invaluable tools for learn-

WINE STORAGE

Proper storage is imperative for the well-being of your wines. Besides keeping your wine healthy, long-term storage, whether at home or at a professional facility, offers the ability to allow your wine to age. It will also allow you to observe the aging process—particularly if you buy in case quantities and have more than a single bottle to test over time. You will read about this aging process in detail, after first reading about wine-storage options for your home.

Keeping your wine at home provides the convenience of having a bottle on hand when an occasion arises.

Using a Cellar

Collecting wine involves a commitment to its proper storage. Depending on your personal goals, a nook in a coat closet that meets the following conditions can serve your wine as well as an elaborate, underground, walk-in wine cellar. You will want to

ing. Writers for wine newsletters and monthly magazines taste more wines than is possible for any collector with a day job. This is a great way to learn about the characteristics of certain wines and to explore wines that may appeal to your palate. Tasting wine alongside a professional critic's note can accelerate learning and experience. (You will read more about tasting wine in Chapter 14.) You should also talk to other collectors, to retailers, and on Internet bulletin boards. There is much to be learned from others and wine collectors tend to be very generous with their experiences.

So then, what to buy? Guided primarily by objective and budget, you can start accumulating a range of different wines. Depending on your focus, the range may be as broad as different wines from different areas of the wine-growing world, or as specific as different vintages of the same wine. Whichever direction the collection takes, it is best to establish a collection's breadth before concentrating on depth. (For more specific examples of wines with which to begin or expand your collection, turn to Chapter 12.)

At the beginning, accumulating wine in full-case quantities can serve investment collections well. For the collector/consumer, on the other hand, full cases tie up both cellar space and finances. Until the direction of the collection is firmly established—something that may take a lifetime—buying wine several bottles at a time is sufficient. You may wish to gather several friends and split a full case of wine.

One of the most rewarding aspects of wine collecting is the relationship buyers develop with various vendors. Whether you source bottles from a retailer, broker, or auctioneer, time spent nurturing these contacts almost always results in climbing further up the learning ladder. Few collections are amassed without a foundation of solid vendor-collector relationships.

Know what you have and know where it is. An accurate inventory of the collection is necessary to avoid senseless duplication and prevent any unnecessary gaps in the focus. An inventory can easily be kept in a notebook or on a personal computer. Several cellar management software and inventory programs are available for the high-tech collector. Any level of complication is obtainable, but the ultimate joy of owning a wine collection is the ability to pull out one of its treasures and pass it around, gently, before pulling out its cork.

consider a temperature-controlled cellar, though, if you plan on keeping quality wine to full maturity or for investment.

Ideally, wine should be kept between 50°F and 70°F. The cooler the wine is kept, the slower it will evolve, but temperatures above or below this range are not good for any wine. The most important aspect of temperature control, though, is stabilization. Any swing in temperature will cause the wine stress as it adjusts from one level to another.

A humid environment is necessary for the health of the cork—but too much humidity, such as in a dank, underground cellar, will wreak havoc on the labels (although the wine itself will not be damaged). Try to maintain around 70-percent humidity.

Darkness is necessary for the wine's health because light, particularly UV rays, can cause a bottle to age prematurely by reacting with the wine's proteins. It is also important that stored bottles be undisturbed by vibrations. Even a standard refrigerator's vibrations can be harmful. Lastly, the storage space should allow for fresh, circulating air.

All of these conditions—horizontal storage, temperature, humidity, darkness, being left undisturbed, and fresh air—are necessary to help guarantee the continued health of your wine. If your cellar meets all these conditions, there is no reason not to buy some quality wine for the purpose of drinking and aging.

Aging Wine

Well-to-do English collectors of the nineteenth and early to mid-twentieth centuries bought wine in large quantities, thinking nothing about keeping a bottle for years, even decades. These wines required years of bottle aging before they were ready to be enjoyed. Collectors kept records as to when a bottle from a certain case was sampled and at what stage it might be ready for regular consumption.

The notion of long-term aging no longer exists in the same way. A typical winemaker of today produces a wine that is delicious early on, able to be enjoyed in its youth. High-quality wines gain depth in character and complexity with age, but today's trends in consumption have resulted in wines that provide more instant gratification for the wine drinker.

The more robust (of strong character) the grape, the greater the advantage of aging in highlighting the complexity of the fruit. Cabernet Sauvignon, Nebbiolo, Syrah, and Tempranillo are generally all long-lived grapes that produce wines best drank at least five years after their release. These wines will not enter the market until two or three years after harvest. Softer red grapes, such as Merlot, Pinot Noir, and

Grenache, offer more character at an earlier age, but also grow magnificent with some bottle age. Their flavors develop and become more intense.

Many wine drinkers mistakenly believe that white wine is not meant to be aged at all. Indeed, most white wines are ready for drinking soon after arriving in the marketplace. Chardonnay, Chenin Blanc, and Riesling, however, are all very long-lived white grapes. The complexity of character developed with age of a white wine is pure magic. When the wine is high quality, it is sometimes a shame to open a bottle of Chardonnay or Riesling younger than five years old.

An easy, general way to consider whether to age a wine is to judge the bottle by its price. Any wine under $20 is probably meant to be opened and consumed right away. Bottles that cost between $20 and $50 can most likely use a year or two of aging before being opened. Bottles over $50 start to require careful consideration. When paying $50 to $150, most experienced drinkers prefer to wait several years before opening the bottle. With wine costing over $150, the aging process should last at least five years from the date of harvest. Exactly how long to wait depends on the type of grape and region. Local retailers of better-quality wines are able to offer experienced opinions on the ideal time to open any bottle. Also, do not be shy about contacting the winery, regardless of its location. Almost all top wineries, châteaux, and *domains*—wine-growing properties in Burgundy—have websites that will accept (and hopefully address) all questions. A winemaker will nearly always be flattered by your contact, because it means that you are interested enough to sample his wine to its best advantage.

> Many of today's wines are best drank shortly after their production and arrival in the market. The majority of wine purchased in the United States, for example, is bought by women and consumed within twenty-four hours.

WINE SERVING

When it is time to enjoy a bottle of wine, there are several considerations to keep in mind. Wine needs to be served at its proper temperature; the bottle needs to be opened; and the wine may need to be decanted. After the wine is poured, you will probably want to evaluate it before downing the glass. Then you will be ready to enjoy your wine with some food. This section will prepare you for all these aspects of wine serving, and includes suggestions on matching your glass with your food for the most palatable results. (Wine tastings will be discussed in Chapter 14.)

The Proper Temperature

I've had red wine served too warm. Flabby and bland, it felt and tasted like unset Jell-O solution. Red wines taste altogether fresher and more interesting when served with a slight chill on the bottle. Whites, on the other hand, don't really taste like anything, let alone tropical fruit, when they are served too cold—as is often the case at many restaurants, where they are served straight from a cooler and put into an ice bucket.

In past centuries, drafty Scottish castles and huge dining rooms of French châteaux provided the perfect serving temperature for wine. Unfortunately, the temperature in today's typical rooms, especially in homes with central heating, far exceeds the room temperatures of yesteryear. Be mindful of the temperature at which you serve wine.

The temperature of the bottle of wine is critical to the drinker's pleasure. Serving a wine either too warm or too cold will prevent its balance, complexity, and finesse from showing. Both red and white wines are best served at cellar temperature (50°F to 70°F) rather than room temperature (68°F to 72°F). Once served, the wine will gradually warm up to room temperature.

If you have a wine-cooling unit or a purpose-built wine cellar, serving the wine straight out of the lower-temperature environment is ideal. If you don't have temperature-controlled wine storage, chill the wine in an ice bucket. The bucket should be two-thirds full of half ice and half water, and the bottle should be left to chill for twenty to thirty minutes. If time is a factor, rock salt can be used to quicken the process.

For those without temperature-controlled storage, an easy rule of thumb to get the temperature right is the 20/20 rule:

- Put red wines into the fridge twenty minutes before serving.

- Take white wine out of the fridge twenty minutes before serving.

Opening a Bottle

With a little practice, it is fairly easy to open a bottle of wine. There is a variety of corkscrews in different price ranges. Find one that works well for you and try to hold on to it. Older corks that crumble offer the most difficult challenge. Even wine professionals have to fudge their way through that situation. If a cork falls into the bottle when you are attempting to open it, so be it. Let the cork bob up and down while you serve the wine.

When opening Champagne or any other sparkling wine, be careful to point the bottle away from yourself and all guests.

To Breathe or Not to Breathe

Opening a bottle some time before serving allows a bottle's contents to mix with oxygen. This process, called allowing the wine to *breathe,* is an attempt to quickly develop its true flavors. The wine relaxes, and the complexity of flavors develop.

Some wines benefit from this aeration while others do not. Most white wines do not need to breathe. Most young red wines (less than five years old) of average quality also do not need to breathe. Older red wine, on the other hand, may or may not benefit from standing open for an hour or so. In this case, a simple taste test should answer the question. Determine if the flavor is tannic (astringent or bitter) or closed (underdeveloped and not yet revealing its potential character). If either tannic or closed, you should probably breathe the wine for at least an hour.

Leaving a bottle open on the counter for a few minutes before serving, however, does little good. There is such a small surface area exposed to air that merely opening a bottle to "let it breathe" offers little advantage. Instead, transfer the wine to a container with a larger opening. Many experienced wine drinkers use a decanter to both *decant*—separate sediment from the wine before serving—and allow the wine to breathe. Frequent taste tests determine how long to allow the wine to breathe. The wine will begin to taste smoother and fruitier as the flavors become more complex. With *really* old red wine that needs to be decanted, the assault on the wine from bottle to decanter or glass is usually enough for a good dose of air to wake it up after years of slumber in the bottle.

Decanting is necessary only with certain wines. Usually, wines that throw sediment are middle-aged and older reds. If you see that a wine has thrown sediment, it is best to address the issue a day or two before serving. Stand the corked bottle upright for a day to let the sediment settle on the bottle's bottom. Then, when ready to serve, pour the wine slowly and gently into a decanter, leaving the sediment behind in the bottle. It certainly is more pleasant to be poured a glass of wine free of any particles, although nothing in sediment would harm you.

Not all red wines will throw sediment, and not all should be decanted. In fact, Madame Bize Lalou Leroy, producer of some of Burgundy's finest, most elusive reds, does not allow her wines to be decanted at all. Many Burgundy producers have followed suit. Madame Leroy does not want her precious juice to be so forcefully hit with all that air after it finally regains its composure from the guy with the corkscrew breaking and entering.

On the other hand, this assault of air is wonderful for top-quality younger wines. The quick mix of air and wine when poured from a bottle into a decanter works like a slap on a newborn's bottom. Many experienced drinkers will pour the decanted young wine back into its bottle for serving. This way the wine really gets sloshed around, in the hopes of softening it just a bit before drinking.

Decanters are extremely useful for serving from large-format bottles. It is fun to have guests stand around for the opening of a large bottle, but pouring small glasses from such a big bottle challenges the best *sommeliers*—restaurant wine stewards. Emptying a large bottle of wine into several decanters makes it much easier to serve. Be careful to know which wine is in which decanter when several different bottles have been opened!

The Proper Glasses

Wine tastes better when drunk out of the proper stemware—stem being the operative word. Holding a glass by its stem prevents body heat from affecting the temperature of the glass's contents.

You can spend a small fortune on fancy, specialized wine glasses, but a standard-shaped, all-purpose wine glass will suffice. The object is to have the wine in a deep bowl that curves inward at the top. This allows even the sloppiest swirlers to keep the wine in his glass. In addition to keeping the wine in the glass, the deep bowl contains the wine's aromas in a concentrated area, making it easier for the wine drinker to analyze or simply enjoy.

Evaluating Wine

Wine can be judged by appearance, smell, and taste. After pouring, first study its appearance. It helps to hold the glass up to something white, while tipping the glass away from you. A glass of wine should look inviting as soon as it is poured into a glass. A beautiful color should hopefully indicate a beautifully made wine.

After examing how the wine looks, swirl it around in the glass. This is when having that inward curve comes in handy. If you have trouble and spill the wine, it helps if you hold the glass by the stem and swirl the wine while keeping the foot of the glass on a flat surface, such as a table. Swirling the wine has the same purpose as allowing the wine to breathe: it helps to oxygenate the wine, releasing bottled-up aromas and flavors which are then contained (to a degree) in the inward curve of the glass.

The aroma will be different depending on the grapes used in its production, but generally, it should smell fresh and clean. Certain bad odors indicate certain bad things—the smell of wet cardboard, for example, often means the cork has become moldy—but a general rule of thumb is that if the wine smells "off" or particularly unpleasant, it is probably bad.

You can learn a lot about a wine from its taste. In initial taste, we look for sweetness, acidity, alcohol, and tannins in the wine. Ideally, most great wines will have *balance*—these four features will be harmonious and even with each other, so none will stand out. Of course you also want to note if the wine tastes good. That will be a subjective observation. A wine's aftertaste, or *finish,* is also important. Some determine the quality of a wine based on how long the finish remains after the wine has been swallowed.

Matching Wine with Dinner

Many winemakers feel that wine is made primarily to be enjoyed with food; no intense swirling and sniffing for them. Entire books are available dealing with the subject of pairing wine with food. *Wine with Food,* by Joanna Simon, and *Red Wine with Fish: The New Art of Matching Wine with Food,* by David Rosengarten and Josh Wesson, are two excellent books on this subject. All begin and end with this basic message: Drink and eat in any combination that tastes good to you.

There are, however, certain combinations that work naturally together. They can be found by considering certain characteristics: flavor intensity, weight, acidity, salt, tannins, and sweetness. Wine should have similar characteristics to the food with which it is being eaten. The better balanced the wine is, the better the chance of enjoying the meal. The "old" rule of red wine with red meat and white wine with fish or white meat has great merit when two things are taken into consideration: the *fruitiness*—the intensity of the flavor—and the weight of the wine.

For a traditional "meat and potatoes" meal, big juicy reds such as Cabernet Sauvignon and Zinfandel work the best with full-flavored grilled meats. As Julia Child taught us, flavor often means fat. The more fatty the cut or taste of meat, the bigger and bolder the wine should be. On the other hand, a lean or delicate cut of meat, such as lamb or pork loin, has a less intense flavor, and would be overpowered by a big red of Cabernet Sauvignon or Zinfandel. Here, a lighter red, like Pinot Noir, would be a better match.

Montrachet, the most famous Chardonnay in the world, has often been paired with certain cuts of lighter red meats. The weight of the Montrachet not only stands up to the weight of the meat, but the wine's richness greatly compliments the more subtle meat flavors. Keep in mind, however, that this pairing only works with Chardonnay that is barrel fermented and has a heavier weight.

Today's kitchens are often home to sophisticated experimentation. There are many individual flavors being combined in the food. In this country, we enjoy Cal-Ital, Tex-Mex, Chino-Latino, and Asian Fusion, to name a few. From sushi to vegetable stir fry, there is one wine to cover most of the new cuisine: Riesling. Medium in flavor intensity, medium in body weight, a nice balance of acids and fruit character, and low in alcohol, Riesling can accompany almost any lighter meal, despite the combination of flavors. For the heavier meal with which a red wine is more appropriate, Cabernet Franc will offer a good match. For meals that are heavier still, drink Sangiovese. Consider these three varietals—Riesling, Cabernet Franc, and Sangiovese—your baseline wines for modern cuisine.

Finally, the order in which to serve the wine at a meal during which many wines will be drunk can be extremely important. White wines should be served before red wines, lighter wines before heavier wines, old before young, and dry before sweet. This gives the palate a chance to enjoy and prepare for the next glass.

CONCLUSION

The study of wine can take a lifetime, and is complicated by the fact that each year brings a new harvest with its own complexities. However, you should now feel ready to begin or continue tasting wines with confidence. You now understand a good deal about differentiating between wines, be it by the general type of wine, the grape from which it was produced, or the region it came from. In the following chapter, we will combine this information on wines with new knowledge on the basics of auctions. These two chapters will supply you with the foundation to succeed at any wine auction.

3

Introduction to Auctions

N ow you understand wine fundamentals, an intregal key to your success at wine auctions. Because achieving your goals at these events will rely as much on your understanding of the auction process as on your knowledge of wine, it is time to look at the auction process in detail. This chapter will provide an overview of wine auctions and explore their pros and cons. It will then discuss a variety of different auction styles and the various ways wine bottles can be organized for sale.

AN AUCTION OVERVIEW

Live modern-day wine auctions are structured on foundations like those of the traditional London auctions. *Consignors*—the sellers—contact the auction house to negotiate selling a collection, either whole or in parts. The auction house estimates the value of the wine and offers the consignor a proposal for its sale. With a few minor exceptions, sales are done on a *consignment basis*—the auction house receives a commission, or a percentage of the sales price, as compensation. If the consignor agrees to the proposal's terms, his wine is shipped to the auction company's temperature-controlled warehouse. Then the auction house inventories the wine, assesses the condition of each bottle, assembles the consignment into auction lots, and creates the auction catalogue.

The auction catalogue is usually printed and distributed to potential buyers two weeks before the auction. The auction company promotes the upcoming event via advertising or special mailings and email blasts. *Absentee bids*—those made in advance by buyers who cannot attend the event—are recorded. On auction day, live bidders are welcomed into the salesroom before the *auctioneer*—the conductor of the sale—begins the auction. (See page 62 to read about the auctioneer's duties.) Each successful bidder is invoiced for his purchases at the close of the sale. The money is processed through the auction company's accounting system before the consignor is paid and the wine is released to the buyer. The seller usually receives payment for the wine approximately one month after the auction. An average of four months pass between the time the agreement is struck with the auction house and the time the consignor is paid.

The majority of buyers and sellers are individual private collectors. Wineries and restaurants, particularly those that offer rare and expensive bottles on their lists, also participate as both buyers and sellers. Restaurants make particularly excellent consignors when the business is closing and the wine cellar needs to be divested.

For those who love acquiring wine, wine auctions are often an exciting option. There are, however, both positive and negative aspects to purchasing wine through the auction process.

BUYING AND SELLING WINE AT AUCTION

Why buy wine at auction? Almost every large town in America has at least one specialty wine shop. Many grocery stores also carry fine wine. Some areas of the country are dotted with wineries that sell their own products. Yet there are several compelling reasons to enter the auction scene as either buyer or seller.

The Benefits

The single most dominating reason to shop at an auction is to acquire wines that are not available elsewhere because they are very old or very rare. These are the wines that keep bidders coming back. When a wine has long since vanished from the retailers' shelves and restaurateurs' lists, the auction arena offers the best chance of its reappearance.

An auctioneer loves the bidder who plans to win at any price, so long as there is an *under-bidder*—any bidder competing for a collection until it is sold to the winner—prodding him on.

Another advantage to auction is that buyers often find these choice wines in quantities larger than a single bottle. Every now and then a retailer may have a single bottle of an older, desirable wine, but if found at auction, chances are good that several bottles or even full cases of the wine will be available.

Buying wine at auction also allows the successful bidder to set the price. After the auctioneer opens the bidding on a lot, the bidder controls what he pays. This takes discipline. Most likely, a bidder is competing against someone with similar goals. The winner will be either the bidder whose predetermined price is higher than his competitor's limit, or the bidder who plans to win the wine at any price. While most experienced auction buyers have stories of great wines bought at great prices, many auction novices can tell you about overpaying for a wine.

For some collectors, the most appealing aspect of the auction process is the effort they themselves invest in the transaction. An auction buyer needs to obtain a catalogue before the sale to study the lots. He has to set his highest bid price for each lot. He must determine whether to bid by attending the auction in person or by *proxy*—

having a substitute stand in for an absent bidder. For many collectors, this time-consuming process is a satisfying part of the game.

Sellers, on the other hand, may choose auctions as an avenue for business for precisely the opposite reason. They often find it appealing to have somebody else do the work. Identifying and advertising the wine for sale, setting a price, finding a buyer, and delivering the wine to the buyer can take a large amount of time and patience—often more than the collector is willing to spend. The wine may also be sold for higher than expected when driven by bidder interest and competition, and the seller does not have to personally oversee the negotiations. Lastly, an auction house can move a large quantity of wine at a single event whereas an independent seller may have to search for several buyers.

Wine auctions are advantageous for these reasons, but they are not without drawbacks. Potential buyers and sellers have to weigh their options when deciding to participate.

The Limitations

The foremost downside of buying at auction is the chance taken with the quality of wine in the bottle. There is little recourse the buyer can take when a bottle of wine is bad. Unlike a retailer or dealer who can offer an exchange or credit, auction houses act as agents and do not have the opportunity to replace a bad bottle. Auction houses explicitly outline this in the conditions of sale in each catalogue and take no responsibility regarding the wine's quality. They do, however, take great care in predicting each bottle's condition, because the quality of the wine they sell reflects upon their reputations. The best advice offered to any auction buyer is "Buyer Beware."

Many buyers are taken aback upon discovering that only a few auction houses accept credit cards as payment, due to surcharges that subtract from the company's profits. For them, the less convenient need for a check or wire transfer is another drawback of the process.

All auction houses accept checks, wire transfers, and, of course, cash.

There is no immediacy of product delivery after an auction purchase. The auction ends, the buyer is invoiced, and the payment is received and processed by the auction house, all before shipping can be arranged and the wines released. It may be several weeks before the buyer receives his wine. On top of that, older wine should be allowed to sit after shipping because of *bottle shock*. Various components in wine can become temporarily altered after travel, and need time to rest and regroup to regain flavor. Because of the delays, a collector who needs a specific bottle for an upcoming date may be better off purchasing his wine elsewhere.

Other would-be bidders simply do not have the time to invest in the auction procedure. The process, so inviting to some, is seen as merely time consuming by others.

Wine collectors who choose not to participate in auctions frequently buy their fine and rare wine through specialized dealers and brokers. Brokers do the work of securing the wine, often from auction, and in turn charge for their time and effort.

Without ambition and a desire to win, you will have only a limited chance to succeed at an auction.

While sellers do not necessarily need to devote the time and energy needed by buyers, there are disadvantages. Perhaps the wine doesn't sell for as much as the seller had hoped or considers the wine to be worth. By setting a *reserve price*, the consignor can choose not to sell if the bidding does not reach his confidential, minimum selling price. However, he will still be responsible for paying the transactional costs attached to the sale.

The Benefits Outweigh the Limitations

The undeniable fact is that some of the world's greatest wines can be found only at auction. Usually, many trophies in well-rounded collections were bought at these sales. The patience and effort required are richly rewarded. Auction regulars know this and keep coming back for more. You are going to read about different auction styles so that you, too, will be prepared to win the bottles you've been eyeing.

TYPES OF AUCTIONS

Most likely, you have seen an auction—either in person or on television. Perhaps, though, you had questions about the fast-paced action. Auctions can be confusing, particularly since there are many different ways for them to be conducted. Fear not. The auction process can actually be quite easy to understand when broken into basics.

Ascending-Bid Auctions

Most auctions use the *ascending-bid* technique. When using this method, each bid must be higher than the one previous to it. The last bid establishes the *hammer price*—the amount of the winning bid. There are several different styles of ascending-bid auctions.

English-Style Auctions

There are two methods that employ both the ascending-bid technique and an auctioneer: the English-style auction and the American-style auction. For both, bidding on a lot is opened at a predetermined dollar amount, and buyers bid by raising a hand or a *paddle*—usually a numbered card. After the first bid, each consecutive bid is higher by a standard increment. Traditionally, each bid represents an approximately 10-percent increase from the previous bid, but the auctioneer uses his own discretion to decide how large each bid step should be. (See Table 3.1 for a list of bidding increments that are often used by auctioneers.)

TABLE 3.1. COMMON BIDDING INCREMENTS	
Starting Bid	**Amount Each Bid is Likely to Increase**
$100–$500	$25
$500–$1,000	$50
$1,000–$2,000	$100
$2,000–$5,000	$250
$5,000–$10,000	$500 or $1,000
$10,000–$20,000	$1,000
$20,000–$50,000	$2,000 or $2,500
$50,000–$100,000	$5,000 or $10,000

In the *English-style auction*, the auctioneer *calls a dollar amount in response to a paddle raise*. Each additional paddle raise is recognized by an incrementally higher price call. The auctioneer can raise the bidding only as quickly as the audience members raise their paddles.

American-Style Auctions

In the often-utilized *American-style auction*, the auctioneer calls out a dollar amount in a singsong chant. In these auctions, *the paddle is raised to meet the call* of the auctioneer. When the auctioneer's plea is met, he immediately starts inviting the next higher price. This auctioneer speaks quickly; he is always calling for the next number. Bidding concludes when there are no more raises. The last to bid wins the lot.

Silent Auctions

The English and American styles of auctioneering rely on the active participation and supervision of an auctioneer, but an auction sale of ascending bids may also be done silently. In these *silent auctions*, an item is displayed directly behind a lined bid sheet. The first person interested in the lot writes down his name and the starting bid, which can be any amount. The next interested bidder adds his name to the list below that of the previous bidder, along with the increased price that he is willing to pay. The bids do not necessarily increase by any specific amount. The final moment of excitement is dictated by a predetermined closing time. At this time, the sheets are collected. The bidder with the last name and highest price on the list is the winner. This type of auction is often utilized at charity events.

A silent auction is called such because bids are written down on paper rather than called out loud. Yet the action can become quite noisy as the closing time nears if two or more bidders desperately want the same lot.

Sale-by-Candle Auctions

A traditional auction method used in early European auctions was *sale by candle*. These auctions relied on an element of random chance to reveal the winning bidder. An inch or so of candle was lit. While it burned, prospective buyers shouted out their ascending bids. The last bid heard by the auctioneer as the candle naturally extinguished itself was the winning bid. There are many records of auction sales by candle in England during the seventeenth century. Uniquely, France's great Hospices de Beaune charity auction is conducted by candle to this day.

Descending-Bid Auctions

A *descending-bid* auction is commonly referred to as a Dutch auction. Here, the auctioneer starts with a price well above the perceived value of the lot. The auctioneer then announces progressively lower sums until a bidder accepts the stated price. In Dutch auctions, bidders must be willing to pay their top price or risk losing the lot.

The methodology of Dutch-style auctions versus ascending-bid auctions presents an interesting business choice. Will bidders pay more in a Dutch auction, fearful that someone else will bid first, or will they pay more in an ascending bid auction, with the spirit of competition goading them on?

TYPES OF LOTS

Auction companies typically stick to one auction method, but the preparation stage of an auction involves other decisions. For example, wines must be grouped together for sale. First and foremost, this is done to maximize profits.

An original cardboard carton *(oc)*.

Most wine auctions are comprised of property from many different consignors. On average, there are about thirty consignors for a sale of 2,000 lots. A *lot*—each unit of wine to be sold—can consist of any amount of wine, from a single bottle to an entire collection. One consignor may be selling several hundred lots while another may be selling only a small handful. Every so often, one consignor offers enough wine to fill an entire sale. The market responds well to the excitement of seeing so much wine come from a single source.

The auction team constructs lots to give the wine broad market appeal. Several factors are considered when building each lot: current market trends, past auction results, and anticipated bidder interest. Auction attendees should be familiar with the following types of lots.

Case Lots

The traditional wine-auction lot is a *case lot* of twelve 750-milliliter bottles. The 750-milliliter bottle is the standard bottle size, and the dozen-bottle case is the standard unit of trade. However, bottles of other sizes are packaged in different quantities, and case lots reflect this. A standard case or case lot can contain twenty-four half bottles (375-milliliter bottles), six magnums (1.5-liter bottles), three double magnums (3-liter bottles), or one imperial bottle (6-liter bottle).

An original wooden case *(owc)*.

The case is usually sold in its packaged condition, either an original wooden case *(owc)* or original cardboard carton *(oc)*. This is stated in the auction catalogue. If there is no mention that a lot is offered in its original case, the bottles may have come from different cases. Collectors pay a premium for wine sold in its original packaging. The full-case quantity will be indicated by the mention of "twelve bottles," "per dozen," or "per doz." When the bottles in question are of a different size, most auction companies will state the bottle size followed by the quantity in paranthesis. For example, three double magnums will be stated as either "3L (3)" or "double magnum (3)" in the catalogue. It is assumed that the reader will realize that this is a full case lot.

Single-Bottle Lots

A bottle of wine that is particularly valuable or rare is often offered as a *single-bottle lot*. For example, an eighteenth- or nineteenth-century first growth Bordeaux is, more likely than not, sold on its own. In this case, both rarity and value factor into the decision to sell the bottle individually.

Market conditions and potential bidder interest drive the decision to offer a single-bottle lot. In 2004, for example, a collector decided to part with his 1996 First Growth Imperial (6 liter) collection of Château Margaux, Château Mouton, Château Lafite, Château Latour, and Château Haut Brion. Collectors pay a premium for large-format bottles because they are rare, with only a limited number produced each vintage (the yield from a vineyard over one season). Collectors also pay a premium for wine from first growth châteaux. (You read in Chapter 2 that the term "first growth" refers to the tier that produces the highest-quality wines of the five levels of Bordeaux châteaux identified in the Classification of 1855.) On top of that, 1996 is a collectible vintage. Should the collection have been sold as one single lot or with each bottle offered individually? Table 3.2 displays the estimated price of each bottle.

TABLE 3.2. VALUE OF FIRST GROWTH IMPERIAL COLLECTION	
Wine	**Pre-Sale Estimated Price**
1996 Margaux	$1,200–$1,500
1996 Mouton	$1,100–$1,500
1996 Lafite	$1,100–$1,500
1996 Latour	$1,200–$1,600
1996 Haut Brion	$900–$1,200

Mixed lots will often be your best bet, because they offer the opportunity for greater tasting experience without the financial commitment of buying too many bottles. You can always trade away the bottles that don't interest you. Of course, there is always the chance that one of the "extra bottles" will end up as your new favorite wine.

Using these estimates, selling the entire collection as a single lot would warrant a value of $5,500 to $7,300, a high price that might reduce the number of interested bidders. But if sold individually, anyone wanting to buy all five bottles would still have the opportunity to do so by bidding on each separately. Decisions like this depend upon many factors, including consignor preference. The objective remains getting the highest price for the wine.

What happened with these bottles? The auction house offered each bottle separately, deciding that the individual estimated prices were reasonable enough to attract bidder attention and competition. They were all sold to the same collector who paid a total of $11,400. We will never know what would have happened if all bottles had been offered as one lot. We do know that sold individually, the bottles fetched quite a bit more than their estimated total value.

Group Lots

Since many sellers are also consumers, they often offer odd quantities of various wines, rather than full cases. Auction houses cannot afford to offer lower-valued bottles individually because high operational costs require a minimum price per lot. For this reason, they often form *group lots* or *mixed lots* of unrelated wines.

Group lots are organized to appeal to a broad market. Yet some buyers will not bid if they want only certain bottles in the group, causing competition and prices to fall. This can make group lots a great value for the savvy bidder. There are several popular types of group lots.

Vertical Collections

Vertical collections are wines from the same producer, but different vintages. Some vintages can be missing, but a consecutive lineup is preferred. Collectors of specific wines are most interested in verticals. These lots present the opportunity to experience a winemaker's style changes through the years. The inset on page 57 illustrates how a catalogue entry for a vertical collection may appear.

A Vertical Collection

This is an example of an auction catalogue entry for a vertical collection. (You will learn more about reading a catalogue in Chapter 5.) As you can see, a vertical collection consists of bottles of different vintages from the same producer. Notice that while the collection includes most years between 1964 and 1985, there are several missing vintages. Next to each vintage year is a short description of the corresponding bottle's condition, including the level of wine in the bottle. The abbreviations describe the levels according to the Ullage Chart, which is explained on page 87. The estimated price of the entire lot is found at the end of the catalogue entry.

Château Mouton Rothschild

Pauillac, 1er cru classe

•1964	us	•1972	ts
•1965	ms, corroded capsule, slightly stained label	•1973	ts
•1966	us	•1974	ts, corroded capsule
•1967	vts	•1976	ts, stained label
•1968	vts, soiled label	•1977	bn
•1969	vts	•1979	vts
•1970	bn	•1983	into neck
•1971	vts	•1985	into neck

Above 16 bottles $3000–4000

Horizontal Collections

A *horizontal collection* is comprised of wines from different producers and the same vintage. The most sought-after horizontals are of wines from the same region and *varietal*—type of grape. These lots offer the opportunity to taste different wine-making styles, techniques, and perhaps philosophies from any given area. The inset below provides an example of a horizontal lot.

A Horizontal Collection

The following describes a horizontal lot of different red Burgundy. The bottles are all of the same vintage, but there are several producers named. The number in parenthesis indicates how many of each corresponding wine is being sold in the lot. The total estimated value for the lot is included at the end of the entry.

Clos Vougeot 1989	(4)
Nuits Saint George, Les Boudots 1989	(2)
Richbourg 1989	(5)
Vosne Romanee 1989	(1)
Above 12 bottles	$1800–2400

A Mixed Lot

Here is an example of a catalogue entry for a mixed lot of Napa Valley Cabernet Sauvignon. These wines were grouped together because they share the same varietal and are from the same region. The number of bottles for each wine offered in the lot is in parenthesis, and the total estimated value for the lot is at the end of the entry.

Sterling Vineyards Cabernet Sauvignon 1991	(4)
Diamond Creek Volcanic Hill Cabernet Sauvignon 1989	(3)
Diamond Creek Gravelly Meadow Cabernet Sauvignon 1990	(2)
Stag's Leap Fay Vineyard Cabernet Sauvignon 1997	(2)
Clos Du Val Cabernet Sauvignon 1994	(5)
Above 16 bottles	$500–700

Other Group Lots

A creative auction specialist will use other commonalities to assemble group lots. Wines of different vintages can be offered together according to varietal, region, appellation, or vineyard. The inset above shows an example of a mixed lot, arranged because all the bottles contain Napa Valley Cabernet Sauvignon.

Parcel Lots

When a collector consigns multiple cases of the same wine, the bottles can be sold in *parcel lots*. A parcel lot is comprised of identical cases of wine that are offered as separate lots, but the winner of the first lot is offered the remaining lots at the same price before they are separately auctioned off to the other bidders.

For example, a collector is selling five cases of 1987 Robert Mondavi Reserve Cabernet Sauvignon. Each of the separate case lots contains this wine in identical condition. The catalogue indicates that the wine is being offered as a parcel. The winner of the first lot can take any number of the remaining cases at the price for which he won the first lot. If the bidder wants all five cases, the auctioneer announces that the bidder has taken the parcel. If he wants only the first case, the auctioneer opens the bidding on the second case. Then, the winning bidder of this case has the option to take any of the remaining cases. This continues until the entire parcel is sold.

There is no sure-fire way to bid for a parcel lot. If a bidder does not act on the first lot, he runs the risk of losing the entire parcel to the first winner. Yet fear of this drives the price of the first lot up. If the entire lot is not taken, subsequent lots are usually less expensive. A bidder has to decide if waiting for a better price is worth the risk of losing the wine. The winner of the first lot can also use the falling costs to his advantage. If the next lot is going for significantly less, he can attempt to win at a lower bid and average his cost. Each parcel lot can play out differently. There is skill involved but also luck, and the only guarantee to getting any of the bottles is to win the first lot.

Super Lots

Sometimes an auction house receives an unusual consignment and has to decide how to best present it to the bidders. A *super lot* refers to a very large and expensive grouping of wine. A super lot can have a big impact on pre-auction publicity, and will no doubt generate excitement at the event. The following example of a super lot held, for a time, the record as the world's most expensive lot.

In 1997, a seller offered fifty cases of 1982 Mouton—the Gold Standard of auction wine—to Zachys/Christie's for consignment. Cases of 1982 Mouton were being sold that year for between $5,000 and $6,000. The auction house realized that it had to offer the cases without diluting the wine's impact on the market.

The company could have held the fifty cases in the warehouse and offered only a small handful at each auction. The rest would be sold over the course of eighteen months. The market was strong and the price per case would most likely increase with each successive auction. However, the consignor did not want to wait for his money, so the auction team had to be creative. It was a bold move to consider offering all the cases at one time. Bolder still was putting a high premium (or selling it above its regular value because it is in scarce supply) on this super lot. The market was never stronger and wine auctions never more popular, so the auction house and the consignor gave it a try. To gauge interest, the Zachys/Christie's team contacted several bidders who they thought might be interested in the lot. The bidders were indeed excited and came to the sale ready for serious bidding. Against a pre-sale estimate of $350,000 to $420,000, the winning bidder bought the lot for $420,500 including the 15-percent *buyer's premium*—the commission paid by the buyer to the auction house for his purchase.

The same super lot reappeared at a Sotheby's auction in New York on November 18, 2006. The price this time was an astonishing $1,051,600 (with buyer's premium)—the new world record of a single lot sold at auction.

CONCLUSION

Even the novice collector knows that a wine auction involves a catalogue, an auctioneer, and a roomful of bidders. But, as you have learned, enjoying and making good use of a wine auction involves a greater understanding of the different forms these sales can take, as well as the various ways that wines can be grouped for sale. These elements can affect the price ultimately paid by the buyer and received by the seller for the wine.

In the next chapter, you will be introduced to the different people involved in wine auctions. This will bring you one step closer to entering the bidding battle and emerging with a great wine, or offering a profitable lot and getting as much as you can from the sale of your wine.

4

The People to Know

There are many people involved with each auction. From the auction bosses to the warehouse workers, everyone involved has to be sure of his role and perform it well for the auction to run smoothly.

There are people involved besides those who engineer the auction. A number of people affect the auction prices. The words of a wine critic can have great impact on general interest in a lot, while wine writers help their readers bid with confidence and wisdom. Critics and writers, along with publications dedicated to wine, can be quite influential on auction day.

To truly understand the energy and dynamics of an auction, you need to be familiar with all the players involved. These are the people who are going to help you make the most out of your wine-auction experience—the people that you will learn to utilize to your best advantage.

AT THE FOREFRONT OF AN AUCTION

Of the many people involved in an auction, those with the most direct influence over the event are the boss, the auctioneer, and the specialists. These people are also the most likely to appear before you at some point during your auction venture.

The Boss

Regardless of an auction company's size, there is one person who is ultimately responsible for each event. Titles vary between auction houses, and this person may or may not be named in the catalogue. The final authority on all matters, the boss can override decisions made by any other auction-team member.

During the standard course of business at some auction companies, many consignors and bidders never meet this individual. Other houses are organized so that the senior authority participates in the company's daily operations. It is important to find out how an auction house is structured and who this senior person is. Because he will likely have the final say on any financial negotiations, having him on your side can offer you a leg up.

The Auctioneer

The auctioneer is at the forefront of the entire auction production. As ringmaster of the grand event, the auctioneer has simultaneous responsibilities to the consignor,

the bidder, and the boss. An auctioneer strives to obtain the highest possible price for each lot because of his responsibilities to the consignor and because auction house revenue is usually commission based. On a more personal level, an auctioneer's measure of his own success is directly related to asking for and receiving "just one more bid."

It is not imperative for the auctioneer to know the details of any given consignment, but better auctioneers find out as much as they can about what and for whom they are selling before they step into the *rostrum*—the podium behind which the auctioneer stands and upon which he places his paperwork and bangs his gavel. Pre-sale conversations with the specialists, although not vital to the auction process, allow the auctioneer to become familiar with

An auctioneer's role off the podium varies between auction houses. Some auctioneers take a full-time, active role in the operation of the auction department. Others work on a contractual basis, hired solely to wield the gavel at a single event.

the consignments in order to more thoroughly portray each lot. (The role of the specialist is explained on page 64.)

The auctioneer should be aware of the consignor's goals for selling his wine as well as whether or not the consignor has agreed to grant him discretion with regard to the *reserve price*—the confidential minimum selling price set by the auction house and the consignor. Does the seller wish for all his wine to be sold, or would he be happy to take back any lots that fail to reach the reserve prices? When the seller agrees to grant *auctioneer's discretion*, he is giving the auctioneer permission to make these decisions as he sees fit. For example, if a consignor's wines are all selling at the top range of their estimates, the auctioneer may allow a lesser wine that did not get many absentee bids to sell below its reserve price. (You will read about the absentee bidding process on page 110.) Similarly, the auctioneer could choose to return a particularly desirable wine to the seller if it does not meet its minimum price. A good auctioneer feels comfortable making these calls because he is prepared for the sale.

The style by which to conduct a sale is completely the auctioneer's decision

The Auctioneer and His Book

The auctioneer juggles many responsibilities. His *auctioneer's book* keeps him organized. This version of the catalogue is prepared prior to the auction and contains important information that must be available to him throughout the sale.

Every wine-auction catalogue includes each lot's number, description, and *estimate range*—a guide to a lot's worth based upon past auction results. The auctioneer's book includes this information as well as the seller's name; the *reserve price*—the confidential minimum price that the consignor wishes to receive for the lot; *absentee bids*—bids placed prior to the auction by people who do not attend; and any special *addenda notes*—information received after the catalogue has been printed.

First, the auctioneer announces addenda items and general salesroom announcements written in his book. Addenda items are announced prior to the sale of the relevant lot, and are also available to each bidder in printed form. Typically, these items include withdrawn lots, vintage or vineyard changes, condition notes, bottles added to or subtracted from a lot, and estimate changes.

The auctioneer uses the estimate range as a guide to determine where to open the bidding on any lot. He will typically open bidding under the low end of the estimate range, although this can fluctuate if there are high absentee bids. He will then either invite an opening bid from the room, or start with a *bid on behalf of the consignor*. The auctioneer can bid on behalf of the consignor in an attempt to meet the reserve price, but once the reserve price has been met, he is not allowed to push the bidding further unless he is executing an absentee bid. If the minimum price is not met, he will announce that the lot has passed, or is unsold, according to the jargon his company prefers. (For more on the bidding process, see Chapter 7.)

There can be any number of absentee bids to execute on behalf of bidders that could not attend the sale in person. Because the auctioneer's book is prepared prior to the sale, all absentee bids must be received at least twenty-four hours before the start of the auction. Each auction company handles absentee bids slightly differently. Some record every bid received on a particular lot, while others record only the highest three. At some houses the responsibility of executing absentee bids belongs to the specialists. (For more on absentee bidding, see page 110.)

(within governing law and regulation). He may accept bids or ignore bids according to his best judgment. He may keep to a standardized set of bidding increments (such as those shown in the table on page 53), or employ his own at any time. Mistakes can be made, but the experienced auctioneer will rectify any situation with effortless panache and keep the auction moving quickly along.

Auctioneers have a responsibility to both buyers and sellers. They must secure the highest price that bidders will pay for a consignment, while remaining fair and unbiased to those bidding. Razor-sharp attention to the drama of each individual lot is required, yet entertaining the crowd and moving the auction at a quick pace cannot take a backseat. Quite a lot of skill is needed to step up on the auctioneer's rostrum, but a great auctioneer can make auction day an exciting and memorable one for everyone present.

There are many circumstances in which an auctioneer may ignore a bid. The most common reasons include a bidder becoming drunk, bidding against his own bid, and bidding on his own property. In these situations, the auctioneer must use his discretion regarding which bids to acknowledge.

The Specialists

Each wine-auction company relies heavily on its team of specialists. Most importantly, the specialists assess the quality and condition of each bottle, price the wine, and represent it in the auction catalogue. Beyond these duties, specialists may take on any number of additional responsibilities to help the other members of the auction team.

A potential seller's first call or fax to the auction company will often be received by a specialist, who will then lead him through the various steps of the auction process. Many specialists arrange the shipping of the consignment into the auction warehouse. The specialist's responsibility to the consignor should continue until the consignor receives payment for the sale of his wine. When the auction catalogue is printed and sent to the buying public, the specialists are available if a bidder desires further description of any lot. Some well-respected specialists become personal shoppers to savvy bidders who rely on the specialists' knowledge, experience, and taste to guide them to the most desirable lots. For this, specialists tend to be under-utilized. Few bidders take advantage of the specialists' eagerness to talk about which wines or consignments are particularly desirable in each auction.

Wine-auction specialists are among the most knowledgeable people in the wine world. They usually enter the field because of their love of wine. The pressures of shipping and catalogue deadlines, on top of difficult customer-service issues, are eclipsed by a specialist's passion for the grape. They love to talk about wine and are an often-overlooked, fertile source of wine information.

> Gone are the days when an accidental wink or wave bought an unwanted treasure—a notion more likely born out of legend than reality. Bidders are identified by the deliberate wave of their pre-assigned, registered paddle. If any gestures are unclear to the auctioneer, he will come right out and ask if the individual is bidding. No auctioneer wants to stick someone with a lot he will not pay for!

BEHIND-THE-SCENE WORKERS

You might get through your first several auctions without having any contact with the warehouse workers, the administrators, the finance department, and the marketers. Yet without them, an auction business can't get off the ground level. These individuals are intregal to the inner workings of the business, and it is every bit as important for them to perform their jobs correctly as it is for the auctioneer to arrive on time with his auctioneer's book in tow.

The Warehouse Crew

Each and every auction company's business relies on the staff of its temperature-controlled warehouse. After all, proper storage of the wine is crucial to auction success. The warehouse staff is responsible for the wine's safe keeping and also assists the specialist team in inventory management.

A consignor or a buyer may never actually speak directly to a warehouse person; inquiries are usually handled by the specialists. However, the ability to accept thousands of cases of wine, while preparing thousands of others for after-sale delivery, takes a top-notch team of warehouse workers. The warehouse team needs to know where each lot of wine rests while it awaits its new ownership. Persistent problems of misdelivered wine, large lists of catalogue corrections, or missing bottles, indicate the need for better warehouse management. Those working in the warehouse are the unsung heroes of a very busy, detailed-oriented team.

The Administrators

The administrative staff is in charge of the details of every auction transaction. They are responsible for the accuracy and neatness of correspondence into and out of the company, including letters, price lists, proposals, and contracts. They often control the flow of inquiries to the team of specialists. When specialists are too busy to answer a general auction query, having the ear of an administrator can be extremely

helpful. The administrative staff also assists callers with questions regarding future sales and auction-related events. They obtain current and past catalogues, as well as auction results, as per request. The administrators may also fill organizational roles of the auction production, such as setting up the venue, registering bidders, selling catalogues at the auction, and executing absentee bids.

Hart Davis Hart employees.

The job of the administrative team is not easy. In the wine-auction business, transposing two numbers can result in a difference of thousands of dollars. When a long list of wines needs to be catalogued and organized, for example, a moment of inattention can result in a troublesome situation. Two bottles of 1988 Château Latour can become eight bottles of 1982 Château Latour; one lot is worth $300 while the other can fetch up to $6,000. If the mistake is carried through the system, a buyer may purchase a lot that does not exist. When preparing for a wine auction, the administrators have to be sure that no detail is overlooked.

The Finance Department

A successful wine-auction company, whether a large, international auction house or a small, privately owned operation, is a multi-million dollar entity. Each auction company has at least one individual responsible for money received from bidders and settlements made to the consignors. A collector looking to either buy or sell at auction should be familiar with the structure of the auction house's finance department. Most auction catalogues outline the details surrounding the collection of payment and its final distribution. If this policy is not clearly explained in the catalogue, a potential buyer or seller should call the company to inquire about the process. Taking the time to go over the expectations of both parties will create a better auction experience for the novice buyer or seller.

Typically, the finance department qualifies unknown bidders, checks absentee bid forms for proper contact information, receives payments from the buyers, follows up with late payers, distributes settlement to sellers, and, sometimes, offers special terms to auction clients. Special terms to buyers may include staggered- or extended-payment options, usually when a consignment is bought at a very high price. Special terms to sellers may include lowered commission fees and special incentives to consign. (See Chapter 10 for more on negotiating these costs.)

The Marketers

The classified section of *Wine Spectator* is a great place to search for a wine-auction company's contact information (which can also be found on page 215).

The auction business's competitive nature and huge annual revenue dictate sophisticated and precise professional attention to marketing. A separate advertising or public relations team, however, is a luxury most auction companies cannot well afford. Christie's and Sotheby's are the major exceptions.

Most auction houses use print ads as a major form of advertisement. Almost every US wine-auction company buys a small boxed ad in *Wine Spectator's* classified section. These ads, written and placed by the marketers, helpfully supply each company's contact information. The larger New York retailers tend to have impressive advertising reach, as they routinely place ads for their retail business in both the top wine publications as well as their local newspaper, often *The New York Times*. These regularly placed ads can include and sometimes even feature the store's upcoming auction activity.

Auction houses often hold special tastings or dinners prior to an important auction. For these events, the marketers have various responsibilities that usually include coming up with a wine-tasting theme, arranging the appearance of wine-world celebrity guests of honor, and advertising the event. Sometimes these functions are open to the public, while other times they are reserved for top buyers and potential new sellers. Getting on the invitation list is a matter of making yourself known to the auction staff and expressing an interest in becoming involved with the company's activities.

At auction houses that do not have a separate marketing department, these responsibilities become additional jobs for the rest of the team, particularly the specialists and administrators. It is crucial to the business's success that these jobs be performed well. This is the department that ultimately brings the consignors and bidders together on auction day.

THE PLAYERS

An auction cannot be pulled off without the attendance of sellers and buyers. These players—who include private collectors, investors, restauranteurs, vintners, and more—are at the heart of the auction process.

The Sellers

Sellers consign their wines for a variety of reasons. Many of the consignors you will encounter have simply (or sometimes not so simply) decided to sell their wine. This category includes wine lovers who find they have collected too much wine for their storage capacity (or drinking capability), collectors who have stopped drinking for any of a number of reasons, and wine aficionados who need money more than cases of unopened wine. There are also drinkers who discover their tastes have matured over the course of their collecting. As novices, they may have started by collecting Napa Valley Cabernet Sauvignon as their wine of choice, and later discovered the wines of Bordeaux or Piedmont or the Rhône Valley more to their liking. They are left with bottles (or even cases) of California Cabernet Sauvignon until they figure out something to do with them. These people may find selling at auction to be their most viable option.

Restaurant owners prefer not to think about the possibility of going out of business, but it happens frequently. When an upscale restaurant goes under unexpectedly, there are often large quantities of wine left in the cellar. Out-of-business restaurants contribute many bottles to wine auctions.

Another key seller to consider is the wine investor. The wine market enjoys the same cyclical effects as the stock market. When times are good, as they were in the mid- to late 1990s, the scramble for hard-to-find, high point-scoring wine is a compelling reason for a collector to sell these wines at auction. Other times, these sellers need to sell to raise money or make room for a new bottle. They might also sell when they believe a prized wine is in its prime condition.

In most auction catalogues, there will be wine from consignors getting rid of entire collections and other consignors thinning out collections for a number of reasons. For the buyer, however, the reason the bottles are being sold is secondary to the condition of the wine.

The Buyers

There are as many types of buyers as there are sellers. The first group of buyers consists of people who truly love wine. These aficionados attend auctions to buy wine unavailable elsewhere. Older bottles from desirable vintages that would not have

Some people attend wine auctions solely for the experience. Often, famous chefs cook the lavish meals, and occasionally there may be celebrities.

been *laid-down*—held—in any one store as well as young, highly prized wines produced in very small quantities can often be found only at auction. These buyers also come to find good values. Not every bidder is interested in every wine, resulting in *bargains*—lots without competitive bidding to push the price higher—at each auction.

Some very fine restaurants take pride in their expansive wine lists. To keep the cellars filled with a broad selection of desirable vintages, representatives attend wine auctions. Like the aficionados, restaurant *sommeliers*—managers in charge of wine service—are searching for good deals and coveted bottles.

Restaurant sommelier.

Investors often attend wine auctions as buyers. Wine auctions are a great source for both good bargains and rare bottles. These buyers usually have their eyes on wines from Burgundy and Bordeaux, but have begun to look outside the Old World wines to make their investments.

At a wine auction, you are also likely to see (and may find yourself a part of) a group of beginning wine appreciators. These people, new to the wine scene, attend to expand their wine education. Auctions are often preceded by invaluable wine tastings that are held by experts in the field and attended by many informed wine drinkers. If a novice is unprepared to enter the bidding battle on his first auction trip, it can still be valuable for him to attend a wine auction because he can learn by sampling wine with experts, studying the catalogue, and watching those around him participate.

Investing in wine can be tricky. Taking a chance on a bottle's condition can work for or against an investor. A good rule of thumb is to never invest more than you can afford to drink.

It can be helpful to understand who you are bidding against because bidders with different objectives can have different bidding strategies. A wine aficionado attempting to expand his beloved collection, for example, may be a high-roller and ready to bid whatever it takes to win the object of his desire. On the other hand, a private wine dealer who is buying for investment most likely has a limit on what he can spend, in order to guarantee a profit on his purchase.

Buyers come to auction to scout out rare wines and good deals. The buyer that comes prepared and remains patient is likely to come away with fantastic wine and a wonderful auction experience.

INFLUENCE FROM THE MEDIA

There are so many types of wine and so many different vintages that auction goers often have to make decisions regarding a bottle based on someone else's experiences. Frequently, they will turn to a renowned wine critic or writer. Taste is personal, but these people can supply you with guidelines to follow, as well as educate you on related issues.

The Wine Critic

Wine critics have tremendous influence over auction prices. Auction catalogues include these reliable wine professionals' critical tasting notes to both educate and entice prospective bidders.

Michael Broadbent, first discussed in Chapter 1, is a wine critic of international repute. His notes, which have appeared in Christie's wine-auction catalogues as well as in a number of books, use a five-star system, with five stars reflecting the wine-maker's very best effort. Broadbent usually includes his opinion as to when a wine should be drunk. His notes on older Bordeaux are considered the definitive record on many of these wines.

Many of Broadbent's contemporary tasters used a twenty-point scale to rate wine. Most twenty-point tasters arrived at the final score after considering and rating sep-arately a wine's color, nose, mouth-feel, and finish, on a scale of one to five. The total score then represented the taster's overall impression. This twenty-point system has been widely replaced by the 100-point system made famous by Robert Parker.

Robert Parker is currently the wine industry's single most influential critical voice. Parker has offered his tasting notes in *The Wine Advocate* newsletter since 1978 and has written fourteen books. He has tasted and stated his opinions on a greater variety of fine wine than anyone else in the world. Parker is a tireless traveler, stu-dious taster, and fascinating writer. His notes and scores are clipped out of his newsletter and pasted on websites, retailers' shelves, and auction catalogues, to authoritatively qualify and quantify wine. A perfect Parker score of 100 points means a home run not only for the winery, but also for any owner of that wine.

Over time, other serious wine enthusiasts have followed Parker's lead into the arena of wine criticism. Auction companies use their notes to enhance the catalogue descriptions. Stephen Tanzer's *International Wine Cellar* newsletter presents critical tasting notes, often including insight into the making of the wine. Notes from the *Burghound*—also known as Mr. Allen Meadows—are considered the ultimate assess-ments of the great and expensive wines of Burgundy. These critiques can be found on his website and in his newsletter. The notes of both these men are also included in some auction catalogues.

The auction house specialists, too, offer their critiques by providing tasting notes in the catalogue. A specialist's note is particularly valuable when written regarding a wine removed directly from a case being sold; the condition of the extra bottle may indicate the overall condition of the seller's other bottles.

A high score affects a wine's value because more people then become interested in obtaining the wine. However, remember that each tasting note is merely a profes-sional's opinion. It is a starting point from which to form one's own assessment.

The Wine Writer

Wine critics write and some wine writers critique. While critics concentrate on evaluations, however, a writer's main objective is to educate. A wine writer's topics can range from vineyards and regions to personalities and histories. The impact of the wine writer on the auction participant is more subtle than that of the wine critic. The more material a collector reads on his area of interest, the more educated he becomes and the more confident he will be buying and collecting wine. The auction buyer will have a more fruitful time perusing an auction catalogue when he can easily research any vintage, vineyard, or producer that is unfamiliar. This makes the wine writer and a basic wine library a necessity.

The British dominate modern wine writing. Starting in the early twentieth century with George Saintsbury's *Notes on a Cellar-Book* (1920), British wine drinkers proved to be thirsty for well-written, well-presented information. The great names in the next era of British wine writing were wine merchants, with André Simon, Harry Waugh, and T.A. Layton at the forefront. Today, the great British wine writing professionals are Hugh Johnson, Jancis Robinson, Clive Coates, and Stephen Spurrier, as well as the auction house stars Michael Broadbent and Serena Sutcliffe.

The American wine literature movement boomed after the end of the Second World War. The first great American wine writers, Alexis Lichine, Frank Schoonmaker, and Alexis Bespaloff, were also wine merchants. More recently, American writers have produced wonderful volumes for educating the beginner. These include Kevin Zraly's *Windows on the World Complete Wine Course*, Karen MacNeil's *The Wine Bible*, and Mary Ewing-Mulligan and Ed McCarthy's *Wine for Dummies* series. Almost every large newspaper devotes some coverage to wine, usually in the food section. Frank Prial's column in *The New York Times* is particularly well known.

The Australian wine writers are a lively bunch. They offer guides to various wine regions and scholarly yet rather informal access to winemaking and wine appreciation. The most famous are Oz Clarke, Len Evans, and James Halliday.

Wine literature educates on a variety of wine-related topics, and there are books for every level of interest. Familiarizing yourself with many different wines through these materials will make you more assertive and confident in the auction arena.

Wine Spectator

Wine Spectator, both magazine and website, is an extremely important aspect of the American auction game. The beautifully designed publication, with its roster of renowned international journalists, is by far the world's best-read wine periodical. The magazine contains research material that covers not only wine, but also wine travel and wine lifestyle. It is educational, like the wine writer, and because the *Spec-*

> Whether by attending classes, reading books, or actually tasting wines, you should learn as much about wine as you can if you plan on becoming a collector. After all, the most knowledgeable collectors tend to assemble the greatest collections.

tator's professional tasting staff offers notes on scores of different wines, it also functions as wine critic. Many auction catalogues use *Wine Spectator*'s tasting notes to augment their lot descriptions.

Wine Spectator's auction expert Peter D. Meltzer reports regularly on the state and results of the US wine-auction market. As part of this detailed coverage, *Wine Spectator* created its own Auction Index, which tracks and averages auction prices after each sale. The Auction Index presents the results as reported to them by each auction house and shows any price fluctuations. Interested readers can draw conclusions about the state of the auction market from these figures, and Meltzer offers his own comments on changes and trends in the wine-auction market.

Alongside the detailed coverage of the commercial wine-auction market, *Wine Spectator* also includes up-to-date information on the vibrant charity wine-auction scene. Both magazine and website include photographs of the colorful galas. Additionally, the magazine's classified section is very important to any collector interested in auction, as almost every major auction house places a small ad in this publication.

CONCLUSION

The wheels of every wine auction are turned by a large group of professionals. While a wine bottle travels from the seller's collection to the warehouse to its ultimate resting place in the buyer's cellar, several months go by. During this time, each member of the team is at some point involved in the auction process. By learning about the people who create the auction, you will gain greater comfort and confidence in a sales process that can be both profitable for the consignor and rewarding for the buyer. You can further increase your confidence by learning as much as you can about wines, both specifically and generally, through the works of wine critics and writers. These people have tasted many wines and are willing to share what they have learned with you.

Now that you are familiar with the people who put the auction together and have basic knowledge of both wine and auctions, it is time to turn your attention to bidding procedures. We will begin by looking at a crucial aspect of the process: the catalogue. The catalogue contains useful information specific to each auction, and should be reviewed before the event so that you are prepared and ready to participate.

PART TWO

The Art of Bidding

5

Understanding the Catalogue

A wine-auction catalogue attractively presents and promotes an auction. The catalogue is excellent for both reading and research and is a significant part of preparation for any auction, as it offers important information about the event and the bottles for sale. This chapter will make the catalogue more accessible by breaking down its code-like symbols and explaining the facts it presents.

FRONT MATTER

Printed auction catalogues are usually 8 inches by 11 inches (203.2 millimeters by 279.4 millimeters) in size. They often have color covers and photographs on glossy pages. Sophisticated and informative, these publications are designed to grab the attention of potential buyers and sellers. The material at the catalogue's start is educational to both newcomers and pros in the world of wine auctions. This is where you will find general auction details and ways to contact the auction house, as well as company rules for participation.

The Cover

A wine-auction catalogue's cover is designed to whet a wine enthusiast's palate. It usually displays an eye-catching color photograph of smartly arranged bottles. The auction house name, the sale date, and the sale location are all printed on the catalogue's cover.

Details such as the auction's title may also be included. The title of a sale may be, for example, *Fine and Rare Wines*. Sometimes the title is more specific—*Fine Bordeaux and Vintage Port*, for instance. If the cover photograph is of a featured consignment, its title might appear as well: *Fine and Rare Wines, Including Extraordinary Burgundy from a Private Cellar*. If the consignor wishes to have his name associated

The first auction catalogue was created by Christie's auction house for a December 1766 sale. Since then, advances in printing and photography have led to impressive growth in design, but the catalogue's main purpose and content have remained the same.

Justifying the Expense of the Catalogue

Printing an auction catalogue is costly, but auction houses consistently shoulder the price. This is largely because the catalogued auction is a long-standing tradition. Also, rival firms are always competing for consignments and big-spending bidders, and the catalogue plays a role in this competitive game. A company that presents its wines in a lavishly produced catalogue has an edge. For a collector selling his entire collection, a fancy catalogue serves as a testament to the time, money, and passion he spent assembling the wines. For a potential buyer, a beautifully designed catalogue is likely to catch and keep his attention, as well as alert him to desirable lots. Although the catalogues are expensive to produce for every auction, they are necessary and worthwhile because of the amount of business they bring in from both buyers and sellers.

Many auction companies offer a free version of their catalogue—which does not include the illustrations—on their websites. This is the best way to have a look at the upcoming sale without committing to the price of the catalogue.

with the sale, this too can be included on the cover: *Fine and Rare Wines, Including the Collection of Dr. Alfred E. Bellows*. Information found on the cover is related to the general sale and should entice you to turn the page.

Introductory Pages

The contents of the inside cover and the first several pages vary between auction houses. Usually, these pages present the auction's location, date, starting time, and any different *sessions*. If there are too many lots to fit into a single day, the lots are divided between different sessions. Session times and division of the lots are listed with the specific auction details. The auction company's address, phone number, fax number, and website address are also included among these introductory pages.

Information needed to contact specific members of the auction team is usually presented a page or two later. Titles and names, along with telephone numbers, fax numbers, and email addresses, are listed here. Some auction companies even include photographs of their staff members, although these pictures may also be placed towards the end of the catalogue. This allows callers to put a face to a voice they first meet on the phone.

Terms and Conditions of Sale

The Terms and Conditions of Sale protect the legal rights of both the auction house and the buyer. They are usually dictated by state and federal regulations. If the auction house is international, these rules must comply with local and national regulations. (See the inset "Terms and Conditions of Sale" on page 77.)

The Terms and Conditions of Sale are usually printed on one of the first few pages of the catalogue, although they do appear in the back of some auction books.

Terms and Conditions of Sale

The exact regulations listed in the Terms and Conditions of Sale are specific to each auction company, but the general rules and precautions are the same from house to house.

■ **Buyer Beware:** Lots are sold "as is." Bidders may inspect merchandise prior to the auction because there is no recourse if purchased products fall short of their expectations. The exception to this is misrepresentation in the catalogue.

■ **Legal Age:** A bidder must be of legal drinking age to bid for alcoholic beverages.

■ **Absentee Bids:** The auction house may execute absentee bids, and is not accountable for errors in doing so. Most houses require that absentee bids be placed at least twenty-four hours before the auction's start.

■ **Reserve Price:** Most items are auctioned conditional on a reserve price, below which the auctioneer does not have to sell the lot. Usually the reserve price is not above the low end of the estimate.

■ **Auctioneer's Discretion:** Any and all disputes are settled by the auctioneer.

■ **Buyer's Premium:** Lots are sold for the *hammer price*—amount of the final bid—plus an added percentage.

■ **Buyer's Responsibilities:** Upon winning a lot, a buyer accepts full responsibility for the item. He also agrees to pay the final bid price plus fees and taxes according to the auction house's stated payment plan.

■ **Shipping Problems:** The auction house bears no responsibility for problems encountered while packing or shipping.

■ **Failure to Comply:** A bidder who does not comply with any of the stated conditions may have any or all winning bids invalidated at the auction house's discretion. If the auction house has to resell the item for less money, the original buyer may be held responsible for the difference.

Buyer, be warned: you owe it to yourself to read through the Terms and Conditions of Sale at least once for each auction company. You may also want to refer back to this page occasionally to see if any rules have changed.

ANATOMY OF AN AUCTION LOT ENTRY

After the front matter, the bulk of the catalogue is devoted to *auction lot entries*. These present detailed information on the wine for sale. Arranged by consignor, auction lot entries are jam-packed with information. We are going to dissect the listings so you can utilize them to your best advantage. Auction houses may present the information in various sequences, but the content remains the same. (See Figure 5.1. "A Sample Lot Entry" for an example of an auction lot entry.)

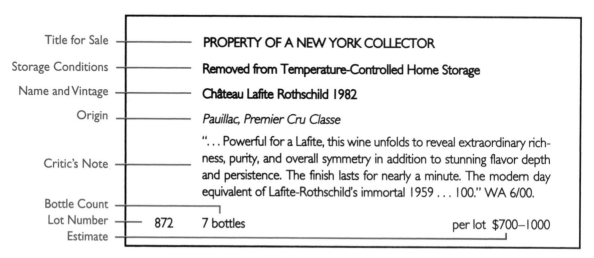

Title for Sale	**PROPERTY OF A NEW YORK COLLECTOR**
Storage Conditions	**Removed from Temperature-Controlled Home Storage**
Name and Vintage	**Château Lafite Rothschild 1982**
Origin	*Pauillac, Premier Cru Classe*
Critic's Note	"... Powerful for a Lafite, this wine unfolds to reveal extraordinary richness, purity, and overall symmetry in addition to stunning flavor depth and persistence. The finish lasts for nearly a minute. The modern day equivalent of Lafite-Rothschild's immortal 1959 ... 100." WA 6/00.
Bottle Count / Lot Number / Estimate	872 7 bottles per lot $700–1000

Figure 5.1.   A Sample Lot Entry

Title for Sale

In a catalogue, a *title for sale* marks the beginning of each new consignment. It is a phrase that can describe the main focus of the consignment, the collection's previous location, or information about the consignor. Let's look at these possibilities.

When the title for sale explains the main focus, it names the wines that make up the consignment's bulk. If named *Bordeaux and Cult California Wine*, for example, these wines are heavily represented in the consignment. However, lots may consist of other fantastic bottles. Read through the entire consignment. You may find a rare catch that competitors have missed because it was not incorporated in the title for sale.

When the title for sale indicates where the wines have been kept, bidders should take notice and perhaps be influenced. For instance, you might be a West Coast bidder at a New York auction who discovers desirable bottles from a consignment labeled *Property of a Long Time Los Angeles Collector*. The wine was probably shipped across the country for the auction, and will be shipped back if you win. That's a lot of unnecessary movement for a new addition to your collection. You may be better off purchasing similar wines from a different consignment. If the wines are unique and

Shipping Wine to an Auction

If you are considering the purchase of wine that has already traveled a distance to the auction, you should ask the auction team for details regarding the manner in which the wine was shipped. The very best way for wine to be transported is via refrigerated trucks. There are several carriers in the United States that will ship wine this way, but it is very expensive. It is usually only reasonable for a consignor to ship via refrigerated storage if his consignment is large (around sixty cases or one full palette). Many sellers choose to transport their bottles to auction by using overnight shipping via commercial carrier. For hearty, younger wines between five and ten years old, second-day air is usually sufficient. UPS or FedEx Ground (which takes around five days) is the last option to consider, and is the least desirable way to ship wine bottles. If you find out that the wines you want have traveled a distance to the auction, you should request the shipping information from the auction team in order to properly consider the consignment's likely condition.

not available elsewhere, you can contact the auction staff about the specific shipment of these bottles. (The inset above describes the best shipment possibilities.) Then you can make an informed decision on their probable condition.

The title for sale can also mention details about the consignor. For example, it might divulge his name. An auction team may urge the seller to reveal his identity if it will have a positive effect on interest in his lots. There is, for instance, a certain mystique to owning a bottle of 1990 Latour once owned by Andrew Lloyd Webber. Ultimately, however, it is the seller's decision whether to make his name public. If he chooses to remain anonymous, general information such as his occupation or kinship to the auction house might be printed here.

Storage Conditions

The storage of a bottle directly influences the wine's quality. A bidder, therefore, should be concerned with the condition of every bottle, regardless of whether an auction company claims that all its wines have been properly stored. Before a consignment is accepted by an auction house, the team questions the owner about the collection's *provenance*—history of ownership, including where the wines came from and how they were stored. This information is invaluable to bidders.

In the catalogue, the collection's provenance is briefly mentioned at the beginning of each consignment's entry. As a reader, you must draw your own conclusions based on this statement. A wine that is consigned to the auction directly from a winery's library, for example, has pristine provenance. It has had limited movement and was kept in a controlled environment. A wine kept in professional storage (also called off-premise storage) has extremely covetable provenance as well. In this case,

The word provenance comes from the Latin word *provenire*. *Pro* means "forth" or "forward" and *venire* means "to come." Provenance is considered by many auction buyers to be the single most important factor in determining whether to bid on a wine.

Storing Wine at Home

For residential collections, the crown jewel of wine storage is a custom-made, electronically monitored, temperature- and humidity-controlled walk-in wine cellar. These spectacular cellars are often the true epicenter of their owners' worlds. There are also great alternatives that require less of a financial commitment. Freestanding, temperature-controlled wine cellars range from relatively inexpensive twelve-bottle refrigerated units to much larger models that can accommodate several hundred bottles. Many new kitchens come with under-counter wine-storage units as standard issue. Today's market has more options than ever before for temperature-controlled wine storage. Turn to page 215 for examples of wine-storage units.

Older wines are rarely removed from the auction house's warehouse to be brought to the auction. Infrequently, an exceptionally rare bottle will be displayed if the auction company is confident that the trip will not affect the wine's quality.

the wine was kept in a rented locker or walk-in cellar in a commercially operated storage facility. It is especially desirable to find bottles owned by only one collector after their release from the winery—providing the owner kept them under temperature-controlled conditions. The mention of any of these storage areas is an encouraging sign. (See the inset "Storing Wine at Home" above for information on residential temperature-controlled storage units.)

Yet many wines on the secondary market do not arrive at auction with such unadulterated histories. The auction team must establish whether the wine's owner regulated the temperature, humidity, angle of storage, and level of darkness. (Chapter 2 described optimal storage conditions.) Occasionally you will see the term *passive storage*. In this case, neither temperature nor humidity was externally controlled. Younger wine kept undisturbed in a crawl space in northern California will most likely be fine. In this area, the temperature does not swing wildly and the natural humidity tends to be perfect for wine storage. On the other hand, wine kept in a garage in Arizona will probably not fair well under passive conditions, even if left undisturbed. There, the high temperatures and varying humidity levels do not maintain a proper environment for storing wine. If you find yourself interested in a lot labeled "passive storage," you should question the auction team about the specific circumstances. This will enable you to make an informed decision.

Lot Number

Auctions may consist of several thousand lots and can be conducted over the course of several days. Each lot is listed in the catalogue sequentially and offered to bidders in numerical order.

The auction company orders the consignments to present them in their best light. An auction of any length is a performance piece. The goal is to hold the audience's interest. The action should flow from beginning to end. There are peaks and valleys of excitement, and high notes should be hit every hour or so. An exciting lot can be an extremely rare wine (such as an 1870 Château Lafite from Glamis Castle in Scotland or a full case of 1945 Château Mouton), an extremely expensive wine (maybe a case of 1985 Domaine de la Romanée Conti), or a wine neither rare nor expensive, but very collectible and able to extract lively bidding from the room (like a young and delicious Burgundy, Rhône, or Italian case). If there is not a sense of impending excitement as each page is turned, the auctioneer's voice can become a drone of numbers.

Lots within a single consignment, on the other hand, are arranged in a traditional sequence. The order was set forth in the post-World War II London auctions and later refined by Christie's Michael Broadbent. It is based on the wines' regions of origin. The order is Champagne, Bordeaux (red then white), Sauternes, Burgundy (red then white), other areas in France, Alsace, Germany, Italy, Spain, California, Australia, Madeira, and finally Portugal. As the list of wine-producing regions grows, there are more departures from the original order. However, you should find consistency within every catalogue from each company. The order of the lots within a consignment does not have any bearing on their value or sale price.

The Wine's Name and Vintage

This line of information provides the name and vintage of the specific wine for sale. If the lot is a mixed lot and contains several different wines, all of their names and vintages will be listed. (More information on mixed lots can be found on page 56.)

If no vintage is listed, the wine is not of one vintage but is a blend of several vintages. Other times the abbreviation *NV* will be used to indicate non-vintage. Port and Champagne are the most common wines to be bottled and released without a noted vintage.

The Wine's Origin

Provided directly under the name and vintage is the wine's origin. If there are different wines, this information is listed under each. A New World wine, named for its grape varietal, has its region name—Napa Valley, for example—listed here. An Old World wine is named after its region of origin, so this line is used to provide further details such as the vineyard, district, appellation, or classification of the wine.

The Wine's Condition

The bottle's physical condition is a very important part of the lot entry. The information given here includes the level of wine in the bottle, appearance of the paper label and lead capsule, and condition of the cork.

Most auction catalogues state that the level of wine in each bottle reaches the bottom of the bottle's neck unless otherwise indicated by designated abbreviations. The explanations for these abbreviations are found on the *Ullage Chart*, located

Sometimes bottles contain different amounts of wine simply because producers do not fill every bottle exactly the same. They must, however, comply with the law that dictates there be at least 750 milliliters of wine in a standard bottle. There are similar laws regarding large-format bottles.

towards the catalogue's end. The level of liquid can indicate the wine's age or storage conditions. It is perfectly acceptable that a wine of any age be filled to the bottom of its neck, while older wines can be expected to have lower levels due to evaporation from cork shrinkage. This is both natural and normal, and wine filled lower than the neck bottom is not necessarily bad. On the other hand, lower levels in a young wine may indicate improper storage or handling. The Ullage Chart can accurately state the level of wine but not the explanation for it. Chance is involved but a risk can pay off. You don't want to miss out on a bottle of matured Burgundy just because its level has naturally gone down! The Ullage Chart is explained in detail on page 87.

The bottle's label is only mentioned in the lot entry if it is flawed. Damage such as slight tears, nicks, or staining will be stated, although not necessarily reflected in the lot's estimate. Completely missing labels or vintage tags, on the other hand, may cause a bottle's value to decrease. The label has no effect on the wine's quality but has become increasingly important with the growth of the wine-auction market. (See the inset "The Condition of the Paper Label" on page 125 for more on the growing desire for labels of quality condition.)

Keep in mind that a wine-stained label can be the result of leakage. At the same time, it can also merely be the product of a clumsy consignor dropping another bottle in the same vicinity. Take note of the catalogued level of wine and whether it is appropriate to the bottle's age when you make this determination. If the label is damaged and the levels are low, you should most likely pass on the bottle. The cause of the damage may be addressed and hypothesized by the cataloguing staff.

A description of the *capsule*—the foil at the top of the bottle that can also be made of wax—will be included here if it is not intact. Sometimes, for example, the capsule is removed in an attempt to uncover vintage stamps on the cork. An auction catalogue will mention whether the staff cut the capsule to reveal the cork, or if the bottle had been consigned with the capsule already cut. Any problems with the capsule should be investigated further by inquiring of the staff cataloguer who wrote the bottle's description. While many young wines will have no ill effects from a damaged capsule, it is a gamble to buy an older wine listed as having an impaired capsule because the company will offer no recourse if there does turn out to be a problem.

If a cork is either protruded or depressed from the rim of the bottle, it will be noted in the auction lot entry. This can occur if there were any temperature or humidity fluctuations during the bottle's storage.

There may be mention of the cork. When you look at a bottle of wine, the cork should be flush with the rim of the neck. If a cork is either protruded or depressed from the rim of the bottleneck, this will most likely be noted. Most auction houses do not take responsibility for corks that shrink and fall into the bottle once sold. At the same time, they do not wish to devalue their reputations by including old and fragile wines without absolute disclosure to potential buyers, so cataloguers are careful to note any visible problems with the cork.

Whether You Want The Wood

You may see the abbreviation of *"owc"* or *"oc"* within a lot entry. This stands for "original wood(en) case" or "original carton," and can affect the lot's monetary value as well as its value to you.

Some wood cases, particularly those from the great (and expensive) Burgundian Domaine de la Romanée Conti, are fortified with metal bands around their exterior. The band serves as extra protection during the shipment from the winery. Policy varies between auction companies, and even debated within auction teams, as to whether or not the bands should be broken and the cases opened for inspection. In the early days of wine auctions, the banded cases were left in their original banded condition. Bidders would pay a large premium for the assurance of their wine's pristine, virginal condition.

Today, cataloguers and inspectors tend to break the banded seal, open the case, and inspect each bottle, to further assure the condition and content of each case. These wines are too valuable for the auction team to take any chances. As a bidder in the sale, you may request that any case be opened and inspected, regardless of whether it means breaking a banded seal. In some instances, the auction company will contact the seller for his permission before they break the seal.

A savvy bidder may be able to save a bid step or two—and therefore some money—by choosing to bid on a case of twelve bottles (or six magnums or three double magnums) that is not offered in its original wood case or carton. Provided that the bidder has read the entire lot description, focusing carefully on the condition of the bottles, this can prove worthwhile because there may be slightly less competition for the lot. This is particularly relevant to the collector

who is planning to enjoy the wine within a reasonably short period of time, or the collector whose wine storage is set up with individual bottle racking. The bidder who plans to lay down the wine long term is better off with the wine in *owc*. The original wood cases are heavy, but convenient to move around without much risk of damage. Store the cases so that the end panels are facing out, so that each case is easy to identify.

If you are buying a dozen bottles *not* in *owc* but are considering long-term storage, it is worthwhile to purchase strong, stackable cardboard cartons in which to store your wine. You can even use the excellent cardboard cartons used by most auction companies to ship purchases to bidders. Once received, opened, and checked for accuracy of delivery, the wine can remain in these cardboard boxes until removed for consumption or bin storage. When keeping your auction purchases in repacked cardboard cartons, write the contents of each case on the outside of the box with a thick marker. Have the case identification facing outward, just as you would with an end panel on a wood case. This brief step can save you hours of searching and frustration when you go to pull a specific bottle.

Auction companies do not air ship wine in the original wood cases. Your *owc* auction purchases will be repacked in cardboard, sometimes with Styrofoam liners. If you want the original boxes, you must arrange with the shipping department to have them sent separately. Otherwise, you can choose not to take the cartons. Usually, the auction houses end up with a stockpile of wood. When the pile becomes too big and takes up too much valuable warehouse space, someone will break apart and dispose the woods.

Although the level of wine and conditions of the label, capsule, and cork are offered to the bidder, there is no judgment as to the wine's quality. It is up to each bidder's experience to use the stated conditions to determine whether the wine is an acceptable gamble. Auction specialists take great care to accurately report these conditions because inaccurate catalogue representation can lead to a potential return.

The Critic's Note

Many auction catalogues include tasting notes from outside wine experts. The most prominent notes come from Robert Parker, the influential wine critic discussed in Chapter 4. Other authorities respected worldwide include *Wine Spectator* magazine, Michael Broadbent, and Serena Sutcliffe.

A critic's description is often extracted from a longer review of the wine. It describes texture and flavors as well as any similar tasting wines or vintages. It ends with his score of the wine and is followed by his initials and the date the note was made.

Notes from these experts give the reader a sense of the wine. This is especially useful if the bidder has never tasted it. These notes are merely opinions but their influence cannot be denied, because a high score and good recommendation often results in a higher price. Sometimes an auction staff member will include a note of his own tasting experience. If it is a wine you are particularly interested in, call the staff member who contributed the note to further discuss the wine.

The omission of a tasting note does not indicate a lesser wine. The staff may not have had time to locate a useable note due to publishing constraints or, although unusual, it is possible no one has yet published a note on that wine.

> Sotheby's has an exclusive relationship with the tasting notes of Serena Sutcliffe. Nobody else in the wine-auction world uses Sutcliffe's notes—and Sotheby's doesn't use any tasting notes other than those of Sutcliffe.

Bottle Count and Size

The catalogue indicates how much wine is sold in a lot. One lot can range from a single bottle to an entire collection. The traditional and most common unit of sale is one case of wine. As we discussed in Chapter 3, some auction catalogues refer to a twelve-bottle case of standard 750-milliliter bottles as "one dozen" or "per doz."

A *bottle* refers to a standard 750-milliliter bottle. If the wine is bottled in any format other than the standard bottle size, it will be mentioned here. (See page 39 for names and descriptions of large format bottles.) For a lot of magnums, for example, this line may read:

6 magnums   per lot $1400–2000

When groups of different bottles are sold together as one lot, the total number of each bottle size will be indicated, as well as a bottle count of each individual wine. For instance, the lot entry may give the following information:

Château Margaux	1982	(1)
Château Mouton	1982	(1)
Château Lafite	1982	(1 magnum)
Château Latour	1982	(2)
Château Haut Brion	1982	(1 magnum)
4 bottles and 2 magnums	per lot $5000–7000	

This horizontal collection of first growth Bordeaux includes one bottle of Margaux, one bottle of Mouton, one magnum of Lafite, two bottles of Latour, and one magnum of Haut Brion. There are four 750-milliliter bottles and two magnums. A bidder interested in these wines must bid on the lot as a whole. (See page 57 for more on horizontal collections.)

The Estimate

The estimated value of each lot guides bidders as they set their limits. It is an educated guess as to what the wine is worth, made by studying recent auction results for the same wine. The auction team uses its own as well as competitors' results, while also considering recent market trends and published opinions on the wine. Up-to-date sales results are readily available because the number of serious commercial wine auctions continues to grow. One of the staff's most important tasks is to keep its records of auction results current.

Both consignors and bidders rely heavily on the accuracy of the pre-sale estimates. It is presented as a low to high figure, such as $1,000 to $1,500. Almost every lot is sold subject to a *reserve price*—a confidential minimum price below which the auctioneer cannot, by contractual agreement, sell the lot (unless the consignor has agreed to grant the auctioneer the right to use his discretion in certain situations). This reserve cannot exceed the low end of the estimated range, according to New York State law and tradition in most other places. Usually, it is set one or two bid steps below the low end. Other consignments have the low end of the estimate as the reserve. Therefore, a bidder looking at a lot with interest must assume he has to spend at least the estimate's lower figure.

The high end of the estimate range is not as important as the low end. It is not the highest possible price, but merely the reflection of recent auction sales of similar bottles. For example, an original wood case of 1982 Château Mouton in perfect condition is estimated between $7,000 and $9,000. Yet three different and recent auctions sold this wine at $7,000, $8,200, and $10,000. As you can see, at one auction, the wine sold for $1000 over the high end of the reserve. This could be a result of the number of bidders, the case's condition, or even the wine's placement within the catalogue.

On average, 75 percent of lots sell within their estimate range, 15 percent sell above the high end of their range, and 10 percent fail to sell.

Ultimately, value is determined by the final bid. The estimate is merely a guide. Websites and reference books list auction results so bidders can research prices. The most comprehensive wine-auction price guide is the *Wine Price File,* a biannual publication of wine-auction prices recorded from the top national and international auction houses, found at www.wineprices.com. Another interesting online source for wine prices is www.wine-searcher.com. However, some of these prices are contributed by retailers; as an auction buyer, you must learn to always be aware of whether the price you are looking at is from retail or auction.

BACK MATTER

The catalogue doesn't end with the completion of the lot entries. Every catalogue includes an index of all the wines in the auction, a Ullage Chart to outline the standards by which each bottle is assessed, an absentee bid form, a pre-registration form, a catalogue subscription order form, and information regarding the collection and shipment of auction purchases. Some companies also include advertisements for other aspects of their businesses, such as tasting events or wine storage opportunities.

The Index

Every bottle of wine in the auction is listed in the catalogue's index. The index is an extremely useful introduction to these wines. Many catalogue readers flip to the index first, either for an overview of the auction or to determine if a certain wine is being sold. The index is organized alphabetically by wine region. The best auction catalogue indexes separately list large format bottles from standard-sized bottles for those bidders interested in big bottles.

Each auction company organizes its index slightly differently. Generally, the wines are organized by their regions of origin, and further divided by vintages. The lot number where a wine can be found is listed to its right. (See inset "A Sample Catalogue Index" for an example.) Interested bidders can use the lot number to reference the body of the catalogue for further investigation of the lot and to determine condition, quantity, provenance, and storage information.

Sometimes a lot number will be in parentheses. This indicates that the wine mentioned is part of a larger lot and being sold with other wines. In the inset on page 87, at least one bottle—and possibly more—of 1945, 1959, and 1961 Margaux are being sold as one lot. If you are interested in Margaux, you could reference the lot entry for Lot 126 to see exactly how many bottles of each vintage are included in the lot. Similarly, Lot 1398 should be referenced by fans of different Port wines from 1963.

A Sample Catalogue Index

This small excerpt from a catalogue index lists the Port and Red Bordeaux wines for sale. Bottles are organized alphabetically by their region of origin. Within each region, bottles are further arranged by their vintages. Within each vintage from a particular region, the wines are alphabetized by name. The lot numbers in which they appear are listed to their right. If the lot number is in parenthesis, the bottle is being sold in a lot with other wines.

Index

Port

1963	Croft	265
	Dow	(1398)
	Fonseca	(1398)
	Graham	(1398)

Red Bordeaux

1900	Margaux	124
1929	Margaux	125
1945	Margaux	(126)
1959	Margaux	(126)
1961	Cheval Blanc	437
	Margaux	(126)
	Mouton	68
	Lafite	294
	Latour	1100
	Petrus	834

The Ullage Chart

The *Ullage Chart* outlines the standards used by the auction company to catalogue the *ullage*—level of wine—in each bottle. This level may indicate how properly the wine has been stored throughout its life. However, as explained earlier in this chapter, wine can evaporate naturally over time. While you should not entirely avoid bidding on a wine that is catalogued with a ullage note, bidding on a young bottle with a particularly low level of wine can be risky.

Because the auction wines are almost never seen by anyone other than the staff

The first Ullage Chart was sketched by Michael Broadbent in 1967. He drew a Bordeaux-shaped bottle as the guide. In 1995, wine-auction expert Kevin Swersey added the additional illustration of a Burgundy-shaped bottle.

member responsible for cataloguing the lot, the description of wine level must be accurate. The Ullage Chart allows bidders to visualize the bottle. It consists of two illustrations: a Bordeaux bottle and a Burgundy bottle. The Bordeaux bottle has a long neck over a uniform cylindrical bottle. Its shoulders are just under the curve where the neck is attached to the body. The levels are described according to where the wine reaches, in terms of the bottle's shoulders and neck. The terms used—bottom neck, top shoulder, upper-shoulder, mid-shoulder, and low-shoulder—are usually abbreviated. The chart explains the abbreviations and clearly states what each is describing. Burgundy bottles are shaped differently, with sloped shoulders. Their levels are measured in centimeters, instead of being described in terms of shoulder height. For both Burgundy and Bordeaux bottles, if the level of wine is not indicated, you can assume the wine sits at the base of or rises into the neck.

Ullage Descriptions & Interpretations

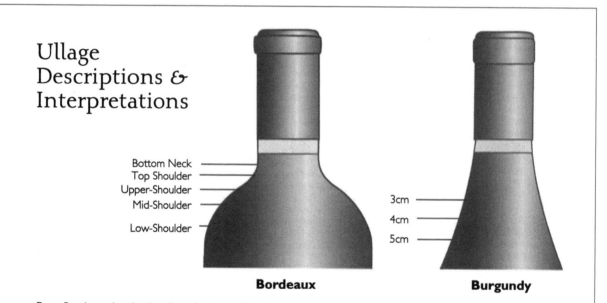

Bottom Neck
Top Shoulder
Upper-Shoulder
Mid-Shoulder

Low-Shoulder

3cm

4cm

5cm

Bordeaux   **Burgundy**

For a Bordeaux bottle, the ullage (or level of liquid in the bottle) is described using the terms below, which correspond to the levels indicated above. For a Burgundy bottle, the fill level is measured in centimeters.

BOTTOM NECK. Perfectly good for any age of wine. Outstandingly good for a wine of 10 years or longer in bottle.

TOP SHOULDER. Normal for any claret 15 years old or older.

UPPER-SHOULDER. Slight natural reduction through easing of cork and evaporation through cork and capsule. Usually no problem. Acceptable for any wine over 20 years old. Exceptional for pre-1940 wines.

MID-SHOULDER. Probably some weakening of the cork and some risk. Not abnormal for wines 30 to 40 years of age. Estimates usually take this into account.

LOW-SHOULDER. Risky and usually only accepted for sale if wine or label is exceptionally rare or interesting. Always offered without reserve and with low estimate.

Fill-Out Forms

Besides presenting information on the auction house and the products for sale, the catalogue offers convenience. The forms included at the book's back give you the ability to place bids from your living room, register before ever stepping foot in the auction room, and purchase an annual catalogue subscription to be mailed to your home.

The Absentee Bid Form

An *absentee bid form* is included in every wine-auction catalogue. (A sample form can be found on page 90.) If you wish to participate through absentee bidding, fill it out and fax or mail it in prior to the auction. The relevant information for doing so is included on the form. Most auction companies have a policy that absentee bids must be received no later than twenty-four hours before the sale. Required information includes name, address, email address, telephone number, and banking information. Sometimes the finance department is satisfied with your bank's name, while other times specific account information is requested. Some companies also ask for credit card information for added security, but they will not place any charges on the card unless you specifically instruct them to charge your auction purchases to that card.

> Although not a requirement, it is a good idea for first-time bidders to call the auction office to establish themselves as potential buyers, especially if they are participating by absentee bid.

There is also sale information found on the absentee bid form. Contact information for the auction company's bid department can be found here. Some include bidding and payment instructions. Some absentee bid forms incorporate a table of bid increments, or bid steps, to make it easier for the absentee bidder to correctly place his bid. We will discuss why you may want to bid by absentee bid in Chapter 6 and explore the actual process in Chapter 7.

The Catalogue Subscription Order Form

Another useful form is the *catalogue subscription order form*. If you know you are interested in a specific company's upcoming auctions, it can be worthwhile to subscribe to their annual catalogue series. The best part of paying for a subscription is that you will not miss an auction because a catalogue will arrive automatically two to three weeks prior to the event. A wine-auction catalogue is usually priced between $25 and $35, with a slight discount offered for an annual subscription. Payment instructions are included on the form. However, if you purchase wine in each or most auctions of a specific company, you should speak with a member of the auction team about having an annual catalogue subscription sent to you free of charge. Almost all auction companies will oblige this request from one of their good clients.

> You can use the catalogue subscription order form, found towards the back of the auction book, to order a single catalogue as well as a subscription.

Absentee Bid Form

Wine Lover's Guide Auctions, Inc.   Sale 001 - February 20th

After filling out bidder pre-registration form, please enter your bids here
and fax both forms immediately to: (123) 555-4568.
Bids must be received no later than 24 hours before the auction.

Name_____ Date _____

        Name of bidder to whom the invoice will be directed

Wine Lover's Guide Auctions, Inc. offers this service without charge as a convenience to our clients who cannot attend the sale. Every effort is made to execute all absentee bids and bidders understand that Wine Lover's Guide Auctions, Inc. takes no responsibility in any errors or omissions in the execution of the bids.

The final bid price is the sum of the hammer price plus a Buyer's Premium of 18%, together with any sales or use taxes when applicable. These bids will be executed at the lowest possible amount and bid up to but not to exceed the Maximum Bid.

In the event of duplicate bids the auctioneer acknowledges the bid that came into the office first.

Only successful Absentee Bidders will be notified by receipt of an invoice. However, all auction results are available immediately after the auction, online or by calling the Wine Lover's Guide Auctions, Inc. office.

Bidders must place absentee bids using these increments. Any bids not following the prescribed increments will be rounded down.

        Up to $200 by $10

        $200–$300 by $20

        $300–$500 by $25–$50–$75

        $500–$1,000 by $50

        $1,000–$2,000 by $100

        $2,000–$3,000 by $200

        $3,000–$5,000 by $250–$500–$750

        $5,000–$10,000 by $500

        $10,000–$20,000 by $1,000

        $20,000 and above by $2,000 or auctioneer's discretion

Wine Lover's Guide Auctions, Inc. • (123) 555-4567 • info@WLGAuctions.com

Lot #	Maximum Bid	# of lots wanted in the parcel

The Payment Instructions and Delivery Form

The catalogue also includes several pages of information that you'll need after the auction. Once your bids are successful, you will need to know how to get your wine. The payment instructions included in the catalogue will state how your payment can be made, when you need to make it, and how long the house will hold your wine until you make arrangements to move it from the warehouse. After your payment is received, the auction house will start the necessary work to deliver your purchases to you.

You can always collect the wine from the warehouse yourself. You may have to make an appointment; information on setting one up will be included here. If that is not an option, use the delivery form provided in the catalogue. You will have to provide your address and telephone number, as well as payment for the shipping and any special shipping instructions. Sometimes auction companies include a chart with the charges for ground shipping. If the auction company has its own temperature-controlled storage facilities, you can probably store your wine with them. Most companies charge $10 to $20 per case per month. Long-term arrangements may also be available.

Bidder Pre-Registration Form
Wine Lover's Guide Auctions, Inc.

Sale Number 001 February 20th   Fax to (123) 555-4568

Bidder Information

Name of Bidder _____ Agent _____ Email Address _____

Street Address _____ City_____ State_____ Zip Code _____

Daytime Telephone _____ Alternate Telephone _____ Fax Number _____

Identification: Drivers License_____ Other _____

Successful Bidder Shipping Information

☐ Same as Address Above   ☐ Different Shipping Address

Name as will appear on Invoice _____ Email Address _____

Street Address _____ City_____ State_____ Zip Code _____

Daytime Telephone _____ Alternate Telephone _____ Fax Number _____

Credit Card Information

Credit Card Information also used for Identification Purposes. Credit Card Purchases not to exceed $25,000. Check, money order, cash or wire transfer may be used to pay the balance. No charges made until 10 days from the date of the auction unless authorized for payment upon receipt of the invoice.

☐ Visa   ☐ Master Card   ☐ American Express   expiration _____

   I agree and am bound to the procedure of bidding as outlined in the catalogue's Conditions of Sale. I also agree that I will not bid on any lot owned by me, and that I am not acting as agent to bid on another's own property.

Signature _____ Date _____

The Bidder Pre-Registration Form

If you plan to attend the auction in person, pre-registering through a *bidder pre-registration form* will save you time on auction day. (See page 92 for a sample form.) This way, your paddle will be waiting for you. The form requires your name, address, information you would like to have appear on future invoices, and payment preferences. Forms of identification and payment vary from company to company. If the auction company accepts payment by credit card, you may be asked to supply that information on the pre-registration form. Instructions on where to send the completed form are located on the form itself.

THE AUCTION RESULTS

After the auction, a printed list of the *prices realized* will be made available. The prices paid for each lot are recorded in numerical order. If a lot number does not appear or if no dollar value follows a lot number, that lot failed to sell at the auction. Check to see if each price reported is the hammer price (the last bid recognized by the auctioneer) or the hammer price plus the buyer's premium (a percentage of the final bid price added to the hammer price by the auction house as a service charge). The prices realized usually appear on the auction house's website a day or two after the auction has ended, and can be downloaded and printed for easy, timely access to the auction results. A copy of the prices realized list should be kept with each auction catalogue for the most accurate record of each auction's results. This is extremely important for the collector who is interested in the most current value of any given wine.

CONCLUSION

Great care is taken to catalogue and present the wine in an efficient and stylish way. The layout of the front and back matter is labored over to make an attractive catalogue. Yet this book is also a valuable research tool. It can teach the serious collector a great deal about the value of collectible bottles. Now that you can read an auction lot entry, you will find yourself making less bidding mistakes and enhancing your collection with better auction finds.

The auction catalogue provides much more than the detailed list of wines for sale. It contains information on both the auction and the auction house as well as the standards used to assess the wines. The catalogue also states the auction house's rules for participation, and includes several forms to make your auction experience as smooth as possible.

Now that you are familiar with the information found in the auction catalogue, we will discuss how to use it to your best advantage as you prepare for auction day.

6

Preparing for the Auction

If you want your day at the auction to run smoothly, you'll have to do a little homework before the event. This chapter explains how to review and mark the catalogue so that you are completely ready when auction day arrives. You will learn how to set bidding limits, an important part of preparation for any auction that will help you maintain good judgment and make quality decisions at the sale. You will also learn how to pre-register, which will save you time on the big day.

There are several ways in which you can bid for the items you want. This chapter will take a look at these options so that you can decide whether to bid in person, by written order, by telephone, or through a representative. Although you will want to attend your first several auctions in person to become accustomed to the scene, there are some advantages to bidding by absentee bid. Once you become familiar with the different bidding options, you will find that lots from all auctions are available to you.

REVIEWING AND MARKING THE CATALOGUE

Thorough preparation for an auction, particularly when working with the sale's catalogue, leads to great wine at great prices. After reading Chapter 5, you should be able to navigate your way from the front to the back of the catalogue. Now is the time to choose the lots you want to buy as well as set spending limits for each. Take notes on wines that spark your interest as you work your way through the catalogue. (You should bid on wines that interest you. However, Chapter 12 will provide suggestions for choosing wines with which to start a collection.) Be sure to take advantage of the catalogue's pre-registration form, which will allow you to avoid the hassle of and possible line at the registration table. Finally, you'll want to review the payment options, which are also found within the auction catalogue.

Setting Maximum Limits

Do your homework before stepping into the auction room. By studying the catalogue and researching prices, you'll make less bidding mistakes. In the auction book, mark the lots that interest you and write the top bid you will pay for each next to its corresponding estimate. Setting limits is the single most important part of preparation because sticking to them will help you avoid making extravagant purchases you will regret later.

Using the Prices Realized List

Use recent auction results to help set your limits. Every auction company releases these figures in a prices realized list. This list, which states the last price paid at auction for the same wine, is a better indication of what you can expect to pay for a lot than its pre-sale estimate. Estimates are educated guesses. Although they are based predominantly on recent auction results, the auction market fluctuates too quickly for them to remain consistently accurate. The prices realized lists are a more immediate reflection of recent sale prices.

For example, let's say that a case of Château Mouton 1982 with a pre-sale estimate of $5,500 to $7,500 sold at a recent auction for $8,500. Chances are that you will not be able to buy an upcoming case at the low end of this estimate. A bidder aware of the latest $8,500 price will set a high limit, bid aggressively, and stand a good chance of winning the wine. Yet not knowing the recent $8,500 auction price may lead another bidder to rely on the estimate when setting his limit. He would bid conservatively and probably lose the lot. If 1982 Mouton continues to sell for around $8,000, the specialists will likely raise the pre-sale estimate to $7,000 to $9,000, or, more aggressively, $8,000 to $10,000, but not in time to help our bidder win his lot. On the other hand, prices also drop, so specialists must use caution when setting estimates and buyers must be aware of this before bidding. The last thing anyone wants to do is overpay at auction.

Taking the time to review recent auction prices before setting your limits will give you a competitive edge, and the prices realized list puts the facts you need at your fingertips.

Figuring Surcharges Into Your Limits

When setting your limits, consider the standard auction charges added to the hammer price. (The hammer price, as you learned earlier, is the final bid and the amount for which the lot is sold.) Auction surcharges include sales tax and the buyer's premium (a percentage of the hammer price that the buyer must pay on top of his final bid). The fixed, non-negotiable buyer's premium is imposed on all auction purchases, from an $8,000 case of 1982 Mouton to a $64.5 million Picasso painting. It is 15 to 20 percent of the hammer price at most auction houses. If you figure the buyer's premium into your limit and stick to it, you will know exactly what you are spending when you bid. If you don't do the math, on the other hand, you may end up feeling ripped off when the buyer's premium is added to your invoice. (This is illustrated in the inset "Accounting for Sales Tax and the Buyer's Premium.")

Sales taxes will vary depending on how the successful bidder takes possession of the wine. Read the catalogue's legal information to determine all costs. If anything is unclear, contact the company's financial department to determine the tax liability.

It takes discipline and practice to stop bidding when your preset limit is reached. Here, a good auctioneer works against you, always trying to get you to bid "one more time." The auctioneer is testing the bidder's will in the exciting but tense moments just before the hammer falls. Although it can be disappointing to lose a lot you have your eye on, most wines will come around again, either later in the sale or at a different auction. It is far worse to come unprepared, get carried away, and spend more than you meant to spend. To help you come prepared to win, we will look closely at bidding strategies in Chapter 7.

Registering in Advance

As discussed in Chapter 5, most auction catalogues contain a pre-registration form. It requires information including identification, invoice preference, and payment plan. Pre-registering supplies the auction house with the necessary data while saving

Accounting for Sales Tax and the Buyer's Premium

A bidder is interested in a lot with a pre-sale estimate of $6,000 to $8,000. After researching the market, he decides that he wants the lot, but for no more than $8,000. Her limit is $8,000. Is he happy to pay the sales tax on top of the purchase price, as with most retail transactions? Is he also willing to add the buyer's premium, 15 to 20 percent of the hammer price, to the $8,000? Or is $8,000 his total limit, including these additional charges?

If the bidder wins the lot with an $8,000 bid, the case of wine will cost $9,200—before taxes—if the auction company levies a 15-percent buyer's premium.

Suddenly his total, including the 7-percent sales tax, comes to $9,844.

As you can see, if the bidder's total limit is $8,000, his top bid must be lower. A bid of $6,500 plus the 15-percent buyer's premium of $975 brings the purchase price to $7,475 before sales tax. If the buyer's sales tax is 7 percent ($523.25), the total becomes $7,998.25 and remains within his budget.

It is personal preference whether to include the additional charges in your limit. Calculating the figures prior to auction day, however, is crucial to making smart decisions at the sale.

you time at the event. The pre-registered bidder can simply arrive at the auction, identify herself, and pick up his paddle. (For more information on the bidding paddle, please turn to page 105.)

There is no downside to pre-registration. There are no charges involved or consequences for deciding not to attend. If you choose to skip the auction, the offered information will remain confidential and unused. (For information on registering at the auction, see page 105.)

Reviewing Payment Alternatives

It is wise to understand your payment options prior to making a purchase. As mentioned on page 91, payment instructions are clearly outlined in the catalogue. The rules vary between different houses.

Most credit card companies charge surcharges for their use; as a result, some auction companies do not accept charge cards. This can be inconvenient, particularly if a buyer is unaware of the rule. The companies that accept credit card payments do so with certain restrictions, often capping the amount that may be charged to each card, typically around $25,000. For these houses, if your purchase is going to exceed their limit, you will have to pay the difference using another method of payment.

You may also want to find out if the company accepts personal checks or bank checks. Again, you'll want to make this determination *before* the auction.

BIDDING OPTIONS

After you receive the auction catalogue and decide that you want some of the wine offered, you'll want to consider your bidding options. The first is to bid in person. You can go to the sale location on auction day, ready to bid on predetermined lots. Alternate ways to compete do not require your attendance. Methods of absentee bidding include written-order bids, telephone bids, and bidding by representative. This section will discuss the benefits and drawbacks of each bidding style.

Bidding in Person

There is no substitute for attending the auction and bidding in person. You have the most control over winning a lot when you are at an auction with a paddle in your hand. Also, by attending the auction, you may have an opportunity to buy a lot on which you weren't expecting to bid. From time to time, the auctioneer may open a lot at a bid that you recognize is under the wine's usual market value.

Another benefit of attending the auction in person is meeting the members of the auction team and other collectors. It will greatly help build and solidify your rela-

If you plan on charging your purchases, you may want to call your credit card company so that it is aware this transaction might take place. Your limit may be able to be raised so a large purchase won't raise an alarm. This will result in smoother dealings when you pay.

tionship with the auction house if the team members can put a face to your name. Additionally, auction events are wonderful for meeting like-minded wine drinkers. Many wine friendships have been established at auctions.

There is only one major downside to attending an auction in person. The chance of getting caught up in the moment and overpaying for a lot is the force working against the live bidder. It is the auctioneer's job to keep everyone's paddle in the air for as long as possible. Some auctioneers are very good at this, and the live bidder who comes to the room unprepared may be an easy victim. Preparation goes far towards avoiding this scenario.

You will become familiar with the usual prices of many wines as you attend wine auctions more frequently. This will allow you to recognize a bargain when the opportunity for one arises.

Bidding by Absentee Bid

Absentee bidders win over half the lots at any given wine auction. As stated earlier, absentee bidders are participants who do not attend the live auction. There is no charge for participating in the auction as an absentee bidder. Auction companies provide this service for customer convenience, and there are many reasons to take advantage of the option.

It is not feasible to attend every large sale because auctions are held several times each month and all over the world. Due to both expenses and time, distance can be a huge motivator to participate as an absentee bidder. Also, many auctions are held on weekdays. It may be impossible for some potential bidders to attend because of work or other obligations. Absentee bids allow buyers to participate in many more auctions than would otherwise be possible.

Many bidders take advantage of this option not only to save themselves time but also because there is almost no chance of an absentee bidder getting carried away by the live action, which can lead to costly mistakes. The exception to this is the telephone bidder who, as you will see, participates in real time and can still have his judgment affected by the heat of the moment, despite not actually being in the auction room.

Yet the absentee bidder must understand that he has less control than live bidders. His bids are placed in someone else's hands. Most auction companies offer a disclaimer stating that, ultimately, they take no responsibility for failure to execute an absentee bid correctly. Because absentee bidders account for a substantial portion of the successful bids at any auction, however, every company takes great care to correctly implement these bids.

Absentee bidders place their bids prior to the auction's start via telephone, fax, or email. Usually, these bids must be placed twenty-four hours before the beginning of the sale. They are then executed by either a member of the auction team or the auctioneer. Chapter 7 will further discuss the execution of these bids.

Written-Order Bids

A written-order bid is made using the catalogue's absentee bid form, described on page 89. A sample form can be found on page 90. This form also serves to register the absentee bidder for the auction.

To fill out the bidding section of the form, first write the desired lot number under the heading "Lot Number." Next, write the limit of what you are willing to spend on the line under "Maximum Bid." It is to your advantage to enter the lot numbers in sequential order, because it will decrease the likelihood of a mistake. It is also of utmost importance to write clearly. An auction company makes every attempt to contact an absentee bidder if it has any questions on the information supplied, but sometimes the intense pre-auction time-crunch results in situations that cannot be clarified or resolved before the sale. Absentee bidders: neatness counts! The form is streamlined and easy to fill out, so avoid confusion by writing legibly. If you have a large number of absentee bids, find a friend to help you double-check the transcribed numbers for accuracy. This extra step can save you from a slip that can drastically alter a bid.

Once the form has been completed, simply fax it to the company. You can also send in the bid by mail, although it has become increasingly less common to do so. Many auction companies now conveniently offer the absentee bid form online. Regardless of the format used, these bid forms should be filled out carefully and neatly to ensure that the auction company understands your exact intentions.

You can even use most absentee bid forms to bid on a parcel lot. As explained in Chapter 3, a parcel lot is several consecutive lots of identical wine from the same consignment. The winner of a lot in a parcel has the option to take any amount of the remaining lots at the same price. If parcel lot bidding is available on the written-order bid, there will be a third line provided, on which you can indicate the number of lots you would like to buy. Begin by writing the lot number on the first line. The next line will have a heading that reads, "Number of Lots Required." Here, indicate the number of lots you would like to buy. Your maximum bid price is listed last. Remember that this price will be applied to the first lot and any additional lots in the parcel you may win. Parcel lot bidding is tricky for even the most experienced auction goers, but the absentee form is usually self-explanatory. If you have questions about filling any part of the form out correctly, call the auction company's bid department. (Read about contacting the auction house on page 76.)

If you have trouble sticking to your limits in the heat of a sale, you may prefer written-order bidding because you won't have the option of spending above your maximum bid. This is a good way to remain within your budget. On the other hand, the bidding may conclude just over your limit. You will lose the lot, perhaps realizing

All absentee bid forms are date- and time-stamped when they are received. This allows the auction company to differentiate between two identical absentee bids. If successful, the bid received first wins the lot.

afterwards that you would have gladly paid the necessary increase. The next chapter will detail steps you can take to avoid this situation, but it is important to always name your top price.

You must also consider the possibility of winning all the lots for which you place bids. When attending an auction in person, you are aware of each successful bid as it occurs. But when bidding by written-order bid, there is no lot-by-lot summary available. You may win none of the lots because your bids are too low, or you may win more than you had expected. Getting too much wine, even at good prices, can lead to financial woe. Be careful not to bid on too many lots. (Turn to page 110 for "Either/Or" and "Global Total" bidding strategies, safeguards against spending too much when bidding by absentee bid.)

Written-order bids are also referred to as *order bids, commission bids,* and *book bids.*

Telephone Bids

The most secure way of bidding in an auction without attending the sale is to bid on the telephone. This allows you to participate in real time and therefore have the most control over your bidding. An auction staff member executes the bids at your command.

A disadvantage to bidding via telephone as opposed to submitting a written-order bid is that you must stay near the telephone during the time of the auction. The staff member always calls the bidder (as opposed to having the bidder call the sale). There is no foolproof way to time an auction, so the telephone bidder needs to be available for a one-hour time frame. The call will be made five to ten lots before the lot in question. If you do not answer or your phone line is busy, you miss your opportunity to win the lot.

Additionally, telephone bidding takes practice because you cannot see the auctioneer or hear his first hand. The bidding goes quickly and you must rely on the relayed messages from the representative. Although the process can be challenging, it becomes increasingly easy with experience.

Telephone bids are arranged with the auction house prior to the sale. There are a limited number of telephone lines and staff members to handle calls, so auction companies use a "first-come, first-serve" system to prioritize these bids. Some houses require that the value of the lot be over a certain dollar amount—usually $2,000 to $5,000—for a telephone bid to be permitted.

In some rare instances, an absentee bidder will book a phone line for a major portion of or even the entire duration of the sale. These clients have a high level of interest in the auction. For example, a bidder planning to buy many lots may want to get a feel for the action in the room. Auction houses interview phone bidders before committing to tying up both a phone line and a staff member for more than a few lots.

Representative Bids

You can send a representative to bid on your behalf. Some collectors employ cellar managers, also called consultants, to attend and bid at auctions for them; others informally get a friend to handle the responsibility. There are no restrictions on who can represent you at the sale. Of course, it may be an advantage if your friend is knowledgeable about wine or auctions.

First, work out your maximum bid for each lot. Then give the numbers to your representative. If you are pre-registering, name the representative on the pre-registration form to circumvent any delays or confusion. If you are not pre-registering, the representative can use his own identification to register at the sale. If successful, you may then request that the auction house redirect the invoice to you. The company's Finance Department can help you determine the most effective manner in which to execute this process.

CONCLUSION

Bidding in person is an important experience when you first become involved in wine auctions, but once you are familiar with the scene, there are several alternative ways to successfully compete when you are unable to attend. Written-order, telephone, and representative bids can be thoroughly rewarding if they are thoughtfully prepared. Some bidders participate through the absentee process not only to save time by not attending, but also to exert more disciplined control. There is little chance of an absentee bidder getting carried away by the excitement of a live auction.

Accomplishment is measured not merely by the number of lots you take home, but also by the amount of savvy you show during bidding. Letting a lot go because competition from other bidders has surpassed your limit is empowering, and setting limits prior to the auction makes this possible. The practiced bidder is in control of the auction process both when he wins and when he loses. Chapter 7 will discuss bidding styles to increase your control of your auction destiny.

7

Auction Day!

Auction day has finally arrived. After reading Chapter 6, you are familiar with the different styles of bidding, and have decided how you wish to participate. With your maximum bids set, you are ready to win some wine!

This chapter will cover auction day from beginning to end, including what to bring, when to arrive, and even where to sit. It will explain how to register at the sale in case you didn't pre-register (which was explained on page 95). You will be prepared for what you will see and what you should do so that your full attention can be focused on the bidding process.

Your bidding skills will improve with experience, but by learning the bidding strategies in this chapter, you will have basic skills at your fingertips from the very start. There are different options to consider depending on whether you are bidding in person or by absentee bid (see Chapter 6 for the benefits and disadvantages of each) and you will be familiar with them all. Some decisions will have to be made on the spot, but you will arrive at the auction with your strategy in hand.

LIVE BIDDING

It is time to dissect auction day, beginning with the role of the live bidder. Be sure to attend your first sale in person so you can acquaint yourself with the auction staff and see personally the details mentioned in this chapter. The bidding guidelines provided will have you participating in the action like a pro from the start.

What to Bring

You will want to bring the information that you've gathered during your auction research to the sale. Some bidders store their notes in laptops that they bring with them. Others arrive with price guides and research books. Any and all material is allowed. You may even want to bring food or beverages if you foresee being there all day without any other refreshments. (Some auction houses offer an optional lunch for auction attendees. This information will be provided in the catalogue.)

If this is your first sale at a particular house, call the office prior to the event. (See page 76 on how to contact the auction house.) You should ask about the room's arrangement before determining what to bring. When bidding is conducted from restaurant-style tables, there is room to spread out and bring whatever you deem necessary. Other auctions, however, are conducted with chairs set up theater style. There, a laptop, research materials, and a catalogue may prove too cumbersome. Inquire about the room's layout in advance so you can prepare your materials accordingly.

If you plan on registering at the event, you will also need to bring a driver's license and a credit card. (See page 105 for registration information.) You may want to bring these cards even if you have pre-registered, for identification purposes.

What to Wear

Although comfort should be your top priority, let the auction venue dictate your clothing choice. If the auction is at Christie's, Sotheby's, or a top-rated New York restaurant, for example, you may want to wear a sports jacket and khakis.

Anything goes with auction apparel. There is no specific dress code imposed at regular commercial wine auctions. It is most important to dress comfortably, because you may be sitting for several hours. Some auctions, particularly charity auctions, may call for a specific dress request, such as formal, black tie, or wine-country chic. These events will mention the dress code on the invitation. Otherwise, be comfortable. The auctioneer is not judging you on your dress.

When to Arrive

Missing a lot because you arrived late is as disappointing as missing one because you were not paying attention. Plan conservatively when setting your time of arrival.

If you are going to arrive after the sale's start, you will have to gauge the timing of the lots so you are present when the lot you want to win comes *on the block*, or on sale. Unfortunately, this can be challenging. Every auctioneer keeps his own pace. One wine auctioneer may sell between 100 and 150 lots an hour, while another may sell more than 200 lots an hour—two lots every minute. The pace is set by personal style, the number of absentee bids, and bidding activity from attending participants, including those at the customer service desk. You can contact the auction team for an opinion as to when you should arrive, but the staff can merely offer an educated guess. It is your responsibility to be present for your desired lots.

Your arriving early helps guarantee that you will not miss a lot that is important to you, while also allowing you time to read the room. As you get into the swing of the sale, take note of the energy in the room. Does the room feel sluggish and sleepy or pumped and charged? Is most of the bidding coming from the telephone bank and customer service? These characteristics may not affect prices, but you should note that each auctioneer and each auction moves to its own beat.

Reading the vibe in the room can provide you with confidence when the auctioneer arrives at your lots.

If you are registering at the event, leave yourself plenty of time before the start of your first lot. Allow at least a half hour for standing in line and supplying the necessary information.

How to Register

Sale-day registration requires the same information that is requested by the pre-registration form: identification, address, shipping information, and payment preference. In fact, the only difference between the two procedures is the possibility of a line at the auction's registration desk. Bring a driver's license and a credit card. After filling out the paperwork, you will be assigned a numbered paddle and can then proceed into the salesroom.

If you plan to register in person, arrive with plenty of time before the start of your first lot. The registration process can take up to thirty minutes if there is a line of bidders ahead.

Picking Up Your Paddle

Bidding at live commercial wine auctions is done with paddles that are distributed upon registration. All paddles share the same basic features. They display a number, which is usually black against a white background, and the name of the auction house. Each bidder is assigned a unique paddle number for the duration of the sale. The successful bidder is identified by this number, facilitating the after-sale billing and transfer of the purchased wine.

What You Will See

All auction rooms are different. Commercial wine auctions take place in hotel ballrooms, restaurants, and purpose-built auction rooms. Yet regardless of where an auction is held, the room's physical setup follows tradition long established by Christie's and Sotheby's. Auction spaces are well-lit rectangular rooms of varying sizes, and the auctioneer stands at a podium at the front of the room.

The larger international auction houses, like Sotheby's and Christie's, post an electronic board known as the *Currency Conversion Board* at the front of the room and to the side of the auctioneer. When bidding is opened and prices rise, the board shows the price in different currencies. It is particularly useful in that it displays the final hammer price for several seconds between lots.

Next to the auctioneer stands a *bids clerk*, also called a *sales clerk* or *sales recorder*. This person records the final bid price and the successful paddle number. Both the auctioneer and the bids clerk are looking at the exact same information: lot number, description, estimate, reserve, and absentee bids. The bids clerk also helps spot bids when they are missed by the auctioneer.

Before You Sit Down

By the beginning of the auction, the specialist team will know the amount of interest expressed in the sale. Although a specialist cannot reveal information about bids already placed, he can tell you how much interest he has seen in a lot. He may even venture an opinion as to how aggressively you will need to bid to secure a lot. Most specialists are happy to assist potential bidders right up to the point that state regulations allow. During the auction, specialists can be found at the customer-service area.

Where to Sit

The most important part of choosing a seat is to pick one within the auctioneer's plain view. He will be standing at a podium at the front of the room. Sitting front and center should guarantee you are seen. You can also stand, towards the side of the auctioneer. On the other hand, you may prefer to see the bidders with whom you are competing. Sitting towards the back of the room will provide you with this view.

Avoid sitting directly in front of the customer-service area. If you sit by this area, you may not be able to tell if the auctioneer has recognized your bid or an absentee bid from customer service. Similarly, if you are competing against another bidder seated directly in front of or behind you, it would be best for one of you—usually the first aware of the confusion—to shift out of the direct line. This will make it easier to determine who has the bid.

When attending the sale with a rowdy group of friends, it is wise to move away from the gregarious group when your lots come on the block. You don't want the auctioneer to miss your bid!

If an auctioneer repeatedly misses your paddle for any reason, get up and change places. This does not happen often, but there are times when an auctioneer and bidder are simply not communicating. For example, a seated bidder wearing a white shirt may raise his white paddle with a subtle gesture, leaving his wrist on the table. The black numbers on the paddle may not be enough to alert the auctioneer to the client's intention to bid. After all, he is standing some distance away. A similar situation may arise if you are seated in an obstructed or partial-view area. You are clearly disadvantaged if the auctioneer cannot see you raise your hand. If an auctioneer becomes aware that he missed a bid, he will usually address the situation with the bidder, who should find a more advantageous seat.

How to Bid

There are two basic approaches to bidding at an auction. Only time and experience will tell if you are an *early-action bidder* or a *late-entry bidder*. We will explore both methods.

Regardless of your bidding style, the best way to execute a bid is to raise your paddle high in the air. Watch the auctioneer to make sure he acknowledges you.

Although he will accept a slight raise of a pen or finger as a bid, it is far too easy for him to miss these subtle gestures. If the auctioneer fails to acknowledge your bid, draw his attention by announcing, "Bidding!" Never be shy about steering the auctioneer's attention to your bid.

The days of stuffy wine auctions are over. It is not uncommon for attendees to ask questions aloud: "What lot are we on?" "Is that my bid?" "What's the price?" Ask questions if you find yourself lost or confused at any time.

Be clear, be direct, and communicate with the auctioneer.

The Early-Action Bidder

Many bidders raise their paddles the minute the auctioneer offers the opening bid, rather than waiting. Immediately jumping into the competition establishes the bidder as a player early on. As bidding continues, the auctioneer is likely to come back to this early-action bidder, even if the price has since eclipsed the bidder's limit. This is a good strategy if you are worried about being overlooked when bidding gets down to the wire. Remain cautious, however, of becoming overzealous and bidding over your limit.

The Late-Entry Bidder

Some bidders choose to hang back from the early bidding burst. After the dust settles, these late-entry bidders keep the action alive. Like the early-action bidders, these players must be disciplined to remain within their pre-set limits. An advantage to joining the bidding in progress, rather than establishing yourself as an early player, is the opportunity to execute a bid on the bidding increment, also called a *bid step*, that enables the bidder to meet and not exceed his limit price. Let's look at this idea more closely.

Managing Bid Increments

Occasionally it is to the bidder's advantage to manage the bid increments. Consider an $8,000 case of wine. You want to buy the lot for $8,000, inclusive of the 15-percent buyer's premium, so you must try to secure the lot with a $7,000 bid. The bidding is opened at $5,000. You raise your paddle and bid $5,500. The bid step is $500. The competition progresses between you and the auctioneer, who is bidding on behalf of an absentee bidder. (There will be more details on the absentee bidding process later in this chapter.) The auctioneer raises to $6,000, and is followed by your $6,500 bid. As a result, the auctioneer will land on the $7,000 price, forcing you (if you choose to keep bidding) to exceed your limit and bid $7,500. Instead of sticking to your limit price, you would pay $8,625 for the $8,000 case of wine ($7,500 hammer price plus $1,125 buyer's premium; see page 94 for more on the buyer's premium).

The auctioneer chooses where to begin the bidding. Usually he starts at a price set in response to either absentee bids he needs to execute (see page 114) or the reserve he needs to meet (see page 52).

Although it is possible you can win the lot for a good price, you will not able to bid up to your limit because you did not correctly manage your bid steps.

As an alternative, you could hang back from the bidding when it begins, and throw your paddle up on the correct bid step, either $6,000 or $7,000. This would give you a greater chance of securing the lot for your top price. This is easier said than done because the auction pace is often too quick to have each intended bid step fall neatly into place. With practice, however, it becomes easier to successfully "land on the right foot"—a phrase traditionally used to refer to this practice.

Once familiar with an auction company's bid increments, some bidders occasionally attempt to cut the increment to their advantage. For example, the auctioneer has opened a lot at $5,000 and continues to announce increases in $500 increments. He calls $5,000, $5,500, $6,000, $6,500, $7,000. The next bid will be $7,500. A bidder can call out to the auctioneer, "$7,200!" Whether this bid will be accepted is up to the auctioneer. If the auctioneer is executing bids on behalf of an absentee bidder with a top bid of $9,000, it is unlikely that he will accept a $200 raise at this point. The auctioneer will address the proposition: "Okay, I'll take that," or "Sorry, I need $7,500."

Sometime the auctioneer himself cuts an increment so that he may be "on the right foot" to execute the top order bid from an absentee bidder. This is an indication that this bid is in fact the absentee's top price. The bidder in the room could ask for the next increment to be cut by same amount, and is likely to outbid the absentee bidder.

All bid steps are at the auctioneer's discretion. He decides when and if it is necessary to stray from the published, standardized increments. At some auctions, a bidder indicates he is interested in a cut increment by slashing the bidding paddle horizontally through the air. This is no longer as common as it used to be, because bidding is usually too fast for the gesture to register and have its desired effect. It is far more efficient to yell out the request. If you find yourself unsuccessful at cutting the bidding increment after several tries, the auctioneer may not be amenable to the reduction. Cutting increments works to the bidder's advantage once in a blue moon, so do not belabor the technique. It tends to be most effective, and the auctioneer is most likely to oblige, when the dollar amount of the lot is in the five-figure range, the increments are larger, and bidding has cooled. Cutting increments is just one of several reasons to approach the auctioneer.

Communicating With the Auctioneer

Address the auctioneer for all practical matters. If you cannot hear the auctioneer clearly, aren't sure which lot is being sold, or suddenly realize you bid on the wrong lot, speak up then and there. An auctioneer can remedy a variety of situations if they are brought to his attention immediately. For example, if you speak up within moments of mistakenly buying the wrong lot, the auctioneer can, at his discretion, reoffer the lot by reopening the bidding. If you wait until later and the sale gets recorded in the system, getting it reopened is less likely. If you are too shy to speak to the auctioneer while the sale is going on, immediately find a staff member, who will also be able to help with any problem. Auctions are vibrant, moving sales and the staff at each company is used to the immediacy of issues. The team is there to help the bidders.

Each auctioneer performs with individual style. Try to observe the differences. Auctioneers offer many useful clues that can help you succeed. For example, an auctioneer may lean forward each time he goes to hammer down a lot. In this case, you can bid just as he leans. Another auctioneer has reached the top of his absentee bids when he picks up his pen or gavel. One may say, "One more?" meaning that one more bid from the room will beat the absentee bidder's maximum price. Some auctioneers plainly state, "One more and it's yours." The key to successful bidding at an auction is to watch and listen to the auctioneer.

Seasoned bidders notice distinct characteristics of auctioneers. Try to be observant—becoming familiar with their small gestures can translate into your greater success.

At the end of each lot, the auctioneer announces both the winning paddle number and the final bid price. If you are the successful bidder, listen carefully to ensure that the information is correct. This is the time to speak up if a different paddle number or the wrong price is stated. The information recorded at the fall of the hammer is entered into the system and transferred to the invoice and shipping departments. Make a note of the hammer price in your catalogue. This will allow you to double-check the invoice when it becomes available. It is also a helpful record for when friends and family inquire about auction purchases.

Prices Realized

A complete list of what each lot sold for—called the *prices realized list*—is available after the auction. Keep the prices realized with the auction catalogue for easy reference and research for the next auction. Many auction companies make the prices realized available online within a day or two of the auction, while others require that you call and request a copy. Regardless of how these lists are issued, they are the most accurate indications of wine-auction prices. See page 94 for more on the value of the prices realized list and using it to set your limits.

When you are reading a prices realized list, be sure to note whether the prices given include the buyer's premium.

ABSENTEE BIDDING

The absentee bidder must go through the same process as the live bidder—carefully picking lots and calculating his limits—prior to submitting his bids. He then provides either the auction team or a representative with the maximum price he is willing to pay for each lot. The advantages and disadvantages of bidding by written-order, telephone, and representative bids were outlined in Chapter 6. All absentee bids are executed as if the absent bidder were in the room.

Written-Order Bids

Written-order bids can be carried out by members of the auction team or by the auctioneer. When team members carry out these bids, also called *order bids*, they use the uniquely numbered paddles issued to each absentee bidder. Like the live bidder, the absentee bidder keeps the same paddle number throughout the entire sale. Staff members responsible for implementing these bids seek to win at the lowest possible prices, just as the client would if he were in attendance.

Using a Bids Notebook to Keep Organized

Most wine auctions include between 1,000 and 2,500 lots. The most efficient way to "shop" is to first go through the catalogue and find the lots that interest you. Then, for each one, write the lot number, a brief description, the estimate, and your bid limit in a spiral notebook. Keep them in lot number order, and bring this bids notebook to the sale. As the lots are sold, record the hammer price next to the catalogue information you've written down. This way, you can later look back at the prices and easily trace them through different auctions.

This list will help make auction day as smooth as possible. Reading a conveniently ordered list is a much easier way to find your next lot than navigating through a large catalogue. You will have a better feel of where the auctioneer is in relation to your next bid, which will help tremendously when scheduling bathroom breaks or socializing with friends. Your notebook will also help you double-check the accuracy of invoices.

A bids notebook can also help you participate as an absentee bidder. You will be able to simply (although still with care) transfer the information to the absentee bid form. The notebook will enable you to neatly and clearly fill out the form without having to flip back and forth through the catalogue, which may cause you to miss a lot. Whether you are a live or absentee bidder, your bids notebook will provide with an instant reference for wine prices and start you on your way to purchasing wines at the prices you want.

If you are unable to transcribe lot information into a separate notebook, you may find it helpful to flag interesting lots with Post-it notes. As you go through the catalogue's index, flag the pages in which interesting lots fall so you will not have to constantly search through the book. Flags of different colors can indicate varying levels of interest. As with the bids notebook, the most important function of these tabs is to help you quickly reference interesting wine.

When the auctioneer is executing the absentee bids, they will be recorded in his auctioneer's book. He considers them as he contemplates where to begin the bidding. If an auctioneer has several absentee bids within the estimate range, for example, it is unlikely that he will start the bidding below the low end of the estimate. To keep the sale moving briskly along, some auctioneers quickly evaluate the absentee bids and start with the highest one.

Let's look at an example. A lot estimated at $600 to $800 has attracted three absentee bidders. These bidders have set limits of $600, $700, and $850. The reserve price for the lot is $550 and the bid step is $50. The $600 bid has already been beaten by the $700 bid, which in turn is beaten by the $850 bid. The most efficient opening price for this lot would be $750 because it is higher than the lower bids while also accounting for the highest absentee bidder's maximum bet.

When an auctioneer executes absentee bids, he may indicate that he is doing so with a number of phrases, including "The commission starts us at . . ." and "I have a bid in the book for . . ." The auctioneer in our example opens the bidding by saying, "Bidding on behalf of the order at $750." When someone in the room raises his paddle, the auctioneer recognizes the $800 live bid. The auctioneer then comes back immediately with $850, again executed on behalf of his absentee bidder. Either the bidder in the room will come back with a bid of $900 or the absentee bidder will win with his top price of $850. If the auctioneer opens the bidding with the $750 bid and is not challenged by any competitive bids from the room, the absentee bidder will buy this lot for $750, despite being prepared to pay $850. The inset "The Written-Order Bid Through the Eyes of the Auctioneer" (see page 114) further illustrates the execution of written-order bids.

It is best to prepare and submit your absentee bids soon after you receive the catalogue, because the winner of absentee bids that are tied for the top price is the bidder whose absentee bid form was received first. You can always cancel any absentee bids prior to the auction's start.

Prepare these bids as if you were going to attend the auction. Go through the catalogue, choose your lots, and set your limits. Then fill out the absentee bid form as explained on page 89. Bidding strategies are easily incorporated onto the form. After recording your limit, you can use the following methods to add flexibility to your bid.

Plus One

As a written-order bidder, you can authorize the auction staff to continue bidding one increment above your top price. For example, let's say you are eyeing a certain lot, and want it for around $500. Next to the bid on your absentee bid form, you can indicate *plus one* by either writing out the words or using the symbol "+1." If the auc-

If, as an absentee bidder, your top bid for a lot is $500, it is possible that someone else will also bid that amount. You could end up losing the lot to someone who is paying the exact amount of your high bid. Indicate "plus one" on your bid form to give your bidder permission to go one bid step higher.

tion team member implementing your bid ends on $450, the wrong bid step, he would be able to bid $550 in response to the $500 bid by the live bidder. By submitting this "plus-one" bid, you give yourself one extra chance to secure the lot and cannot lose it for the amount of your top bid.

The "plus-one" bid is, in fact, your maximum bid and should be figured including the buyer's premium and potential sales tax, as with any bid. "Plus-one" bids do not give the absentee bidder any sort of advantage or control. They simply provide one more chance to secure the lot. Remember that a "plus-one" bid does not mean that if you bid $500 plus one, you will have to pay $550 for the lot. The staff member or auctioneer will bid $550 only after $500 is bid. This "plus-one" bid results in a potential $600 purchase price (due to taxes and surcharges). These bids are usually executed by a member of the auction team because it is too much for the auctioneer to have to consider this strategy on top of everything else involved in the sale.

Either/Or

Another option that offers some leeway in the absentee bidder's strategy is the *"either/or" bid*. The "either/or" bid is exactly as it sounds. You want either lot number 4 or lot number 5, but not both. On the absentee bid form, fill in the information for Lot 4 and Lot 5, and write "or" between the two lines.

This strategy can also be used for lots that are not sequential. To indicate this, you can break away from keeping the bid form in strict numerical sequence. For example, to indicate that you would like to buy either Lot 4 or Lot 328, record the information for each on adjacent lines and write "or" between the two lines. You can also request to purchase one of several lots. List the numbered lots and write "or" between each number. You can add "only one please" in the margin to reiterate. Be sure your writing is clear and logical. The auction team will do its best to follow your wishes, but will not be able to if your directions are illegible.

The auction staff will then execute the bids according to these instructions. This strategy is particularly helpful if you want one case of a particular wine. If there are several similar cases offered during the course of the auction, you can fix your price, and patiently wait to secure one of the cases without paying dearly on the first attempt.

Either/or bidding offers the greatest amount of flexibility to a written-order bid. If, as an absentee bidder, you want one case out of several in the auction, indicate this near the appropriate lot numbers and make a note of it elsewhere on the form to clarify your instructions to the auction staff. The absentee bid form will pass through several staff members' hands up until the point of execution, and it never hurts to reiterate anything apart from standard procedure.

Global Total

One way to exert control over the absentee bid process is to set a *global total*—a total dollar limit for the entire sale. A bidder's eyes can often be bigger than his budget. There may be many lots that you would like to add to your collection, but perhaps you have almost fulfilled your annual wine allowance. Having done your homework and set the top limit prices for many lots in the upcoming auction, you know it is unlikely that you will be successful with each and every bid, but you simply cannot afford to win all the lots on which you are bidding.

By setting a global total of $10,000, you are informing the auction team that you wish to spend no more than that amount on your total auction purchases. To remain within this budget, the staff member will keep a running total of the lots you successfully purchase. He will cease bidding for you when the global total has been spent. These instructions can be written directly on the bid form. After filling out the form with each lot number and dollar amount, clearly and boldly write something to the effect of, "The total of all successful bids not to exceed $10,000." The auction house will call you if they have any questions.

Properly using these bidding options makes the absentee bid form one of the most disciplined ways to win any auction lot. It will provide you with the opportunity to win some excellent wine, without the chance of getting caught up in the competition.

Telephone Bidding

When *bidding by telephone*, you will book the phone line prior to the sale day. Your pre-registration and bid information will be given to the staff and you will be identified by a unique paddle number. You will already have chosen the lots in which you are interested and you will have set a limit for each one. It helps to have your top bids written down. As mentioned in Chapter 6, the call is given an approximate time. Answer in a quiet place where the process will not be disturbed. The auction staff member will call and proceed along the following lines:

"Hello, Mr. Telephone Bidder. My name is Ursula from WLG Auctions. How are you today? The auctioneer is now on Lot 50. I understand that you would like to bid on Lot 55. When the lot comes up, I will repeat the opening prices the auctioneer has already received, and if you are still interested in bidding, instruct me to bid by simply saying 'bid!'"

At this point, the staff member will explain any differing methods or styles he prefers. He may conclude, "I am going to put the telephone down and pick it back up at the start of Lot 54. Okay?"

The staff member may set the telephone down or continue to chat. As the

The Written-Order Bid
Through the Eyes of the Auctioneer

We first discussed the *auctioneer's book*—the catalogue belonging to the auctioneer—in the Chapter 4 inset "The Auctioneer and His Book." Now let's look at the absentee bid process from the perspective of the auctioneer. Written-order bids are handled slightly differently by each auction company. Some record every bid received on a particular lot, while others record only the top three. Some have the auctioneer execute these bids, while other companies rely on other team members for this job. The auction house in the following example records only the top three, and the bids are executed by the auctioneer. Recorded in the auctioneer's book solely for his eyes, the information may look like this:

Lot	Estimate	Reserve
Lot 34.	$5,000–$7,000	R. $4,500
absentee bids:	$8,000	#111
	$7,000	#372
	$5,000	#264

As you can see, absentee bidders are identified by registered paddles just like live bidders. The three absentee bids have already met the $4,500 reserve. The auctioneer will consider these bids before he begins.

Each auctioneer will chart his own course towards the top absentee bid. In the above example, the top bid is $8,000. If time is of the essence, the auctioneer can open the bidding at $7,000, knowing that someone is willing to pay more. He can open the lot with paddle #372's bid of $7,000; a bidder in the room may raise to $7,500; and the auctioneer can call his next absentee bid, $8,000 from paddle #111. At this point, absentee bidder #111 will win the lot for $8,000, or a live bidder will bid $8,500—after which this new bidder will proceed to either compete with another bidder in attendance or win the lot.

A different scenario will occur if the auctioneer opens the bidding on this lot at $7,000 to no response from the room. This amount is equal to the limits of bidders #111 and #372, so the auctioneer will jump to $7,500 on behalf of paddle #111. If still no bids come from the room, paddle #111 wins the lot for $7,500. A problem can result for the auctioneer if a late-entry bidder (see page 107) jumps in after the auctioneer has executed a $7,500 bid for paddle #111. He cannot continue with the $500 bid step, because the bidder in the room will be at $8,000, matching his remaining

desired lot grows near, so does the seriousness of the call. The staff member will often give the details of the lot prior to the one you are waiting for so you can get used to his speed and style. "Okay, Mr. Telephone Bidder. The auctioneer is starting the bidding on Lot 54, the 1978 Mouton. He's starting the bidding at $1,000, $1,200, $1,400, $1,600, $1,800. $1,800. $1,800, he's stalled at $1,800. He just sold the lot for $1,800. Now it's our lot, Lot 55, the 1982 Mouton. Here we go—he's opened at $5,500, $6,000, $6,500. $7,000. $7,000. Would you like $7,500?"

absentee bid. To rectify the situation, the auctioneer can cut the bid steps and offer the bidder in the room a $7,800 or $7,750 price, so he can counter with #111's bid of $8,000. This can also work to the advantage of the bidder in the room if the auctioneer then offers to cut the next bid increment as well. In other words, after executing #111's bid for $8,000, the auctioneer should offer the competitor the next bid of $8,200 or $8,250. The auctioneer's discretion would come into play.

Let's look at a similar lot with no absentee bids.

Lot	Estimate	Reserve
Lot 34.	$5,000–$7,000	R. $4,500

Here, the auctioneer would start the bidding under the $4,500 reserve, hoping to get a bidder from the room to meet the minimum price. The auctioneer could choose to open the bidding at $4,250 in anticipation that a bidder in the room will jump in at $4,500, or the auctioneer could invite the room to start the bidding at $4,500. Some auctioneers may even start well below the reserve price and chant up to just under the minimum to build up steam that may entice a bidder to throw up his paddle. Until a bidder raises his paddle, these bids are executed on behalf of the consignor's reserve, which is perfectly acceptable. It relies on the auctioneer's style.

A different situation with a similar lot may look like this:

Lot	Estimate	Reserve
Lot 34.	$5,000–$7,000	R. $4,500
absentee bids:	$8,000	#111

The auctioneer has only one absentee bid, paddle #111's $8,000. Without any other absentee bid to rival paddle #111, the auctioneer must start the bidding on behalf of paddle #111 at the reserve. He can announce that he has a "bid in the book for $4,500." Bidders then respond to #111's opening bid. The auctioneer keeps bidding on #111's behalf until the room dies out or the price of the lot becomes more than $8,000. If there is no bidding in the room at all, paddle #111 would win the lot at the reserve price of $4,500.

It will become increasingly easy to predict an auctioneer's next move as you attend more auctions. Since the execution of absentee bids depends on the auctioneer's discretion and style, you may find yourself more comfortable at an auction conducted by a certain auctioneer. Learning the style of a conductor is key, but make it a point to become familiar with several auctioneers. As you observe their differences, you will improve your auction skills.

If you are willing to pay this price for the lot, you can say, "Yes!" or "Bid!"

"Okay. It's ours at $7,500. $8,000 has been bid—would you like $8,500?"

You can repeat, "Yes!"

"It's ours again at $8,500. $8,500, it's still ours, it's still ours, SOLD, ours at $8,500! Congratulations!"

The staff member will then tell the auctioneer your paddle number.

You can choose to stop bidding at any time. Once the price has surpassed your

When the lot on which you are bidding has sold, you may have questions regarding other lots in the sale. Ask the auction staff member if anyone is free to speak with you. This particular staff member probably needs to assist another telephone bidder with an upcoming lot, so this will ensure better service.

limit or if you don't want to bid higher for any reason, simply say, "No!" or "I'm out!" The staff member will most likely keep you on the line until the lot is sold so you can hear the final successful bid price.

As with every type of bidder, the telephone bidder sets his maximum price before the call. Some auction companies require that the telephone bidder provide the staff member with this number in case the call is lost. It is a good idea to tell the team member your limit so that he can bid up to it, at which point you can always choose to continue bidding. This will make it easier for the staff representative, who can then bid confidently up to that amount before starting the interaction with you, the telephone bidder. This way, the bidding relationship with the auctioneer can be set without knocking the auctioneer off his pace. The auctioneer may be more patient with a telephone bidder after it has been established that he is an experienced bidder or a serious newcomer.

Telephone bidding can be intimidating at first. A savvy auction employee will take charge of the situation and you win your lots. If you have worked comfortably and successfully with a certain employee, you may wish to request his assistance for your next telephone bid.

Representative Bidding

As you learned in Chapter 6, you can *send a representative* to bid on your behalf. Make sure the representative completely understands your auction goals and limits. He will follow the live bidding procedures.

If you send a representative and your information appears on the registration form, the lots he buys will be charged to you. Once your representative registers with your name and billing information, it will be impossible for you to say, "I didn't tell him to buy that," after the auction. Be very clear with your directions to anybody bidding on your behalf.

CONCLUSION

With your limits clearly set, you are ready to jump into the action. At the auction, your blood starts pumping and your heart races as your lot approaches—but don't let the excitement carry you away! At all times, stick to your pre-determined limits.

You will gradually become more comfortable and confident with live auction bidding as you implement this chapter's strategies and attend more auctions. Mastering various skills—including those for absentee bidding—will ensure that no auction need pass you by. Like victors at most competitive endeavors, auction winners are the players who are the best prepared. Chapter 8 will address what happens after you win!

8

Collecting Your Wine

You may or may not win wine at your first auction. But if you keep attending sales and set reasonable limits, you will soon be adding to your collection. Your preparation and patience will pay off when you win a prized lot at a price within your range—but that doesn't mean the auction game is over. You will still have to pay for and receive your wine, and carefully examine both the invoice and wine for any inaccuracies or problems. This chapter explains in detail what you will be checking for, as well as what to do with the wine immediately upon its arrival.

NOTIFICATION OF SUCCESSFUL BIDS

The items you win and their costs will be listed on an invoice. This itemized bill can usually be generated at the check-out desk when you leave the sale, whether the auction has ended or is still in progress. Some auction companies are even prepared to take payment immediately. If you do not request an invoice at the auction, one will be generated a day or two after the event's end and mailed to the address you gave on the registration form.

Checking Your Invoice

Verifying the information found on the invoice should be a top priority after the sale. The invoice will contain your name, your paddle number, the sale name and any identifying codes, and the sale date. For each purchase, the hammer price will be listed as well as the price including the buyer's premium. Check that all your purchases have been recorded accurately. It is important to keep a record of your successful bids at each auction so you can be sure everything you won appears on the invoice.

At some auctions, the company allows bidders to pay for their purchases immediately, even before the end of the event. If this is convenient for you, speak to an auction team member for details.

If any mistakes have been made, contact the auction house immediately. Post-sale, the auctioneer's book and the sales clerk's record serve to double-check any discrepancies. All auctions are tape recorded in case any final verification is needed.

The invoice will include the name of the sale and any identifying codes. These codes are used by auction houses to track specific auctions.

The initial invoice may or may not include state taxes, local taxes, and shipping charges. This depends on the information provided on the registration form, because bidders can choose to supply delivery details later, but taxes and charges cannot be calculated until the auction company receives these instructions. If the shipping information has not yet been supplied, a second invoice will be generated when it can be completed. The specific rules and regulations for each auction company's taxes and charges are outlined in the catalogue's conditions of sale.

Paying for Your Wine

Each company requires payment within a specific time frame outlined in its catalogue. Some companies want to be paid upon receipt of the invoice. Others specify a number of days (generally from seven to twenty-one) within which the payment must be remitted. All auction houses require payments to be made in full. To entice successful bidders to pay quickly, some auction firms offer a small credit that can be applied to future purchases in exchange for quick remittance. Be aware that some auction companies charge interest on late payments. This and other payment procedures are explained in the catalogue. Once payment is received and cleared by the auction house, you can begin preparations for collecting your wine.

CHOOSING A STORAGE FACILITY

Before deciding how to transport the wine, you have to determine where you are going to store it. Often, the choice will be between a long-term storage facility and a wine cellar or storage unit in your home.

Many auction companies offer long-term storage arrangements. This can be a great option if you have not yet formed your own storage plan. Perhaps you are in the process of or have not yet started building your home cellar. Maybe you have outgrown several rented storage lockers and already have wine in more than one location. Rather than moving a purchase more than once, you can pay to keep the bottles at the auction warehouse. This way, they can remain there until you are prepared to give them a permanent home. Remember, you are trying to move your wine as infrequently as possible.

There is a particular advantage to long-term storage at the point of purchase for the investor-collector. Besides removing the tiresome hauling of heavy cases of wine from cellar to cellar, this option gives an added boost to the wine's provenance when the time comes to resell the stock. (You can read about provenance on page 79.) Potential bidders will be pleased to know that your wine was not moved from the time of its original auction purchase.

Home-storage units and long-term storage facilities are described on page 80.

Unless you decide to store your wine at the auction company's warehouse, begin preparation for the bottles' arrival once arrangements have been made for their transportation. If you need time to set up or find a storage unit, you may be able to leave your purchases in the auction warehouse for a short while. Each house has its own policy as to how long purchases will be held after an auction before a storage charge is imposed. This time frame and subsequent storage charges are explained in the catalogue.

TRANSPORTATION OF THE WINE

You have several options for taking possession of your wine. The decision will most likely be based on the proximity of the sale to the rest of your collection, whether it is stored at your home, a warehouse, or elsewhere. If it is nearby, you may decide to pick up the wine yourself. If you are unable to do so, have a large distance to travel, or would rather have the process handled by professionals, you can have your wine shipped. Regardless of how you decide to collect your purchases, you are responsible for informing the auction company of your intentions.

Picking Up the Wine

You can always pick up your purchases at the auction warehouse. Directions to the warehouse and procedural instructions—including warehouse hours and whether an appointment is necessary—are listed in every auction catalogue. Some companies charge a small fee per case or per lot, which may be waived or reduced by request for large orders. Local taxes are collected from buyers who pick up the wine in person. The invoice must be satisfied in full before any wine is released for either local delivery or in-person pick up.

Many auction companies will allow you to store your purchases in their warehouse for a monthly fee. If you choose do so, you do not need to arrange for the bottles' transportation. This option is good for the wine's provenance.

When driving your new auction purchases home, turn on the air conditioning, don't leave the car parked for any length of time, and avoid any sudden temperature changes. It is always best to drive straight home.

Shipping the Wine

Many companies, particularly those associated with retail businesses, offer complimentary or inexpensive local delivery service. When the wine has to be shipped a large distance, however, the shipping process involves a bit more money and forethought.

Shipping charges will be calculated once your instructions are given to the auction house. Most auction catalogues list the estimated charges for both local delivery and out-of-state ground and air carriers. Read the section carefully and discuss it with a member of the auction staff to make sure you fully understand the costs and can calculate an estimation before the wine is moved. All reputable wine-auction houses will have individual policies regarding the shipment of wine during undesirable weather conditions, or to certain states where there may be regulatory restrictions.

Ask the auction house if there are any packing or handling charges. There may, for example, be a *repacking charge*. Ground carriers store deliveries on wrapped palates and are able to move bottles in their original wooden cases. When the wine is being shipped by air, on the other hand, these woods cannot withstand the rigorous journey, so the bottles are repacked into cardboard cartons. Per-case repacking charges cover the cost of extra materials, such as cardboard cartons and Styrofoam inserts, and the original woods are shipped separately, usually through a less expensive service. Many auction companies publish the cost of shipping the original wooden cases on the shipping or registration form. Not all wines require repacking but many do. The auction staff can help you choose the best route for your particular purchase.

In addition to handling or repacking charges and the cost of the freight, most auction companies impose an insurance charge on outgoing shipments. Usually one percent of the sale total, this charge covers any loss or damage that occurs while the wine is in transit. The auction houses automatically include the nominal charge on each shipping invoice—but you are not required to take this provision. Upon signing a waiver, you can decline the insurance charge and take your chances with the wine traveling uninsured.

The decision to ship auction purchases via temperature-controlled carrier is based on the fragility of the wine and the philosophy of the purchaser. If the wine you have purchased is old, fragile, or expensive, this service is probably necessary. The auction specialists can help you make this decision. With offices based out of New Jersey and California, Western Carriers is the national leader in the auction-related industry of temperature-controlled shipping. (See the Resource section for contact information.)

In the United States, the vast majority of wine is expedited through common commercial carriers UPS and FedEx. These services help assure that the wine is not compromised, provided the weather conditions are not unfavorable to its transfer. They offer the best options of overnight and two-day delivery.

Less expensive—but at times more risky—is ground shipping by common carrier. Not recommended for costly or rare wine, ground service is generally considered fine for young, hearty reds or whites from Bordeaux or California, provided the weather refrains from a heat wave or cold snap. The wines will be fine in transit, but may have to sit on a shipping dock to transfer trucks at any point during the journey. When in doubt, spend the money and ship fine wine overnight, or, at the very least, through a two-day service.

Wine should not be subjected to large temperature swings during the move. (You learned in Chapter 2 the ill effect temperature changes have on wine.) The large wine-

Not all purchasers want the original wooden cases. Their wine is repacked in heavy-duty cardboard boxes. The woods that remain at the auction company are destroyed or used as garbage cans or decorations.

Unfortunately, there is the possibility of loss or damage to the bottles while in the auction warehouse. Every company has a different policy regarding the insurance of bottles prior to their shipment. A conversation with the staff will clarify who is responsible if anything happens to the wine after the fall of the gavel and before the wine leaves the warehouse.

auction companies constantly monitor the nation's weather conditions and will alert you to conditions that make it prudent to postpone shipment. When everything is "good to go," overnight delivery of wine is the best, most economical option, provided you are shipping a small number of cases. On the other hand, when you are shipping a large number of cases, it is worthwhile to ship your wines by temperature-controlled ground carrier. A "large number of cases" is relative, of course, but I would consider twenty cases enough to ship by ground. Keep in mind that a standard palate of wine is sixty cases.

If the wine is being shipped, have someone available to receive it in person. This can be easily accomplished by having the wine sent directly to a professional storage facility with experience in accepting wine shipments. Most reputable places handle these shipments for little or no charge. If the wine is being sent to a residence, on the other hand, someone of legal drinking age must be present to sign for and receive the boxes. (Most companies require a signature.) This person can then bring the wine directly into the house, even straight into the cellar.

If you have not made other arrangements, you may be able to store your wine in the auction warehouse for an extended period of time. For more information on storing your wine at the auction warehouse, turn to page 118.

RECEIVING AND INSPECTING THE WINE

Your bottles have been bid on, paid for, and shipped or picked up. What now? Wine—a living, breathing thing—needs time to recompose after the agitation of traveling from the auction warehouse to your cellar. It should lay undisturbed after any journey. The older the wine, the longer the bottle should sit before it is stood up and attacked with a corkscrew. A recent vintage of a fine wine should rest a day or two—although preferably a week—before being opened. Red or white wines older than eight years old should sit for two weeks and then be stood up in the cellar for a day before opening. Ideally, wine over ten years old should sit still for three weeks before being served. As with so many aspects of the wine-collecting game, patience is greatly rewarded. Unfortunately, there may be a further delay if there are problems with any of the bottles you receive, so thoroughly checking your purchases should be a top priority.

Purchasers have recounted times when a case, repacked in a Styrofoam shipper, arrived the following morning from a warehouse across the country, and still had a chill from the warehouse's cellar.

As soon as possible, open each box of wine. Match the contents against the original invoice and the packing or shipping list—an itemized list of the products being shipped that will be enclosed with your purchases. Then check the bottles received against their catalogue descriptions to make sure you have been given exactly what you bid on. If you purchased many cases at a single auction, this can be a time-consuming process. Some collectors leave it for a day when several hours can be carved out. However, if you wait too long, cases can add up until the task is daunting and no

Whether dealing with a refrigerated unit, a walk-in cellar, an interior wine closet, or a basement, space should be cleared ahead of time to ensure the boxes have a place out of harm's way. Don't allow the cases to become a permanent fixture in your entryway.

longer fun. The little bit of discipline needed to avoid this is one of the most important aspects of successful wine buying and collecting.

Alert the auction house immediately if anything appears to be different from either the catalogue description or the invoice. The auction house needs to be made aware of problems as soon as possible because the consignor may need to be contacted. Unlike a retailer, an auction house does not own its property and, therefore, may not have the opportunity to instantly replace any given bottle of wine. We will look at ways a company may rectify certain situations as we discuss the problems you should immediately bring to the company's attention.

Wrong Bottle

Perhaps you have received the case you ordered and most of the bottles are exactly as you had hoped. Unfortunately, there is one wrong bottle in the box. There are two possible explanations. The mistake may have occurred when the wine was being prepared at the auction house, or the wrong bottle may have been in the case all along and been miscatalogued.

Once the problem is brought to the auction house's attention, the company will attempt to find the correct bottle, whether by returning to the consignor or by finding a duplicate through a third party. Replacing the bottle is the ideal solution, but can be complicated if the bottle is difficult or even impossible to obtain. If this situation occurs, the auction house will probably make an adjustment to the purchase price. As with most bottle discrepancies, this will be dealt with on an individual, per-bottle basis since the value and rarity of wines differ so wildly.

Faulty Cork

A corked bottle from a wine store or restaurant can be brought back, but there is no recourse for one bought at auction.

Cork-related problems can be quite a headache for a wine collector. There are two common signs: a wine level differing from the catalogue description, and visible signs of wine seeping out through the cork. A slightly decreased level of wine happens naturally over time, due to evaporation through the porous cork. Yet a level that is more dramatically lowered can be an indication of *cork shrinkage*, because this problem can lead to wine leaking from the bottle. A cork will shrink substantially when not kept in the proper temperature-controlled environment. If caught in time, evidence of some seepage may not be indicative of a bad wine, particularly if the wine is less than ten years old. The only test is to open the bottle and taste the wine. In extreme instances, the cork can drop into the bottle, resulting in an entirely worthless bottle.

An even more frustrating problem with corks is *cork taint*. A musty, wet-cardboard, off-putting smell pinpoints this silent killer. Infected bottles are referred to as *corked bottles*, and contain an offending compound called 2,4,6-trichloroanisole (TCA). Each year, up to 5 percent of wine bottles are affected by TCA.

Regardless of the cause and its effect on the bottle, a faulty cork is not a legitimate reason to return the wine to the auction house. Most catalogues explicitly state that the company does not bear any responsibility for cork failure. After all, the cataloguer has no way of knowing about this problem when he accepts a bottle into the sale. Rarely is compensation offered. Seasoned collectors accept this as an unfortunate aspect of their hobby, but it is never a pleasant experience.

> TCA, which causes cork taint, originates in the winery. Even a tiny amount of TCA can ruin the wine's aromas and flavors, but it is not dangerous to ingest. Some wine drinkers are more sensitive to the unpleasant aroma than others.

Inaccurate Description

Auction companies do their best to accurately describe the condition of each bottle, particularly as it pertains to the level of the wine, the condition of the label, and the quality of the capsule. But occasionally you may receive your wine and disagree with the auction book's description. Resolution can be tricky because the differences are sometimes slight. The catalogue's description and the company's methods of cataloguing will be referenced to settle disputes.

Level Disputes

The Ullage Chart, introduced and discussed in Chapter 5, illustrates the company's cataloguing standards and is located towards the back of every auction catalogue. It is important to familiarize yourself with it so you can form accurate and reasonable expectations of the wine's condition. If you receive wine and believe it is not filled to the level represented in the catalogue, your first step should be to consult the Ullage Chart to confirm that your expectations actually reflect the auction book entry. If you determine that the level is in fact lower than indicated by the catalogue, it is time to contact the auction company.

Label Problems

Whether the label's condition affects the bottle's desirability is a matter of preference. (See the inset on page 125.) As you learned in Chapter 5, the catalogue should state problems such as tearing, discoloring, ripped edges, and mold. If you believe your purchase's label is of a lesser quality than described in the auction book—and label quality is important to you—bring it to the auction team's attention.

Capsule Concerns

As you learned in Chapter 5, the *capsule* covers the cork. Made from a variety of materials including lead, wax, plastic, and foil, it helps protect the wine from contamination. Damaged or missing capsules are noted in the catalogue, although the

A cracked wax capsule on a large-format Burgundy bottle is not unusual because the bottle has probably been moved several times. It is also natural for the capsule's color to have faded, particularly when the wine is older.

quality of the wine is often unaffected by capsule imperfection. If nothing is mentioned, the capsule should be intact and, ideally, snug. If the wine arrives with a cracked or missing capsule that wasn't mentioned in the catalogue, you may want to report back to the auction as soon as possible. However, as long as the cork does not appear compromised, the wine within the bottle is probably fine.

If the delivered wine is notably different from the catalogue description with regard to the wine level, label, or capsule, call the company immediately. Although an auction sale is represented to potential buyers as an "as is" transaction, the top auction firms actually uphold an "as described" motto instead. This remedy is an important part of the customer-oriented auction process. The companies will usually take returns or offer credits when the wine received does not match the description in the catalogue. As a savvy collector, address any problems as soon as possible, before the auction specialist moves on to the next sale and your wine is a distant memory.

Bad Wine

The top auction houses pride themselves on their assessments of quality and condition for all the wine they offer for sale. Each bottle must pass a pre-inspection, which includes a pre-consignment interview. The potential sellers are asked questions addressing their consignments' quality and condition, and there may be random sample tastings. (We will look at some of the questions a seller may be asked in Chapter 10.) But occasionally a bad bottle slips through.

There are different types of bad bottles, and different methods of settling with the buyer. For the auction process to be successful, the buyer must trust that an older bottle will be of a fine quality when a reputable auction house solidly attests to the provenance of the collection from which it came. In most cases, the buyer is well rewarded. As for the few unfortunate cases when an older wine has simply died in the bottle despite indications to the contrary, the purchaser must chalk it up to bad luck. Experienced collectors of older, classic vintages are aware of this unfortunate risk. If you buy an older bottle that turns out to be bad, contact the auction house. The company will not usually refund any money, but the specialist in charge of that particular consignment would be interested to know of your experience, and it should be brought to his attention. This is also a great way to develop a relationship with a specialist at an auction house.

The bad bottle of a younger wine is more serious and requires a different approach. Most collectors have experience drinking younger wines and know what to generally expect of each bottle's quality and condition. Personal taste is a separate matter, and certainly no credits or refunds are issued if a buyer doesn't like the way a wine in good condition tastes. But if something is wrong with a younger bottle that gave no indication of having gone bad, you should contact the auction house. The specialist in charge may ask you to taste another bottle from the same lot (if one is available) before making any compensatory decisions. The specialist will then return to his notes involving the consignment to ensure that the wine came from proper storage conditions and provenance prior to the sale. When a level is well into the neck and the bottle has a fresh, clean label but something is clearly wrong with the wine, the auction house will have to decide how best to serve the customer. Although some catalogues state that no returns for any reason will be accepted, most auction houses will fashion some type of arrangement to retain the customer.

Unlike retail shopping, buying a bad bottle—young or old—at an auction will most likely not result in a refund or credit. Auction purchases fall within the Buyer Beware category. Wine-auction companies carefully state this in various places in every auction catalogue. They usually include a note that they take no responsibility as to the quality of juice in the bottle. If the auction house has already paid the consignor, the consignor is not going to supply a remedy. Unlike the retailer, who goes back to the distributor, who goes back to the winery for a refund or credit of returned bottles, the auctioneer cannot easily go back to the consignor.

No auction house wants any purchaser to suffer the disappointment of a bad auction purchase. But sadly, the nature of wine collecting includes the random disappointment of a bad bottle every now and then. However, the rewards of great bottles more than compensate for the few "sour grapes," keeping collectors continually on the hunt. And auctions are by far the greatest, most exotic hunting grounds to be found.

The Condition of the Paper Label

The earliest American collectors did not consider the condition of the paper label when assessing a wine bottle's value. These collectors searched for old, classic vintages and expected bottles to come complete with cellar dirt. The bin-worn labels gave the wine character. Collectors valued the juice in the bottle much more than the bottle itself, and it is extremely rare that the condition of a label will have any bearing on the quality of wine inside.

Yet the paper label's condition has become increasingly important as wine collecting grows in popularity and wine cellars grow in sophistication. A gentleman with a recently constructed, state-of-the-art home cellar that includes the ability to showcase certain bottles wants to show off only clean bottles with pristine labels. Likewise, a restaurant sommelier does not want to offer a bottle with a yellowed, torn, or tatty label to a client drinking fine and expensive wine. Suddenly, the condition of the label affects perception—and therefore value—of a bottle.

CONCLUSION

From receiving the catalogue weeks before the sale to receiving the wine weeks after, every step of being a buyer at an auction is a triumph in itself. Few other buying transactions require the attention to detail involved in buying wine at auction. If the process seems inefficient at times, remember that wine is not like any other commodity. The attention it demands for its existence is an equal challenge to buyer, seller, and auctioneer.

At the same time, the rewards are unparalled. Because some wines are so old that most of their counterparts have long since been consumed, and because other wines were produced in such small quantities that only a few lucky collectors can obtain bottles, auction lots spark the imagination of collectors and drinkers. Bidders continue to search catalogue after catalogue, hoping for the chance to win something that can't be won anywhere else.

PART THREE

The Science of Selling

9

Choosing the Right Auction House

Now that you are completely versed in the process of buying wine at auction, we will explore how you can become a successful seller. Being a *consignor*—the owner of property to be sold at auction—can be as rewarding as being a buyer. There is also just as much work to be invested.

The first step in the process is choosing an auction house. It is to your advantage to sell through an established company. As you may remember from Chapter 1, the two big international auction houses, Christie's and Sotheby's, have the most experience selling wine at auction. The large New York retailers, Acker Merrall & Condit, Morrell & Company, Sherry-Lehman, and Zachys, entered the field more recently but with great panache and large lists of long established fine wine buyers. Hart Davis Hart Wine Co. of Chicago and Bonhams & Butterfields of California, the two largest regional wine-auction companies, are successful in large part because of their loyal clientele. With such a large selection of auction houses, how do you, the consignor, decide where to place your wine?

In the first part of this chapter, you will become familiar with the characteristics of a successful auction house. Then, you will concentrate on questions and answers for your initial conversation with a specialist. After reading this chapter, you will be prepared to choose a house with which to conduct your auction business.

THE FOUR P'S

I have been an auctioneer for many years and for several different companies. From my experience, I believe there are several important qualities that you, the potential seller, should consider when choosing an auction company. I refer to these elements as "The Four P's to Choosing an Auction House." They are professionalism, proposal promises, price comparisons, and payment options. When you find a company that satisfies these criteria, you will have found the house to sell your wine. Let's look at the P's in detail.

Professionalism

The first P is professionalism. You can judge a house's professionalism by the ease you have contacting a knowledgeable staff member; the competence shown during initial conversations; the response time to telephone calls and consignment-related inquiries; and the frequency and effectiveness of promotional materials. Most importantly, note the company's reputation in the marketplace and the staff's attitude towards its customers. These distinguishing features will help you determine if you are dealing with a reliable, professional auction house.

Make a note if it is difficult to get a person on the phone without having a specific contact name or extension number. An electronic receptionist, for example, may not be able to immediately direct you to an appropriate staff member. If you, a potential seller, cannot easily reach a knowledgeable auction professional, the same is likely to happen to a buyer with specific questions about your wine. This is a great way to judge the effectiveness of an auction house office. Reaching a professional quickly and easily is a good sign.

The customer-service aspect of the industry is an important key to success. Once connected to a member of the auction team, evaluate whether the staff member seems knowledgeable and helpful or harried and bothered. Similarly, if you leave a voicemail message either for a staff member or in a department mailbox, is the call promptly returned? How a company interacts with its customers is important in separating one firm from another. A company that doesn't incorporate appropriate skills and tactics into everyday communications should probably not be given the opportunity to conduct your business. (The second half of this chapter will prepare you with questions and answers for these initial conversations.)

After contacting every auction house of interest, you will have to submit an inventory of the wines you want to sell to each company. (Chapter 11 will explain what to include in this list.) Then the auction teams will complete the list by supplying their pre-sale estimates and reserves. (Turn back to Chapter 6 to learn how buyers use these estimates to form their bid limits.) Each company should offer a time frame within which the list will be returned to you. Waiting for the finished list can be frustrating. Successful companies tend to be the busiest, and your inquiry may end up beneath a pile of forty or so other lists. The processing of potential consignments is dealt with on a first-come first-serve basis. All you can do is ask the auction specialist for a realistic indication as to when your estimates will be available. Then, be patient.

This wait will allow you to see how the company operates. Again, are your calls returned promptly and efficiently, regardless of whether your list has been completed? Does the auction specialist know who you are when you call? Is your list returned within the specified amount of time? These pre-sale procedures indicate how much attention to detail will be paid by the company throughout your entire experience.

Be sure to review each auction house's advertisements, press and editorial appearances, and auction catalogues. Every printed word should communicate the company's desire to win your business. The frequency of well-placed ads, particularly in wine-trade publications, exemplifies the company's financial commitment to making wine collectors aware of its auction efforts. Note, too, whether these ads make it easy for people to contact the house. You want your wine sold through a firm that buyers will know about and be able to reach. Sponsorship of regional wine events promote and highlight a company's enthusiasm for its business, while editorial coverage suggests a serious house that journalists turn to for reliable and expert information. A professionally presented auction catalogue is also extremely important, because your wine will potentially appear within its pages and should be presented with sophistication.

Top auction companies have good reputations. When you are shopping for an auction house to sell your wine, discuss your options with collectors who have previously bought and sold at the companies you are considering. Even though you are primarily interested in the best consignor customer service, it is important that buyers have an easy time working with the auction house, too. After all, as soon as a contract is signed and the auction house has your wine, your biggest concern will be with the buyer's end of the process. You can ask around at tasting groups or wine retailers, or request that the auction house supply past-consignor references.

Does the auction specialist assigned to your consignment convey that he wants and appreciates your business? Attitude is everything in this business, which is a combination of high-end customer service balanced with constant deadline pressures. It is a fast-moving, ever-changing scene in which the faces change from auction to auction, and you do not want to be swept aside by the lightening-quick turnover aspect of the auction process. You want to work with a professional auction house that cares about your business.

Proposal Promises

When an auction company wants to sell your wine, you will be mailed a written proposal. This letter will contain your wines' pre-sale estimates, the date of the auction, and any associated deadlines. Some proposals are elaborate and costly hard-bound volumes. Others are word-processed documents or even form letters. This presentation is an indication of the company's interest in your consignment. The attention given to the proposal may reflect the attention that will ultimately be given to the consignment itself.

> Although lists are normally reviewed in the same order they are received, an exception may be made for a million-dollar list. However, even if your list represents a fantastic selection of wines and adds up to a significant amount of money, there may be other lists that are just as important in the pile. Be prepared to wait for the results.

The most important information in the proposal includes the following: How much does the auction team believe the consignment is worth? When will the consignment be sold? And when will you be paid? The rest of the proposal will essentially outline how this auction company plans to realize higher prices for your wine than its competitors. Let's look at the topics that will most likely be included in the proposal.

Deadline Dates

The date of the auction will be stated in the proposal. (The inset on page 133 explains how wine auctions are scheduled.) It is more important for you, however, to look at the date by which your wine must be in the warehouse. Determine if this deadline is realistic for your schedule. If your wine is spread out in several different storage areas, for example, you may have trouble assembling your consignment by the date given. This is not the place to ask the auction house for leniency. These dates are set to meet the printer's requirements, and the printer's requirements are set to make sure the finished catalogues are in the bidders' hands well in advance of the auction. You must get your property to the auction house by the established deadline, so make sure the date given is feasible for you.

Sale Venue

The auction venue should be a selling point in the proposal. You want your wine to be sold in a place that attracts bidders. Sotheby's and Christie's both have purpose-designed facilities that make this an easy sell. Other auction companies rent restaurant or hotel facilities in which to hold their events. The location chosen speaks to the care and attention that the company gives to the bidders and their comfort.

Restaurant venues are currently popular. Bidders can relax at a table while being served food and drinks throughout the day. Sometimes bidders pay for the food service; other times the bill is covered by the auction company. Yet it can be difficult to maintain the professional administration of the auction and set up computers for bidder registration and checkout at a restaurant. Some companies handle this better than others. If possible, visit different auctions to get a sense of each sale's mood. Upon entering a venue, you want to find a relaxed, friendly, and animated environment.

Catalogue Presentation

Traditionally, photographs were used to illustrate the condition of older wines, especially in showing their ullage (the level of wine in the bottle's neck). Now, photographs tend to highlight rare bottles and ones in particularly good condition. Specialists usually decide which bottles to photograph during the inspection and cataloguing stage.

Auction Scheduling

Most of the auction market—including sales of art, jewelry, books, and other collectibles—follows the same schedule as the traditional school year, starting in September and ending in June. Rarely are important auctions held over the summer. The two big international auction houses, Christie's and Sotheby's, traditionally schedule their biggest New York and London art and jewelry sales in November and May.

The wine-auction market, on the other hand, does not follow quite the same schedule. These auctions deal with multiples of the same items, whereas the other sales sell unique objects. Because of this, wine-auction companies deal in volume, and therefore schedule their sales according to the number of lots they are able to process over the course of the year. Several auction companies have monthly sales, but it is more common to hold a wine sale six times a year.

The houses want to pack the room with bidders, so auctions—for wine and other products—are usually held when the most bidders will be able to attend. As a result, few auctions are scheduled for holidays or school breaks. The companies also try not to hold any events in the same city on the same day as a competitor's event, although occasionally this cannot be avoided. The absentee bid process is extremely useful in these circumstances. (See page 110 for more information on absentee bidding.)

If you want the auction catalogue to contain pictures of any of your collection's bottles, have the company commit to include these photos in the proposal. Photographs are important. They can brighten up and draw attention to any consignment. Some companies charge for photography. Others use it as an incentive to consign, and will photograph your wines for free. An important consignment will typically not incur any photography charges.

Other cataloguing procedures, such as any additional text, should also be agreed upon at the proposal stage. With unusual wine, extra copy may be added to make the wine more appealing to bidders. This can include comments from outside sources, as well as in-house essays and reviews. Any top scores given by significant critics—particularly Robert Parker, *Wine Spectator*, Michael Broadbent, or (in Sotheby's auctions) Serena Sutcliffe—may also be used. Bidders read the auction catalogue carefully. The more enticing your lots appear in the catalogue, the better chance your consignment has of receiving high bids.

Lot Duplication

Auction houses have a duty to each consignor to present the bottles to their best advantage, but lots will inevitably be duplicated because of the large amount of wine offered in every auction. Make sure there are not *too* many other bottles that are identical to your wine in the auction. If you have a large collection of 1982 Bordeaux, for example, you do not want to sell at an auction at which many other large quantities of 1982 Bordeaux are being sold. Ask the auction specialist if there are many similar consignments slated for the auction and, if so, whether he would advise you to wait for the next sale. If the specialist suggests you stay with this sale, he may be able to assure you that the next similar consignment the company receives will be held for a future sale. It is important you feel confident that the auction specialist has the best intentions for your collection.

Past Success

The auction company will use the proposal to outline its preceding achievements and explain how it brings buyers to its auctions. Different proposal styles include statistics and highlights of past auctions, press releases from important publications, and testimonials from buyers and sellers. The proposal will most likely state how many catalogues are printed and sent to prospective bidders for each event, as well as list past advertising placements and promotional initiatives such as tastings, dinners, or lectures, to illustrate the possibilities for the upcoming auction. You need to know how the firm is going to attract attention to your wine to determine that it intends to sell your wine for the highest possible price.

Extra Perks

When you consign valuable wine, don't be shy as you make requests of the auction company. More than likely, the team will be willing to do whatever it takes to keep your business.

When presented with a potential blockbuster consignment, an auction team will go to great lengths to retain the seller. It might promise that its best auctioneer will lead the sale. Occasionally it will offer to fly the consignor to the auction. Breakfasts, lunches, dinners, and various types of entertainment are routinely in the offering. There are no limits to what an auction house will do to win business. In this sophisticated and competitive marketplace, the owner of a valuable collection calls the shots. If you find yourself in this position, ask the auction house to consider any and all of your requests. Conversations with potential sellers are always valuable to the auction team because new ideas may win the next consignment. The team will try its best to deliver.

House Charges

The *terms of the sale*—commission charges—are outlined in the proposal. Any special terms, such as reduced (or even waived) commission or associated charges (such as shipping or photography) will be noted as such, and most likely compared with the company's standard charges. Here, you can compare apples to apples as each competing company makes its pitch. Take the suggested reserve price of the collection (which will appear on your returned list) and subtract the proposed charges to find your way to the bottom line: the fair market value of the collection. When presented with different figures, you can return to each competing house, where the charges will be compared and possibly adjusted. (You will read further about these costs and their negotiations in Chapter 10.)

By the end of the proposal stage, you will have learned a great deal about each auction company and what it is prepared to do to keep your business. Remember to also look at the proposal itself: a simple one-page printout should tell you very different things about the company and its intentions than an elaborate proposal would. One of the things it may indicate is the effort the company plans to put forth towards realizing the highest price for your wine. Now let's take a look at predicting these final sale prices.

Price Comparisons

There are a variety of reasons why you may be selling your beloved bottles. Regardless, the money you receive for doing so should ultimately be your most important objective. Auction houses, operating on a commission-based fee structure, are similarly interested in realizing the highest price for each bottle offered. But that does not mean that each company will achieve the same results. An important aspect of picking an auction house is comparing what you can reasonably expect each company to realize for your wine.

Estimates and Reserves

As you have read, you will submit a list of the wines you wish to sell to different auction companies. (Tips on writing this list start on page 155.) Gradually, these lists will be returned with pre-sale estimates and reserves. To set these figures, all auction companies use the same market materials—most notably the comprehensive, annually-published *Wine Price File*, along with a variety of other reference materials. In addition to these sources, they use their own past auction results, oftentimes also turning to the results of their competitors.

Every wine with a history of being traded at auction has an established market price. Yet different auctions often yield different prices for similar wines. Let's look at three lots that each contain one case of 1982 Château Mouton. At three different New York auctions within one month, these lots may sell for $8,000, $8,500, and $10,000. Presented with these varied results, an auction specialist would need to identify and interpret the factors that influenced each price in order to determine the pre-sale estimate he should provide to a potential consignor of this case. One auction company may offer an estimate of $7,000 to $9,000 for the 1982 Mouton, while another house might estimate it at between $8,000 and $10,000. (Remember, however, that the case is ultimately worth the amount of the winning bid, regardless of the pre-sale estimate.)

When you receive your list back from competing auction companies, the house-to-house pre-sale estimates for the entire consignment will usually vary from one another by around 10 percent. This estimated total value is a more meaningful figure than the individual per-lot estimates. Although you may be attached to particular bottles, it is important to look at the big picture.

Yet the most important aspect of the pre-sale estimating process is not the high-low range, but the reserve. (The reserve, as you learned earlier, is the confidential minimum price below which the wine will not be sold.) Remember that estimates are guesses. There are no set upper limits for any wines, so final selling prices are impossible to predict. Experienced consignors ignore estimates except to acknowledge that these figures will be used to determine the reserves.

The reserves are set at or below the low end of the estimate range. They are most often one or two increments under the low estimate. The only way to value a consignment prior to auction is to deduct the associated charges and fees from the collection's reserve. This will show the lowest potential amount you will receive when the wine is sold.

Auction houses of great repute take the estimating process seriously and work hard to stay current in the ever-changing market, but different companies have different philosophies in setting these figures. Some companies give aggressive estimates in order to win a consignment, and then place the reserve prices far below the low ends. As a result, a company that gives the highest estimates for a consignment may also provide the lowest reserve prices. Other houses give conservative pre-sale estimates, trying to generate bidder interest with appealing lots and low opening prices. This, too, is a rather dangerous game to play because low estimates result in low reserve prices. In turn, low reserve prices can result in low realized prices.

> To calculate the pre-auction value of your consignment, subtract the various fees from the total reserve of the entire collection. A realized amount higher than this value should always be considered a bonus.

When shopping for the best auction company, ask the specialist at each house to explain the company's philosophy for calculating pre-sale estimates. When it comes time to compare the estimate lists, this answer may help you understand any differences in estimates for the exact same wine.

If the majority of a house's lots sell for either far above or far below the estimated prices, the pre-sale estimates won't have much meaning. You want to sell your wine through a company that has a solid, proven track record of realistic estimate-to-hammer-price results. Now you will learn how to examine and compare this aspect of the different companies.

Prices Realized

Auction companies trumpet their successes by publishing any record-breaking prices achieved at their auctions. Other results are available in prices realized lists. These lists are public record, so don't rely solely on the prices presented to you in the auction company's proposal or promotional material. The highlights the company will want you to see are used to illustrate successful results and may not correctly represent the company's overall auction performance. Instead, read the prices realized lists thoroughly, because they include all the lots in a sale.

Price records are very valuable tools in your decision-making process. You want to accurately compare the different companies so that you can make an educated guess as to which house consistently produces the highest hammer prices for specific bottles. As you learned in Chapter 5, prices realized lists become available shortly after the auction. You can call the auction office to request a copy. Additionally, some auction houses make the lists available on their websites as soon as possible.

For each potential company, gather prices realized lists from several auctions. Various circumstances—such as the provenance of the wine sold, the number of bidders in the room, and the timing of the auction—can affect a wine's price from one auction to another. The results from a single auction, therefore, are not an accurate representation of the business the firm conducts. Look first at prices of the same wine over several auctions at one house, and then at prices for the same wine achieved at different companies, to get an accurate picture of the fair market value of that wine. Then use these figures to determine which auction house tends to be the most successful.

> Estimates are simply guesses and bidders will often pay whatever is necessary to win the lot. Rely on other factors when choosing an auction house if a company's estimates fail to reflect its realized prices.

Payment Options

Be sure to ask all potential auction companies about their payment schedules before you sign on the dotted line. Most will have similar systems that involve a delay in remittance. If you are consigning valuable wine, you may be interested in a financial incentive such as a cash advance or a guarantee. If receiving one of these considerations is important to you, be sure to request it. This may help you choose a house because these offers are often quite different from one company to the next. Your ability to receive these financial options depends directly on the quality of and desire for your consignment.

Traditional Payment

When dealing with most auction houses, you will be paid for sold lots thirty-five business days after the auction. Most companies will pay only after they have collected their money from the successful bidders. As a result, payment is often not made in full on the first payment date. If the auction company is paying only when proceeds are received and processed, you should keep diligent records of the payment process.

As consignor, you will receive your payment in the form of a company check, which will be mailed to the address on file. These proceeds can be paid out to whomever you wish. These arrangements should be discussed with the auction house

> Many bidders pay in a timely manner, but some do not. Even when payments are remitted on time, there may be a delay while they are received and processed by the company. Ultimately, the seller suffers the consequences. Some auction companies allow bidders to pay up to a certain amount with a credit card, which speeds up the process and results in faster payment.

well in advance of the thirty-five-day payment target. Speak to the finance department of each auction house to redirect the check. Your auction team contacts can help put you in touch with this department.

Cash Advance

Occasionally, after the specialists estimate the value of the consignment, the auction house offers the consignor a proportional cash payment, to be paid prior to the auction, as an incentive to choose this firm. A seller trying to choose between several companies may be swayed by this advance.

Cash advances are given as loans, and interest is paid to the auction house. For example, let's say that you own a collection with an estimated value of $500,000 to $700,000. The auction house may offer you a cash advance of $100,000. This money will be paid after the contract is signed and the wine is received in the auction warehouse. This amount, plus the pre-agreed interest, will then be deducted from your proceeds for the sale. The amount of interest on the advance is usually prime plus several points, but varies from house to house and from consignment to consignment. If you are offered an interest-free advance, the auction house clearly has an intense desire to win your consignment.

Pre-Auction Guarantee

When an auction house makes a *guarantee*, it promises to pay the consignor a certain amount of money after the auction, regardless of the final results. Hotly debated since their use by Christie's and Sotheby's in the late 1980s, guarantees are yet another financial incentive offered to clinch important collections. In today's more closely regulated climate—New York State, for example, stipulates that auction companies indicate guaranteed lots in the catalogue—auction houses tend to offer these rather conservatively.

In states such as New York, where auction companies must indicate guaranteed lots in the catalogue, a symbol will precede the lot number to designate the guarantee. These lots are sold subject to the same regulations as every other lot but the symbol informs bidders that the auction company is selling this lot with different financial considerations.

Let's look again at the collection valued between $500,000 and $700,000. The auction house may guarantee a payment of $400,000 on a specified date, regardless of the auction's final results. Proceeds over the $400,000 will also be paid to you (minus the pre-determined commission percentage). In the case of a more aggressive guarantee—such as $600,000 for this consignment—any proceeds over and above the guaranteed price may be split fifty-fifty with the auction house. Each guaranteed consignment has an individually structured agreement.

As you contact each auction house, think about the Four P's. These attributes will help you choose among the companies. Deciphering the Four P's, however, is impossible without posing certain questions to the auction team. When you call for the first time, what are you going to say and ask? Will the person on the other end have questions that you should be prepared to answer? What will be the actual purpose of his questions? Now we will take a look at some of the questions you will be asked when you approach an auction house about selling your wine, as well as certain questions you should pose to help round out your research into the company. At that point, you will be completely prepared to decide between the different houses.

THE INITIAL CONVERSATION

Now that you know what to look for in an auction house, the next step is to contact the team. The specialist will have questions for you when you call, so this section will help you prepare your answers, as well as your own questions to ask him. The answers you receive should provide you with the final information you need to decide which auction house is right for you. At all times, keep the four P's in mind.

When you make the call, tell the person who answers the telephone that you are interested in selling your wine at auction, and he will direct your call to a specialist. It is important to find a good personality fit with your auction specialist, because the team member in charge of your consignment is the key to your successful auction experience. You will be working with this person for several months, from start (this initial phone call) to finish (the payment for your wine). You do not want your wine to get lost in the shuffle of consignments, tight deadlines, and general auction customer-service stress. At the same time, the specialist will have a handful of other clients. It is, therefore, important to have a professional yet solid relationship with your specialist, so that your consignment will be treated as a priority.

Questions from the Auction House

Some or all of the following questions will be posed to you during your initial conversation with the auction house. Being ready and willing to answer them all will improve your chance of having your consignment accepted by the company.

> *What are you interested in selling?*
>
> *Have you bought or sold with us before?*
>
> *Where did you buy these wines?*
>
> *Where and how has the wine been stored?*
>
> *How long have you had these wines?*
>
> *What are your expectations of selling at auction?*

Even if you are already confident answering each of the above questions, this section can be helpful. To make sure you are prepared to show your consignment in its most positive light, you should consider the specialist's intentions as he delivers each question.

Answer each question honestly. Answering dishonestly will hurt your wine-selling reputation. The truth will eventually emerge, either when your wine arrives at the warehouse or after it has been sold to a buyer; the later it does, the more damage your reputation—and future in the business—will incur.

One Man's Method of Choosing an Auction House

A Japanese businessman owned four incredible Impressionist paintings: one each by Alfred Sisley, Paul Cézanne, Pablo Picasso, and Vincent van Gogh. When he decided to sell these great works of art, the gentleman contacted both Sotheby's and Christie's, asking for a proposal from each. The proposals came back, with each house pulling out the stops in order to win the business.

The businessman studied the competing offers. Each proposal mentioned its company's superlative record selling similar works of art; its firm's unrivalled expertise in the area of Impressionist paintings; the house's huge, loyal clientele who would come to bid on these paintings; and the comfort of its clients while bidding in its state-of-the-art auction room. Both Christie's and Sotheby's claimed to be the absolute best firm to handle such an important consignment.

The Japanese gentleman was suitably impressed and could not decide between the two. He asked the houses to take the matter into their own hands—literally. The potential consignor asked that Sotheby's and Christie's play one round of Rock, Paper, Scissors. The winner would win the opportunity to sell his paintings.

Christie's chose scissors. Sotheby's chose paper. Christie's won the right to sell the paintings.

The paintings were sold for a total of $17.8 million.

What Are You Interested in Selling?

When you are asked this question by the auction specialist, tell him all the details of your bottles. Be sure to include vintage and bottle size (if other than the standard 750 milliliters), as well as the number of bottles you want to sell. If the consignment is in full-case quantity, confirm whether it is in the original wood or cardboard box.

The auction specialist will begin with this question to get a general sense of your potential consignment. If you and the company are incompatible for business, both parties can save a good deal of time and aggravation by recognizing this immediately. Not all wines are traded at auction. The market is limited to wines that bidders want; typically, such bottles are unavailable elsewhere. Your consignment may consist of very recent vintages still available in stores, and therefore may not be the type of wine in which most auction houses deal. In this case, you will most likely be informed that the company is not interested in your bottles at this point in the market cycle.

At the same time, auction companies have different guidelines as to what they will accept. For example, some houses may impose a minimum consignment value, usually between $10,000 and $25,000. If your wines do not meet this value criteria, the auction specialist may recommend you go elsewhere. By determining right away what each caller is interested in selling, the specialist can quickly eliminate potential sellers who are not a good fit for his company.

Have You Bought or Sold With Us Before?

If you have already sold through or bought from the company you are contacting, the auction team will probably have a record of your contact information as well as your previous transactions. The specialist will be able to see the type of wine you bought or sold. As a seller, repeat business may be rewarded with more favorable commission terms. However, there is no disadvantage if this is your first experience with the auction house. It is never too late to begin the relationship!

Where Did You Buy These Wines?

As you learned in Chapter 5, the provenance of a collection is extremely important to prospective bidders. Since where you obtained your wines speaks directly to their provenance, the auction specialist will get to this question not long after the call begins. If you purchased the bottles at auction, be prepared to tell the specialist when you bought the wines, from which auction house you bought them, and any important details about the consignment from which they came. It is always to your advantage to provide this information, but it's especially important when the wine is of a very old, classic vintage. Prospective bidders are more interested in a bottle whose history of ownership can be traced.

At a recent London sale, Christie's had a rare offering of Château Latour consigned directly from the château. A case of 1961 Latour was at the château for the entire forty years of its life, and sold for £31,000 ($43,400). Later that same year, a full case of 1961 Latour from an unknown source sold for £15,000 ($21,000). Bidders were willing to pay twice as much for the case with flawless provenance.

The auction specialist will also inquire for more details if you say you bought your wines from a retail store. When you purchased the bottles from the retailer (the wine's primary source), was it upon their release or soon after? If so, there will be a mention of this in the auction catalogue, so that bidders can note that your wine has been moved only minimally during its lifetime.

Where and How Has the Wine Been Stored?

Top auction companies will only accept wines that have been properly stored. This requires cellaring the wine under controlled conditions, whether in a home or at a professional facility. Tell the specialist details such as if the wine has been kept in a walk-in subterranean wine cellar or in an under-the-kitchen-counter-top unit.

Most houses will also accept wine kept in passive storage situations from certain areas of the country, including northern California, Oregon, and western Washington state. The climate at these locations allows for excellent passive storage that is particularly appropriate for young wine. The auction specialist will most likely verify the wines' condition by requiring sample tasting bottles from the collection. The passive conditions will be mentioned in the catalogue so that buyers are fully aware of them and can make informed decisions.

Bidders are informed of the storage conditions of each consignment regardless of the situation. The line "Removed from Ideal Storage" is an auction company's seal of approval and a potential buyer's green light to bid. Ideal storage means a temperature- and humidity-controlled environment (with the temperature set anywhere from 55 to 65 degrees Fahrenheit and humidity kept around 70 percent).

Potential consignors who have properly stored their wine are proud to offer this information. An experienced wine-auction specialist can usually tell when a collector is not being completely honest about these conditions, particularly as the telephone conversation continues.

How Long Have You Had These Wines?

Although this question is frequently posed to potential sellers, it satisfies the auction professional's curiosity more than his notes for the catalogue. Your answer will not affect the wine's final selling price, but it can indicate how much you originally paid for these bottles. An experienced wine-auction specialist, who has been through several market cycles, will be able to easily guess at your profit margin after confirming if the wine was purchased several decades ago or within the last five years. Although this has no relation to the market value of your wine, the question implies that the specialist is interested in you and your collection. This can indicate your ability to forge a good relationship with this particular specialist and auction house.

What Are Your Expectations of Selling at Auction?

This is a very important question if you are a novice seller. As a prospective consignor without any prior auction experience, you may have some preconceived ideas of the process. With this question, the experienced auction professional will make sure that you both share the same outlook. You may have read about huge prices and blockbuster auctions in wine publications, but not every auction is a record breaker, and most bottles are not worth many times what their owners paid for them. Unrealistic expectations on a consignor's part are nothing short of disaster for any auction company.

Every bottle has a certain value, which is the price set by the auctioneer in conjunction with the final bidder. The auction company sets the stage to encourage bidders to compete for your wine. You want to work with the auction company that will best create the environment for this competition.

Questions for the Auction House

Now it is your turn. The following are questions you may want to ask the specialist. Some answers will be the same for every auction house, while others will be unique to each individual company. Make sure you understand each issue before signing any contract.

Will You Take All the Wine I Want to Sell?

If you have not discussed the company's guidelines for acceptance of a consignment in the first half of your conversation with the specialist, start by asking if the wine you have is best suited for an auction sale, as well as best suited for a sale by this particular auction house. There is no point taking the time to submit a list and wait for the reply if the auction company is not going to offer your wine. His answer should indicate (and if it doesn't, ask) whether he and his company are interested in your entire collection or only certain bottles from it. This may not matter to you, or it may be the deciding factor that results in your finding another company. This is a personal decision that depends solely on what you want for your collection.

Will You Come and Look at My Collection in Person?

This is important for you to know for scheduling purposes. You need to know if—and when—a representative from the auction company will come to inspect your cellar, so you can arrange and clean the space. A neat, well-organized cellar shows that you are respectful of the time and expense taken by the specialist to make the visit, and also represents your commitment to your collection. Although the bidders will not see your cellar nor know if it is tidy and organized, the specialist's opinion of your collection's organization may make it into the catalogue. Understandably, the consignor who takes proper care of his wines tends to realize the highest possible prices for his bottles.

How Are the Estimates Determined?

The auction team will use your list to prepare the estimates for your consignment. (As the companies return these lists, use them to further differentiate between each house. See page 157 for more on interpreting the estimate lists.) These are the same estimates that will eventually appear in the catalogue. The process for arriving at these figures is standardized. The specialists study recent results from past auction sales and current market trends. Other potential consignors with the same wines will receive the same initial estimates. They may be adjusted to reflect the bottles' condition or a sudden market change once the wine is received in the warehouse.

After you receive a specialist's evaluation, you can discuss the estimates with him or choose whether to have his company sell your wine. But the actual realized price will always be set by the highest bidder.

Can I Set the Reserve Price for My Wine?

The reserve price (sometimes called the minimum price) is the lowest amount that the auctioneer will accept for a lot. The auction house sets it, usually no higher than the low end of the estimate. The reserve protects your wine from being sold below its value. The auctioneer indicates that bidding has not reached this amount—and will therefore not be sold—by saying "pass" instead of "sold."

What Happens to Bottles That Are Not Sold?

Any lots that are not sold at the auction will be returned to the consignor, reoffered at a future auction, or sold immediately after the sale. As seller, you will choose among these options if and when the situation arises.

Usually, the unsold lots are rolled over into the next available auction for no additional charge. If you know you want any unsold lots to be returned, on the other hand, determine who will pay for the return shipping *before* the auction. The consignor usually pays, but this can be negotiated at the proposal stage. The third option is to allow the auction house to make an outright sale of any unsold lot. After the sale, most auction houses like to sell remaining lots for their reserve prices if any collectors express interest. Commission is then deducted as if the lots were sold at auction.

Regardless of which action you would take, find out prior to the auction if the house charges an *unsold lot fee*—a small fee on a lot that fails to sell at auction. This fee will be further discussed in Chapter 10.

> With realistic estimates and professional catalogue presentation, the vast majority of consignments —around 90 percent— are sold in their entirety the first time they appear at auction.

How Much Is This Going to Cost Me?

Auction houses typically work on a commission-based schedule of charges, so a percentage of the sale total is deducted from the final proceeds. Each auction house has a standard rate of sellers' commission, ranging from 10 to 20 percent of the earnings. There are a number of charges in addition to the commission. Expect to pay for insurance and for shipping your wine to the auction house, while the cost to include a photograph of your wine in the catalogue is optional. Some companies levy an unsold lot fee, while others may charge you the cost of having your unsold wine returned to you.

As you will see in the next chapter, many of these charges are negotiable. Once the value of your consignment is determined, you and the auction team will enter into a discussion of the various charges. Before signing the contract, you can determine how much the auction process will cost you by subtracting the commission rate and associated charges from the total reserve price of the consignment.

How Long Will This Take?

After the initial telephone conversation, the first step is to submit your wine list. The time it takes to organize the inventory and prepare the list is up to you, the collector. When your list has been submitted, the auction house may keep it between two weeks and two months before responding. Occasionally, the wait may be even longer. Estimating a collection's value is a time-consuming process because the wine-auction market fluctuates quickly and the estimate databases are under constant revision.

After receiving the estimates, you can negotiate the contract terms before sending your wine to the warehouse.

The auction house needs your wine in its warehouse approximately three months prior to the auction. (A deadline will be set at the proposal stage to ensure you are aware of when your wines need to arrive.) This allows for proper inspection and cataloguing of the consignment. The catalogue information is usually sent to the printing company two months before the auction so that the catalogue can be printed and sent to potential bidders three to four weeks before the sale.

Depending on the length of time spent by the consignor to get the wine into the auction warehouse, the process from estimates to payment can take anywhere from three to six months.

When Will I Get the Money?

Make sure payment terms are outlined in the contract or consignment agreement. Traditionally, payment is made thirty-five days after the auction, provided that the auction company has collected from the buyers. In the event where one buyer has not yet paid for the wine out of a multi-lot consignment, the auction company settles only those lots for which payment from other bidders has been received and processed. The auction house will then personally contact any late-paying bidders by telephone, urging them to send in their payment. In more cases than not, late-paying bidders settle immediately upon the reminder.

When Will My Wine Be Auctioned Off?

Auction companies accept consignments for specific upcoming auctions and will advise sellers about the best potential auction dates. When a company recommends a sale date, ask for the associated deadline. Although not standard practice, you can request the deadline in writing. At the very least, make your own note of the date so that you can be sure to uphold your end of the deal and get your bottles into the auction for which they are best suited.

How Do I Get the Wine to the Warehouse?

Ideally, you can drive your wines to the warehouse if you live close enough. Of course, this is rarely the case, so the auction company will most likely guide you through the shipping process. Because bottles come from all over the country, each auction house has solid relationships with various temperature-controlled trucking companies. Your auction specialist will make shipping recommendations and assist in the arrangements. If you do not have proper containers within which to ship your bottles, request that the auction house send these cartons to you. These costs should be negotiated before the materials are sent out.

Can I Change My Mind After I Have Sent My Wine?

Once the contract is signed, you should not expect to remove any bottles from the consignment, particularly if the catalogue has already been printed and includes your wine. However, reasonable requests are usually honored by the auction house. This largely depends on both your request and your relationship with the auction house.

Who Is Responsible for My Wine?

A percentage of the wine's value will be deducted from your earnings as an *insurance fee*. Once the estimate list is supplied, your wines will be insured for the value of the mid-range estimate. Therefore, you should not move your wines to the auction house until either a list of estimates is supplied or an understanding of the replacement value is agreed upon. The insurance fee will be discussed further in Chapter 10.

How Will My Wines Be Promoted?

This is an important consideration when you are choosing between different auction houses. How much advertising and promotion has the company provided for past auctions? How many bidders subscribe to its catalogue? Will there be additional promotional events—such as dinners, tastings, and lectures—prior to the auction? If a company is planning a blockbuster sale due to a special consignment, the promotion of the overall sale will benefit your lots. Ask the specialist if there are any mega-consignments scheduled for the same auction.

Conversely, ask the specialist how many other consignors in the sale are selling the same wine you are offering. If it already consists of ten other lots of your best wine, it may be worth your while to wait a sale or two so you can be the first consignor in with that particular wine. You could then make a request—which may or may not be granted—that your consignment be towards the front of the catalogue or that the team limits the number of these similar lots. You do not want your lots to have to compete with others for attention.

What if a Buyer Reneges?

The auction house decides what action to take with a reneged buyer for future sales. It is likely to either restrict or completely blackball the negligent bidder.

If a buyer reneges within the allotted payment time, you will probably not be paid for the lots he has purchased. With your permission, the auction house would reoffer the wine at the next auction. This is one reason why most companies make payments to their sellers only on the wines for which they have received payment.

There are times, however, when the auction house pays the seller in full, regardless of the fact that all monies have not been received from the successful bidders. If the buyer then backs out of the agreement, the auction house takes legal possession of the wine and decides whether to reoffer it for their account. Although rare, it has happened that an auction company contacts the consignor for return of money paid prior to the default of payment. This is a very important point to review with your specialist.

CONCLUSION

A comfortable, professional relationship develops when each party understands the expectations of the other. If you are new to the auction game, you need to understand your responsibilities and those of the auction company so you can be in full command of the process. The questions in this chapter are designed with this in mind.

When it comes to professionalism, proposal promises, price comparisons, and payment options, you should choose the auction company that best anticipates and promises to fulfill your expectations. The auction process is a long, detail-driven endeavor. To ensure the best possible working relationship, a pleasant pre-auction atmosphere, and a positive auction experience, you need to forge a comfortable and confident relationship with the company with which you choose to work. Assessing the firms' performances by addressing the Four P's should guide you to the auction house with which you can achieve the most success.

In addition to discovering these essential facts, however, you should be looking for the company that understands you, your wine, and the best way to market your collection. This will be a gut feeling. You will sense that the auction house and proposal are speaking to your consignment individually, rather than presenting the material in a cookie-cutter manner. Only you will be able to recognize this when it happens.

10

Auction Fees and Their Negotiations

I n Chapter 9, you read about the importance of having a professional relationship with the auction team. For most sellers, this crucial aspect is overshadowed only by the bottom line. The final proceeds can be approximated by deducting the consignor charges from the reserve prices. To properly determine this figure, you must have a clear understanding of the various charges.

It's important to become familiar with the following charges and review their costs with the auction specialists during the proposal stage. There is often room for negotiation before the contract is signed and the final deal is closed. (You will learn more about the contract in Chapter 11.) As you read the description of each charge, you will see which costs are flexible and which are not. This will help you obtain the best possible deal with the auction company.

VENDOR'S COMMISSION

Most wine-auction companies employ a commission-based fee structure. As the seller, you will be charged a *vendor's commission*—a percentage of each lot's hammer price paid to the company in exchange for its selling your wine. It is usually charged on a sliding scale, in response to the total dollar amount the consignment earns at the auction. Table 10.1 illustrates standard commission rates for a typical seller. As the table shows, the commission rate decreases as the dollar value increases. Each auction company decides what dollar value merits a lower commission, so this chart varies between houses.

However, commission rates are often negotiable. The flexibility of these figures is directly related to your consignment's value to the auction house: the more a team desires your wines, the more likely it will be to lower the charges in an effort to win your business. When it receives your inventory list, the auction company will immediately judge the type and quality of the wines to estimate their values, but it will look at other key factors as well. For example, the team will consider the amount of

TABLE 10.1. STANDARD VENDOR'S COMMISSION RATES	
Hammer Price of Consignment	**Commission Rate**
Under $50,000	15 percent
$50,001– $100,000	12 percent
$100,001–$250,000	10 percent
$250,000–$500,000	8 percent
$500,001–$1,000,000	6 percent
Over $1,000,000	4 percent

Because a wine consignment of $50,000 represents a solid piece of business, most houses charge a lower commission rate for the right to sell its bottles than they will for a consignment worth $10,000. A consignment valued at over $100,000 will garner even more aggressive attention from both auction houses and bidders, so its seller will be charged an even smaller percentage.

work it will have to invest to sell these bottles, such as the effort needed to transport the wines to the warehouse and whether working with you appears to be easy or difficult. The staff will also determine if your bottles can possibly headline a sale or be highlighted in pre-sale advertising and promotions. These factors all weigh in when the team considers what they will charge you to sell your products.

Wines that are valuable, rare, and in high demand are more aggressively chased by auction teams because they often inspire competition among bidders. A house is more likely to negotiate the vendor's commission for such bottles. Each company also looks for and strives to include wines that are particularly popular with its specific bidding base. An auction team will usually shave a point off the standard commission for a high-value consignment of these easier-to-sell wines.

On the other hand, if your consignment is of less value but includes a salesroom favorite, you might still be in a good position to request a better commission rate. For example, a top vintage of Château Petrus; a small collection of the best California Cult wines; a super-elusive Burgundy, Rhône, or Italian lot; or any other hard-to-find flavor-of-the-month bottles may receive a lowered commission rate, because auction houses really like including these wines in their sales. In fact, an auction house will probably accept one of these consignments even if it is beneath its standard minimum lot value.

Another effective way to receive a better offer is to court competitive houses. Your receiving a particularly low charge from one house may encourage a different company to offer you an even better deal. When comparing competitive offers, however, be sure to look at the entire picture. Some auction houses offer a 0-percent seller's commission and then pad charges for cataloguing, handling, and insurance costs. Some auction houses impose a vendor's commission and then waive all other costs, making the commission an all-inclusive final charge. To accurately compare figures, chart out the terms offered by each competing house and determine the total that will be deducted from your proceeds.

Wines outside of traditional offerings will be unlikely to yield a lower commission rate. These bottles create risk because they may fail to sell. Unsold lots reflect negatively on the final sale results, and also create more after-sale work for the staff. A team member must then take time to determine whether the wine should be rolled over to a future auction or returned to the consignor, as well as to complete the extra paperwork involved. This prevents the staff from quickly moving on to the next auction.

The auction team will often consider how much work will be involved with a new consignment. Property consisting entirely of wines in their original cases and cartons, for example, takes significantly less work (when being unpacked, organized, and catalogued) than a consignment of single bottles that needs to be grouped into lots. If your consignment is in its original woods or cardboard box, you are in a better position to ask the auction company to consider a commission reduction. You can—and should—point this out to the specialist with whom you are dealing if this is to your advantage.

It is necessary to consider what the company sees as the positive and negative aspects of your consignment before approaching the team to discuss a commission rate. Showing the staff members that you understand the process as well as their point of view will open the doors to negotiation.

> You are in the best position to negotiate costs when the auction house actively wants what you have to offer.

INSURANCE CHARGES

Most houses routinely add a 1- to 2-percent charge for insurance. The auction company will become responsible for your wine and the insurance will begin coverage once your consignment is in the company's possession. If the bottles are being delivered by a shipping company, this will start when they are picked up from your cellar. If you are dropping them off yourself, the company will become responsible when the wines are received in its warehouse. The wines will then be insured for the amount of their mid-range estimate until they are sold at auction.

Insurance typically covers loss and damage. Cork failure—when a loosened cork slips into the bottle—is not covered. Each auction catalogue clearly states that the company takes no responsibility for cork failure because it is natural for a cork to shrink with age.

If you have already insured your wine and can produce a certificate that insures your bottles for the duration of the auction, you can choose to waive these charges. Most collectors, however, do not independently insure their bottles, and are therefore required by the auction house to protect the wines under the company's policy.

Most companies prefer not to waive this charge, as the cost of coverage is more than offset by each buyer's and seller's 1-percent charge. They often view insurance as a small revenue center. You are better off agreeing to pay the insurance charge while looking for a reduction of charges elsewhere.

> When the hammer falls, the wines become the successful bidder's property. As you learned in Chapter 8, he is usually charged a percentage of the wines' new values to insure his new bottles until they are in his possession.

SHIPPING CHARGES

The least expensive way to get your wine to the auction warehouse is to drive it there yourself. If you do not live close enough to the warehouse to deliver the wine or are unable to travel with it in a temperature-controlled environment, you can hire a professional third-party shipping company. Most auction firms have close ties with several shipping companies. They will usually be happy to recommend one for your use.

This charge will most likely be your second largest expense (less than only the vendor's commission). The cost per unit almost always decreases when more bottles are shipped, although rates vary depending on the distance the bottles have to travel and the company used. Shipping charges can usually be paid either by you directly to the shipping company at the time of pickup, or by the auction house and later deducted from your final sale proceeds. This should be discussed, agreed upon, and put in writing before any wine is moved.

There are additional costs that may be added to this charge. If the wines are not in shipping-appropriate cases, you may have to pay for packing materials such as styrofoam inserts and cardboard boxes. An auction staff member will assist in making the shipping arrangements and should be able to estimate the total price before any wines are moved—but you may end up having to pay for his services as well.

If you have a valuable collection, you should ask the auction company to forgo or reduce the shipping charges. The house will recognize the additional cost of any packing materials as it considers the reduction of these charges, and may offer to pay for these extra costs. Regardless of your particular collection, you should always discuss the shipping charges and the possibility of a price reduction with the auction specialist before committing the collection to auction.

Some auction catalogues include an outline of shipping charges. It is meant as a guide for successful buyers, but it can be used to estimate the cost of shipping your consignment to the warehouse as well.

CATALOGUE PHOTOGRAPHY COSTS

Many auction companies produce catalogues with beautiful color photographs. In some cases, the cost of the photography will be passed along to the consignor. Auction houses that charge for photography will have set fee scales for these services. The charges can be deducted from the final proceeds.

Any specially promoted or particularly valuable lots should be photographed for free. Including exceptional wines in its auction is as important to the company as to the seller, so the company should not charge you to promote them. If your wine is particularly valuable, you may want to request free photography.

Often, however, you will not be offered this service for free, and you will have to decide whether you want to spend the money to have your wines highlighted in pictures. Remember that a vast majority of consignments are sold without any visuals. On the other hand, color photographs bring the catalogue alive, and a picture of your consignment will make it more noticeable. Photographed lots tend to sell particularly well. You may want to ask the specialist to compose a group shot that includes several of your lots: maximum exposure for a minimum price. If you do agree to pay for a selection of your lots to be photographed, make sure you get to approve the pictures. You do not want to pay for poor photography! (Turn back to Chapter 5 for more information on the auction catalogue.)

If an important collection is being shipped to the warehouse, the auction company may send one of its specialists to oversee the packing and shipping of the wine. This is reserved for the most valuable wine collections.

HANDLING CHARGES

Some auction companies levy a per-lot handling charge, collected from consignors to help absorb some of the auction houses' large overhead. Usually several dollars per lot, this covers everything from the cost of temperature-controlled storage to the price of repacking the wines as necessary for the sale and the staff needed to physically move the wine through the auction process. Usually deducted from the proceeds and not hugely significant to a consignor's bottom line, handling charges are negotiable.

UNSOLD LOT FEES

The final charge is on any lots that remain unsold at the auction's end. You first learned about the unsold lot fee in Chapter 9. It is usually a percentage of the estimate. Because it costs the same amount to process a lot through the auction system regardless of whether it finds a buyer, many auction houses use this charge to cover their pre-sale expenses.

However, finding a buyer for each lot is the responsibility of the auction house, not the seller. When you are bargaining the unsold lot fee during the proposal stage, tell the specialist that if every measure, including accurate estimates, is properly taken to well represent your collection, there should not be any unsold lots. The auction house should offer to waive or reduce this charge as an indication of confidence in its ability to sell your wines better than its competitors.

If the lot is sold immediately after the sale to a collector willing to buy the lot for its reserve, the unsold lot fee is not charged. An auction house may even refund this fee if the lot is sold before the next auction.

You must also consider the return shipping cost of any unoffered or unsold lots if you think you might want them returned. Keep in mind that although it is not unusual to be left with some wine that does not sell, the auction house wants to find a buyer for each and every lot. The team should be motivated to sell 100 percent of your wine the first time it is put up at auction—so this should be a fairly easy point to negotiate in your favor. The cost to return the few lots that fail to find a buyer is not significant, and the auction house will realize that offering to pay for their return is a gesture of good faith. However, the company will probably not offer this unless asked.

CONCLUSION

Auction houses receive a fixed revenue on the sale of each lot: the buyer's premium. Successful bidders pay the company 15 to 20 percent of the hammer price for each lot they win. Unlike the vendor's commission, this charge is not negotiable. This guaranteed revenue is the key factor that enables the house to negotiate the consignor's terms.

Determine whether or not your consignment is such that the house would negotiate a better deal for the opportunity to sell it in its auction. The greater the interest an auction house has in a particular consignment, the more likely it will be to negotiate the charges. On the other hand, most companies tend to stick to their standard fee schedules when they are dealing with low-value consignments. The high cost of storing and selling wine precludes the auction houses from otherwise making money on these bottles. Yet regardless of your consignment's value, you can always ask the company to consider a lower rate.

Sometimes the company knows its costs and cannot afford to compromise. Regardless of these charges, selling wine through a professional auction house is the best way to ensure that your goods will be traded at a fair price. If the houses you approach will not budge from their standard vendor's commissions and other costs, look at the pre-sale reserves and subtract the selling charges. Use these figures to determine whether you still wish to sell your wine.

Keep in mind that the auction professionals work hard to produce the catalogue and bring bidders to your wines, while taking on much necessary overhead to successfully put each auction together. The 10- to 15-percent charges are hardly exorbitant. Most sellers will still come out ahead after selling their fine and rare wines at the standard auction costs, provided they have purchased their bottles wisely. At the same time, it can never hurt to ask the specialist for the most favorable terms available. Remember, everything is negotiable.

The Seller's Paperwork

Each auction house generates paperwork that reflects its individual procedures. As a seller, you should become familiar with these papers. Paperwork provides documentation of your consignment as well as a record of negotiations between you and the auction specialist. In the event of any confusion or discrepancy, accurate paperwork is invaluable. From the inventory to the receipt and from the contract to the final check, the paperwork discussed in this chapter is important at every step of the auction experience.

THE INVENTORY

Your first step towards becoming a consignor will be to submit a list of your wines to an auction house. The time needed to assemble this list is directly related to the level of organization in your cellar and the thoroughness of your previously itemized lists. If you do not already have an inventory of your collection, take one immediately or hire someone to complete the job. Account for every bottle.

In the past, each collection had a *cellar book*—a handwritten volume, remaining at the cellar's entrance, in which wines were logged in as they were laid down and out as they were removed to be drunk. Today, many collectors keep their inventories on computers. A variety of cellaring programs are available. (See the Resources on page 219 for a list of computer programs.) Regardless of how and where you choose to keep this list, it is an important aspect of wine collecting.

The type of wine, vintage, bottle size, and quantity of bottles should be supplied on your inventory list—whether it is being prepared for your own records or for an auction company's review. A basic inventory list is shown on page 156.

When your list is reviewed at the auction house, the specialist's pre-sale estimates will be based on the given information and the assumption that the wines are in good-to-excellent condition appropriate to their ages. It is important to

A neat and organized cellar enhances the experience of wine collecting and drinking. Have you ever gone to open a specific bottle, but couldn't find it? Within a cellar of any size, wine can be lost. Minimize the likelihood of misplacing wine by keeping your collection organized.

Year	Wine	Size	Quantity
1982	Ch. Mouton	750 ml	12 bottles, owc*
1982	Ch. Mouton	1.5 l	6 bottles, owc*
1983	Ch. Margaux	750 ml	6 bottles
1989	Ch. Haut Brion	375 ml	24 bottles, owc*
1990	Ch. Latour	750 ml	8 bottles
1987	Mondavi, Reserve CS	750 ml	12 bottles
1994	Colgin, Herb Lamb Vineyard	750 ml	3 bottles
2002	Colgin, Tychson Hill	750 ml	3 bottles
2002	Colgin, IX Estate Cabernet	750 ml	3 bottles
2002	Colgin, IX Estate Syrah	750 ml	3 bottles
1998	Claredon Hills, Astralis	750 ml	12 bottles

* original wooden case

A Basic Inventory List

Auction companies look for high-quality wines that their bidders will want to win. But not every lot can be a record breaker. Auctions should be well balanced, with something for every bidder. A good sale, for example, will include medium-priced wines that collectors seek for drinking stock. So include every wine on your inventory list, regardless of its value.

include all information that is available for every bottle, because distinguishing factors can affect the wines' values and are necessary for the specialist to make accurate evaluations. The description for each bottle should include any of the following that apply:

• producer (such as Mouton or Mondavi),

• proprietary name (a label, such as Astralis, owned by the wine's producer and used for a particular blend of grapes),

• varietal (a single type of grape from which the wine is made, such as Syrah or Cabernet),

• any special bottling (such as a *named cuvee*—a blend of grapes that make a quality wine), often designated as a *reserve*, and

• vineyard designation (such as Herb Lamb Vineyard).

These specific details help the specialist determine exactly which bottles your consignment contains, so be as accurate and clear as possible. Be very careful to distinguish, for example, between Château Latour and Latour a Pomerol. They are both excellent Bordeaux, but the former is from Pauillac while the latter is from Pomerol. La Tour du Pin and Château Le Pin are two very different wines with similar names, as are Château La Tour Carnet and Les Forts de Latour. Provide the specialist with the necessary clarifying information to pinpoint the exact wines in your collection, so he can correctly calculate the worth of your consignment.

Top auction houses receive significant numbers of inventory lists for their review. Specialists prefer to work with complete, well-organized lists, and potential consignors who provide such inventories often receive top priority. On the other hand, if any of the proper information is missing from your list, it may be shuffled to the bottom of the pile, and you could miss the next available auction. Most collectors submit inventories as Word documents or Excel spreadsheets, and you may find the organization of these programs helpful. Nevertheless, the auction team can work with any style of list, provided it is neat, clear, accurate, and complete.

> A specialist's professional life is comprised of lists and numbers and lots, and lots of lists and numbers. Make your inventory thorough and accurate so it won't be stashed at the bottom of the pile.

THE APPRAISAL

As you have read, the auction house will evaluate the products listed on your inventory list. If the team wants to sell the bottles you are offering, a specialist will prepare your consignment's pre-sale estimates. The results are returned to you as the *appraisal*. Until the actual price is established at the fall of the gavel, the appraisal is the main indicator of your collection's fair market value. You can determine this pre-sale value by deducting the proposed charges from the appraisal's total estimate. Use this figure to decide whether it is worthwhile for you to sell your wine at auction.

The pre-sale evaluation is also an inventory of the product that the auction house wants to sell. If the specialist decides that some of your wines are not suitable for auction, he will indicate this by stating it on the list or by omitting the wine from the list altogether. If none of your bottles have been accepted by the auction house, you may receive a polite thanks-but-no-thanks letter. Feel free to contact the auction house for an explanation if the refusal of your wines is not explained.

The Appraisal

Year	Wine	Quantity	Estimate
1982	Ch. Mouton	12 btls, owc	$8,000–$10,000
1982	Ch. Mouton	6 mags, owc	$8,000–$10,000
1983	Ch. Margaux	6 btls	$3,000–$4,000
1989	Ch. Haut Brion	24 half, owc	$6,000–$8,000
1990	Ch. Latour	8 btls	$3,000–$4,500
1987	Mondavi, Reserve CS	12 btls	$2,000–$3,000
1994	Colgin, Herb Lamb Vineyard	3 btls	$1,200–$1,500
2002	Colgin, Tychson Hill	3 btls	$1,500–$2,250
2002	Colgin, IX Estate Cabernet	3 btls	$1,000–$1,500
2002	Colgin, IX Estate Syrah	3 btls	$900–$1,200
1998	Claredon Hills, Astralis	12 btls	$2,400–$3,600

THE CONTRACT

No reputable auction company will sell your wine without a signed contract. At the same time, the agreement is also important for you. Don't expect any perks that are not included in its clauses.

Each company sets its own policies regarding the length of time for which a contact is valid. Some contracts apply to one specific auction. Other contracts are honored for different consignments over the course of a year, while still others may allow an agreement to extend over the entire course of its relationship with the seller.

After receiving the specialist's appraisal of your consignment, you have several decisions to make. First you need to determine if this company is right for you. In Chapter 9, you read hints for choosing an auction house. Then, Chapter 10 explained how to determine and understand the bottom line after you receive your estimates and negotiate the charges. If you decide you want to do business with the auction house and believe that its estimates are fair and appealing, you are ready for the auction team to draft a contract.

The standard wine-auction agreement outlines the various charges, as well as the auction company's responsibilities to the seller and the seller's responsibilities to the company. Read the contract carefully. Contracts are often written by legal teams, and can be lengthy and time-consuming to read. If you are uncomfortable or unsure about any part of the document, have an attorney review it before you sign. Your signature means you agree to all the clauses and to have this company sell your wines.

Make sure all the charges are accurately recorded as they were negotiated during the proposal stage; that deadline and payment dates are included and reasonable for your schedule; that you understand how insurance issues will be handled; and that you are aware of the company's policy for dealing with non-payment from a buyer. Any items not covered in the standard contract can be added before you sign, provided that you and the company can come to an agreement. You and the auction representative should both initial any changes made to the original contract.

Although small adjustments can often be made, most auction agreements follow standard provisions. The inset that begins below shows a typical contract. Keep in mind that the order in which the included clauses appear is likely to differ between companies. When you receive a new contract, take your time and read it in its entirety. You will see that despite various changes in wording and order, the information found within the clauses will be similar to that in the sample contract.

A Sample Contract

Every auction house drafts agreements differently. Some reuse the same contract, cutting and pasting information in a cookie-cutter manner. Others have lawyers draft every contract individually. The most notable changes are in the layout and order of clauses. However, each agreement will address the same information.

The following is a wine-auction contract between an unnamed seller and the fictional company Wine Lover's Guide Auctions, Inc. Although the contract with which you will eventually be presented may look or be arranged differently, it will contain most of the same points—but, of course, with details that relate specifically to you and the deal you made with the auction company.

Always read the entire contract, and never sign anything if you don't completely agree with and understand every clause.

WINE LOVER'S GUIDE AUCTIONS, INC.
123 Going Going Gone Avenue • Sold, NY 00001
Ph: (123) 555-4567 • Fax: (123) 555-4568

Date:

Seller: _____ **Agent:** _____

Address: _____ **Address:** _____

CONSIGNMENT CONTRACT

This introductory paragraph does not have a formal heading. It names the parties involved and defines them using terms by which they will be referred to throughout the contract.

This Agreement (this "Agreement"), dated as of the date set forth above, is by and between WINE LOVER'S GUIDE AUCTIONS, having an address at 123 Going Going Gone Ave, Sold, New York 00001 ("WLG") and the above-referenced Seller, having an address as set forth above ("Seller").

Introductory Paragraph

1. The seller gives permission for the auction company to sell those products listed in his inventory list. The list can be amended later only if both parties agree.

1. Consignment. Seller appoints WLG as the sole and exclusive sales agent to auction the products listed on Schedule A hereto (the "Products") which Schedule A may be amended or supplemented from time to time upon mutual agreement of the parties (the "Products"). Seller hereby consigns to WLG the Products for auction by WLG in accordance with this Agreement and the Conditions of Sale and Information for Buyers in effect at the time of any applicable auction.

Clause 1 Consignment

2. The vender's commission, as agreed upon at the proposal stage, is stated here as a percentage of the hammer price. Turn to page 149 for more on the negotiation of this charge.

2. Commissions. Consignment Commission will be 15% of the hammer.

Clause 2 Commissions

3. This clause acknowledges a deadline for the wines to be delivered to the warehouse, and specifies which party will be responsible for all related costs and liabilities.

3. Product Delivery. Seller shall deliver the Products to such location as WLG shall designate, or shall make the Products available for pickup, no later than 60 days prior to the scheduled date of the initial auction in which WLG intends to include the Products. Upon request, WLG may recommend a carrier/packer; provided, that WLG shall have no liability therefore, and all packing, transporting, delivering and insuring of the Prod-

Clause 3 Product Delivery

ucts will be at Seller's sole expense and risk. WLG shall arrange for storage on behalf of any Products delivered to WLG, and at no expense to Seller (except as provided in paragraph 9(b)). If WLG agrees to pick up Products, Seller will pay WLG all costs and expenses associated therewith including the cost of all packing materials, plus all trip expenses incurred by WLG for onsite inspection/inventorying, all of which will be deducted from payments owed by WLG to Seller. Seller will also be responsible for all costs of boxes needing to be replaced to ensure proper storage as WLG sees fit.

4. The auction house has complete discretion in making all sale decisions, both general and as they relate to this specific consignment.

Clause 4
Method of Sale

4. Method of Sale. WLG shall have complete discretion as the place, date and manner of sale, the Conditions of Sale, the illustration, and/or the description of the Products in its catalogues or other literature, and the combination or division of the Products into such lots and/or separate auctions as WLG shall determine.

5. The auction house does not guarantee that each lot will be sold at its estimated price. Also, estimates may be adjusted prior to the auction to reflect market value.

Clause 5
Estimates

5. Estimates. Any appraisal, estimate or other statement of value by WLG or its representatives with respect to the estimated value or selling price of any Product ("Estimates"), whether made orally or in any writing, are opinions of WLG based on recent market value for Product in Excellent Condition. Estimates shall not be relied upon by Seller or any third party as a prediction or guarantee of the actual selling price, and in no event shall WLG be liable for the failure of any Product to be sold at any such Estimate or the reserve price therefore. WLG reserves the right to change Estimates at any time before a sale based on any considerations deemed relevant by WLG. Following physical inspection of inventory, WLG will provide Seller with notice of any items not previously represented; provided, however, that any such Estimates will be subject to the provisions hereof.

6. The auction house can sell a lot below its reserve price. However, the company will then be responsible to pay the difference to the seller.

Clause 6
Reserves

6. Reserves. All Products will be sold subject to a reserve, which is the minimum price below which the Product will not be sold. If bidding does not reach the reserve on any Product, the auctioneer will withdraw it from sale. Should WLG sell any Product at a price below the Reserve, WLG will be responsible to Seller for the difference between the hammer price and such Reserve.

7. The seller cannot bid on any lot in his own consignment.

7. No Bidding by Seller. Seller shall not, directly or indirectly by or through any of its representatives or agents (other than WLG), enter or cause to be entered a bid on any of Seller's Product being offered for sale.

8. Withdrawal of Products.

8(a). The seller can withdraw his items from the sale only if the auction company agrees. If this occurs, the seller may be charged a fee.

(a) No Withdrawal by Seller. The Seller may withdraw no Product after the date hereof. If WLG consents to a withdrawal by Seller, the Product may be withdrawn upon payment of 10% of (i) the reserve price, or (ii) if the reserve has not yet been set, the valuation base (as defined in paragraph 14 hereof), in either case plus all out-of-pocket expenses incurred by WLG for packing, shipping or delivery.

8(b). The auction company, on the other hand, may withdraw items from the sale for any of the listed reasons.

(b) Withdrawal by WLG. WLG reserves the right to withdraw any Product at any time before actual sale if in WLG's sole judgment (i) there is doubt as to the attribution, authenticity, quality or potability of the Product, (iii) there is doubt as to the accuracy of Seller's representations or warranties set forth herein in any aspect, (iv) Seller has breached or is about to breach any provision hereof, (v) there is doubt as to Seller's title to the Product, or (vi) for other just cause. In any such event, WLG will return to Seller the Product withdrawn at no penalty to Seller, but at Seller's sole cost and expense.

9. Unsold Products.

9(a). The company's rights regarding the sale of unsold lots are outlined here.

(a) Unsold Product. For any Product offered but not sold during the auction, WLG may, in its sole discretion, sell any such Product in a private sale for no less than the reserve amount, provided that such sale occurs within five days of the auction's conclusion. Unless otherwise instructed by Seller in writing as set forth below, any Products not sold in auction or pursuant to such private sale shall be retained by WLG and will be placed in a future sale. Any such future sale (i) may or may not be the sale immediately following the one in which the Product did not sell, (ii) may be live or via internet, (iii) shall be at such prices, including reserves, and upon such terms and conditions, as WLG shall determine in its sole and absolute discretion. There will be no service charge with respect to unsold Products, and there will be no charge to Seller for the storage of unsold Product, except as provided below. The proceeds of such subsequent sale shall be remitted to Seller in accordance with the terms of this Agreement.

Clause 7
No Bidding
by Seller

Clause 8(a)
No Withdrawal
by Seller

Clause 8(b)
Withdrawal
by WLG

Clause 9(a)
Unsold Product

9(b). If a seller wishes to have any unsold lots returned, the steps he must take as well as any possible charges he would incur are stated here. These charges were discussed in detail on page 153.

Clause 9(b)
Reclaim of
Unsold Product

(b) Reclaim of Unsold Product. If Seller wishes to reclaim unsold Product, (i) WLG must receive written notice from Seller within 30 days of the auction in which the Product was offered for sale, and (ii) any such Product must be reclaimed by Seller and removed from WLG warehouse, at Seller's sole cost and expense, within 60 days from the date of such auction. Thereafter, Product will be transferred to a public wine storage facility, and Seller will incur a storage charge of $2.00 per month for each case of Product, plus 1.5% annual insurance charge. Seller shall not be entitled to reclaim any unsold Product until all commissions; expenses and other amounts owed to WLG have been paid in full.

10. After the sale, the seller can expect to receive his payment within a certain number of days, stated here. Reasons why the seller would not receive payment are also listed.

Clause 10
Settlement
of Account

10. Settlement of Account. WLG will pay Seller the net proceeds received and collected from the sale of Seller's Products, less any commissions, reimbursable expenses and any other amounts due WLG from Seller (whether arising out of the sale of the Product or otherwise). WLG will make such payment to Seller within 35 calendar days after WLG has received and collected payment in full from the Buyer, unless, prior to the expiration of such 30 day period, (a) WLG shall have received notice of the Buyer's intention to rescind the sale or any other claim relating to the Product or its sale, or (b) WLG shall have for any reason refunded such proceeds to the Buyer. All payments shall be made in US Dollars.

11. A sale can be canceled if a buyer does not pay for items won. The auction company includes a clause stating that it cannot be held accountable for this situation.

Clause 11
Non-Payment
by Buyer

11. Non-Payment By Buyer. In the event of nonpayment by the Buyer, WLG may cancel the sale and return the Product to Seller, enforce payment by the Buyer, or take any other actions permitted by law, as WLG shall determine in its sole discretion. In no event shall WLG be liable for any incidental or consequential damages resulting to Seller as a result of any breach or failure by the Buyer.

12. The buyer will be allowed to return an item won under certain circumstances explained here. If this occurs and the seller has already been paid, the seller will be expected to return this money to the company.

12. Rescission of Sale. WLG is authorized to accept the return and rescind the sale of any Product at any time if WLG, in its sole judgment, determines that there is a genuine issue as to quality, authenticity or title of the Product, or there exists any other circumstance which, if not remedied, could, in the sole opinion of WLG, result in liability to WLG therefore. In such event, WLG is further authorized to refund or credit to the Buyer the purchase price of such returned Product, and if WLG has already remitted to Seller any proceeds of the rescinded sale, Seller shall, immediately upon notice by WLG, pay to WLG an amount equal to the remitted proceeds; however, in no event shall Seller reimburse WLG more than the Seller received from WLG for the rescinded sale Product.

**Clause 12
Rescission of Sale**

13. If the buyer finds that an item he won was incorrectly described in the catalogue, the auction company will determine the appropriate course of action, and the seller must comply with its decision.

13. Buyer's Claim. After the sale, if within 30 days following receipt of Product, a Buyer notifies WLG in writing of a claim that the lot is short or ullaged or that any statement of opinion in the catalogue is not well founded, WLG in its sole and absolute discretion will decide such claim as between the Buyer and Seller. WLG may decide that the sale stand or be rescinded and that the purchase price be refunded in whole or in part. WLG's decision will be final and binding on Buyer and Seller, and no action shall be brought in connection with any claim, except on and in accordance with WLG's decision.

**Clause 13
Buyer's Claim**

14. The cost of insurance, as well as a detailed explanation of the insurance coverage, is described. For more information on insurance costs, turn to page 151.

14. Insurance. Insurance coverage of all Product will be furnished by WLG as follows: Product will be insured by WLG for any loss or damage commencing (a) in the case of a pickup by WLG at a location designated by Seller, from the time of such pickup, and (b) in the case of Product received at WLG's premises or a warehouse designated by WLG, from the time of receipt, and in each case such coverage will cease upon the fall of the hammer during the auction. Insurance coverage shall be for an amount not to exceed (i) if the Product has been sold, the hammer price, or (ii) if the Product has not been sold, an amount equal to the mean of our estimates at the time of loss or damage. Either such amount shall be referred to herein as the "valuation base." WLG's liability to Seller resulting from loss or damage of any Product shall not exceed the above-mentioned insurance coverage of such Product and will exclude any damage or loss caused by earthquake or flood. Seller shall, without exception, be charged at a rate of one percent (1%) of the hammer total of the Products being offered at auction in respect of

**Clause 14
Insurance**

insurance coverage. Any claim will be less the deductible required by the insurance company for the policy in effect at the time. ALL INSURANCE CLAIMS SHALL BE LIMITED TO THE PHYSICAL INVENTORY TAKEN BY WLG AUCTIONS, NOTICE OF WHICH WILL BE PROVIDED TO SELLER PROMPTLY UPON COMPLETION.

15. The auction company has the right to photograph consignments. The copyright ownership of any such pictures as well as the additional catalogue material will be addressed. Additionally, the company acknowledges the seller's right to privacy, although the seller can forfeit this right if he wants his name attached to his consignment.

Clause 15
Rights to Images
of Products

15. Rights to Images of Products. WLG retains the exclusive right to videotape or photograph the Product for catalogue advertising purposes. WLG retains the exclusive copyright to all catalogue text, illustrations and descriptions of the Products. WLG shall not use Seller's name in its catalogues or advertising, or disclose Seller's name or identity to third parties unless Seller has placed its initials after this paragraph.

16. The auction team may taste sample bottles out of the consignment to determine the condition of a consignment.

Clause 16
Tasting & Capsules

16. Tasting & Capsules. With permission from the Seller, WLG may taste a sample bottle or bottles of the Product determined by the quantity of the consignment. Bottles also may be opened with the consent of the Seller for prospective bidders at pre-auction tastings. WLG may cut capsules in order to inspect cork and markings to confirm authenticity.

17. The auction company will be responsible for collecting all appropriate taxes from the buyers.

Clause 17
Sales Tax

17. Sales Tax. WLG shall collect from Buyers all sales taxes due, if any, and will timely remit to the appropriate agencies all such sales taxes.

18. The seller must agree that the consignment belongs to him and that he has the right to sell it at auction, at which point he will transfer the title of ownership to the buyer.

Clause 18
Seller's
Representations
and Warranties

18. Seller's Representations and Warranties. Seller represents and warrants that (i) Seller has the right and title to consign the products for sale, (ii) the products are, and until completion of sale by WLG, will be, free and clear of all liens, claims and encumbrances of others ("liens") or restrictions on WLG's right to offer and sell the products at auction, (iii) good title will pass to the buyer of all products free and clear or any such liens of restrictions. These representations and warranties shall survive the completion of the transactions contemplated hereby. Seller shall notify WLG promptly in writing of any events or circumstances that may cauce the foregoing to be inaccurate or breached in any way. If seller is acting an an agent for a prinipal, seller and principal, jointly and severally, assume all of the obligations under this agreement. Seller agrees that the intended beneficiaries of this provision include all buyers of the products.

19. Additional Representations and Warranties.

19(a). The seller must be able to legally enter into this agreement.

(a) By Seller. Seller represents and warrants to WLG that (i) it has full power and authority (if Seller is a legal entity) or legal capacity (if Seller is an individual) to enter into this Agreement and perform its obligations hereunder, (ii) if Seller is a legal entity, this Agreement has been duly authorized and validly executed and, upon execution by WLG, constitutes a legal, valid and binding obligation of Seller, enforceable against Seller in accordance with its terms, and (iii) if Seller is a manufacturer of Product, sale by the Seller of the Product through WLG is for promotional purposes and is not being done to circumvent applicable laws regarding distribution of beverage alcohol.

Clause 19(a) Additional Representations and Warranties By Seller

19(b). The auction company must be able to legally enter into this agreement.

(b) By WLG. WLG represents and warrants to Seller that (i) it has full power and to enter into this Agreement and perform its obligations hereunder, (ii) this Agreement has been duly authorized and validly executed and, upon execution by Seller, constitutes a legal, valid and binding obligation of WLG, enforceable against WLG in accordance with its terms, and (iii) it is licensed and permitted under the laws of the State of New York to sell the Products in the State of New York.

Clause 19(b) Additional Representations and Warranties By WLG

20. The seller will compensate the company for any losses derived from claims made against his products.

20. Indemnification. Seller shall indemnify, defend, and hold harmless WLG and its affiliates, and their respective officers, directors, shareholders, members, managers, attorneys, agents, consultants, employees and other representatives (collectively, "Indemnities") from and against any and all claims, liabilities and expenses (including, without limitation, interest, penalties and attorney's fees and amounts paid in investigation, defending or settling any of the foregoing), whether in an action between the parties hereto or between or among any Indemnities and any third party, arising out of or related to: (a) any acts by or omissions of Seller, its agents, employees, or representatives, relating to or affecting the Products, (b) any breach or inaccuracy of any of the representations, warranties, covenants or agreements made by Seller in connection with the transactions contemplated herein, (c) the claims of third parties claiming or challenging title to any Product consigned hereunder, and /or (d) any claims of Buyers, persons claiming for Buyers or for any other person resulting from WLG's offering for sale or

Clause 20 Indemnification

selling any Product consigned hereunder, whether or not the Product has been offered, sold, or returned to WLG.

21. The seller and auction company agree to take any unresolvable issues to the appropriate court system. Also, this contract will supercede any prior agreements between the auction house and seller.

**Clause 21
Miscellaneous**

21. Miscellaneous. (a) This Agreement shall be governed by the internal laws of the State of New York; (b) any disputes arising in connection herewith shall be exclusively resolved in the State of New York before a panel of three arbitrators of the American Arbitration Association (the "AAA") in accordance with its rules on commercial arbitration; (c) the parties hereby irrevocably consent to the exclusive jurisdiction of the State of New York, waive any objection to personal jurisdiction, and waive the right to trial by jury. In furtherance thereof, if Seller is not a United States citizen, Seller hereby appoints _____ as its Authorized Agent for service of process in the State of New York with respect to any matter arising out of or relating to this Agreement, and represents that such party has agreed to serve as Seller's Authorized Agent in such regard; (d) any notices hereunder shall be in writing and shall be deemed given if delivered either personally, by overnight delivery or sent by certified or registered mail, postage prepaid, to a party at its respective address as set forth above; (e) this Agreement, together with the Schedules hereto, as they may be amended from time to time as provided herein, contains the entire agreement of the parties concerning the subject matter hereof, and supersedes any and all prior agreements oral or written among the parties hereto concerning the subject matter hereof, which prior agreements are hereby cancelled. This Agreement may not be amended or terminated orally; (f) WLG has the sole right to amend or replace any of the foregoing Schedules, which, as so amended, shall be deemed incorporated by reference herein and made a part hereof.

Both the company and seller will sign and date two copies of the contract. The seller will receive a copy for his records.

Signatures

IN WITNESS WHEREOF, the undersigned have duly executed this Agreement as of the date and year first written above.

Wine Lover's Guide Auctions: Seller:

By: _____   By: _____

Date: _____   Date: _____

THE RECEIPT

After signing and receiving your copy of the contract, you will either personally deliver the bottles or have a delivery service ship them to the company's warehouse. (See page 152 for details on transferring your collection to the warehouse.) At that point, the specialist will generate a receipt. The information on the receipt will be similar to that on the initial appraisal. The name, quantity, bottle size, estimate, and reserve for each and every bottle received and stored in the warehouse will be listed. The receipt will then supercede the appraisal. Because the receipt will become the official list of the wines sitting in the auction warehouse, you'll want to immediately check it for accuracy and contact the specialist regarding any discrepancies.

The receipt supercedes the appraisal as the official list of bottles in the warehouse because you can alter your consignment by adding or withdrawing several bottles after the appraisal is produced and before the contract is signed. You should always inform the auction company of changes to help things run smoothly.

Some auction companies will not issue a receipt until the consignment has been inventoried and catalogued. The receipt will then be taken from the actual catalogue page. If this is the case, you must have your initial inventory list updated to reflect what has actually been sent to the warehouse. Have the specialist sign an amended company-generated evaluation to serve as a temporary receipt. This will protect both parties from any discrepancies between bottles sent and bottles in the warehouse.

All consignors should receive a copy of the completed catalogue. This, too, can serve as a receipt. Review the appropriate pages carefully. If you notice any errors or omissions, now is the time to speak up!

AFTER-SALE NOTIFICATION

After the auction, the company will issue a list for each consignor with the hammer price of every lot the seller has sold. If you have not attended the auction, this *after-sale notification*—record of your auction results—will be an anticipated and exciting piece of correspondence.

The computer-generated list will be mailed or emailed to each seller. Cross reference the after-sale notification with your receipt, being sure to account for every bottle of wine. If there are any discrepancies, immediately notify the specialist in charge of your consignment. Then make a note of any unsold lots and notify the house regarding whether these bottles should be reoffered at a future auction or returned to your cellar. You will usually have a limited number of days (stated in the contract) to ask for your bottles back, so make this decision as soon as possible.

SETTLEMENT STATEMENT

Many auction companies generate *settlement statements*—second after-sale notices that outline the charges and state the final payment amounts. The settlement statement includes a per-lot breakdown of hammer prices, all charges owed to the auction company, and a final total for your consignment. Always check your settlement statement very carefully. Make sure that the charges match the agreed-upon amounts, and that your lots and their hammer prices were accurately recorded. Errors must be brought to the auction house's attention immediately. It is much easier to have changes and adjustments made before any payment checks are issued.

THE FINAL CHECK

The last piece of paperwork you will receive is the payment. It should be sent on the date specified in your auction contract, depending on timely payment by the successful bidders. It may, however, be split into installments, in which case you will receive the first check around this date. You can choose to receive your payment by mail or wire. For more information about and options for receiving your payment from the auction company, turn back to Chapter 9. You may also request via written instruction that the auction company direct final payment to a third party.

CONCLUSION

For a smooth consignor experience, you must prepare for the paperwork that will be generated during the process. Earmark a folder specifically for these documents so that they will all be kept safely together. The papers will track each bottle of wine through the auction system and should be checked for accuracy at every stage. From the very beginning of the process, you will need to make sure that all your bottles are accounted for by the auction company. Discrepancies and changes are easier to remedy the sooner they are discovered.

It is also important for you to verify that the contract is thorough and reasonable, and complies with your proposal negotiations. At the auction's end, you will use this agreement and the receipt to verify the after-sale notifications. Having properly organized paperwork will further guarantee the safety of your bottles and the promptness of your payment.

The lessons in this chapter, however, relate not only to the paperwork but to the entire auction process. While each auction company consists of wonderful people who will assist you every step of the way, it is always important for you to keep yourself abreast of all situations dealing with your bottles. The workload may seem tedious at the start, but it will soon become second nature. Your full enjoyment of the auction process begins and ends with being an informed seller.

PART FOUR

The Fruits of Your Labor

12

Expanding Your Collection

Wine auctions are valuable for improving a budding wine collection, but amassing a great collection requires more than simple attendance and payment. In this chapter, you will read specific advice on advancing your collection to the next level, whether you are starting on the ground floor or with some experience as a collector.

There are countless types of wine, from all over the world and from many different vintages. Beginning a wine collection without first narrowing your field of vision can be overwhelming, while providing your new collection with direction can save you time and money that may otherwise be misspent. Regardless of your budget and level of experience, this chapter is your first step towards the wine collection you have always wanted.

BEGINNING YOUR COLLECTION

Every great collection starts with a keen interest in wine and a single bottle. As a wine enthusiast, you probably purchase bottles (or cases) that simply taste good. Bottles will accumulate and one day, without realizing how easy the transition from consumer to collector can be, you might discover that your drinking stock has become a collection.

Try to envision how large you want your collection to grow before you arrange a home for your bottles. This way, you can prepare an area of appropriate size. (See page 41 for details on storing wine bottles.) Very few collectors begin with adequate temperature-controlled storage, though, and you can always seek out additional storage space as it becomes necessary.

The main goal of your collection should be to develop your overall appreciation of the world of wine. The exact focus may shift direction as your appreciation matures, but your wine knowledge will continually expand in proportion to the size of your collection. The following sections, which offer suggestions on what purchases to make and when to make them, were written with your wine education in mind.

Learning About the Classics

A varietal is the type of grape used to make the wine. For the varietal to be named on the label, at least 75 percent of the wine must be made of that grape.

One way to begin collecting is to concentrate on the classic varietals. These are the wines of which every serious collector must have basic knowledge. If there are many wines discussed here with which you are not already familiar, check them out regardless of whether they are going to factor significantly into your collection.

Discussions of quintessential wines tend to begin with France. After all, the wine-auction market—as well as the entire world of wine—is historically based on a foundation of red Bordeaux. Chapter 2 explained that the wines of Bordeaux are divided by quality into different growths, from first to fifth, according to the Classification of 1855. (All the first growth wines are named in the inset on page 56.) Wine auctions offer the best opportunity to obtain these great red wines, which are often the most sought-after auction lots. The inset on page 174 lists examples of top-notch bottles and their particularly delicious vintages, from Bordeaux as well as other regions.

The contribution of Bordeaux to the world of wine is singularly important, as can be seen from its influence on the New World. New World wines either attempt to emulate those of Bordeaux—like Robert Mondavi sought to do in California in the 1960s and 1970s—or blend Bordeaux varietals with the local region's traditional fruit—like the Italian Super Tuscan wines, which are created by adding Cabernet Sauvignon to Sangiovese.

You should have experience tasting both first growth Bordeaux and Bordeaux from the great vintages. A bottle of 1982 Château Latour is both a first growth and from a great vintages, so you can taste both qualities in one fell swoop with a bottle of this wine.

Two other extremely important wine regions are Burgundy in France and, particularly for American collectors, Napa, California. If you haven't already done so, taste the great examples of each. The inset on page 174 gives several examples of quality wines from the most important wine regions. (For more information on these regions, refer back to Chapter 2.)

The best classic wines of Bordeaux, Burgundy, and Napa are expensive in any vintage, so try buying them in mixed lots. (Turn to page 54 to read about different types of lots.) Read the descriptions of mixed lots carefully, looking for any first growth bottles among a group of other red Bordeaux. Do the same for great wines from other regions. You and some wine-drinking friends may want to share the cost of a group lot and divide the bottles among yourselves. Better still is buying a lot with a group of collectors to taste through the bottles together in a somewhat serious setting.

Online auctions can be useful for finding these expensive bottles, because you can often buy a single bottle out of a larger lot. This will allow you to stay within your wine budget while still adding great wines to your collection.

Buying What You Like

When you identify a wine that you enjoy drinking and sharing, you will want to find it often and at its best price. You are most likely to locate these favorite wines at auction, particularly if the vintages are no longer stocked at retail.

You may also be able to stock up on a preferred younger wine at auction. Young wines are often offered by the case. Maybe on a recent tasting trip in Napa, you found the new wines from Pine Ridge to be especially delicious. Auctions are great for finding odd lots of Pine Ridge—and because the majority of bidders do not come to auction for these young bottles, you may be able to secure some real bargains.

If you particularly enjoy a wine from a certain producer, try an older variety of the same wine. You will probably be able to find these older vintages at auction. Browse through several catalogues from different auction companies to find out how often these bottles appear and to gauge how aggressively you need to bid. If you discover that your tastes lean toward the rare and expensive, you will be hard-pressed to find a deal—but you will know to set aside a larger part of your budget for these bottles.

Look for value when buying in case quantities. Large mixed lots and group lots tend to offer the best values. Because of the great bargains these lots can offer, some auctioneers refer to them as drinking stock or drinking lots. Figure out the average price per bottle in the lot and bid as your budget allows.

Whether you are at a live or online auction, bid on bottles in the best available condition. Eventually you will pull the corks and taste the wines—and bottles in excellent condition provide the best experiences. It is not worth buying a bottle of lesser quality just to save a little money.

Trying Different Wines

To further advance both your wine knowledge and your pleasure of the wines with which you are already familiar, it is a good idea to mix it up from time to time. If you are a California Zinfandel drinker, why not try some Australian Shiraz? And what about comparing an Australian Shiraz to an Australian Grenache? If you only drink red Burgundy, aren't you curious to taste Oregon Pinot Noir? Sophisticated wine drinkers can look anew at California Pinot Noir. Have you sampled the highly regarded Tempranillo from Spain? Try various bottles from different areas so you can fully realize the complexity of wine. Drinking different wines from all over the world will also sharpen your senses of smell and taste. Experiencing wines of different grapes, different styles, and different prices will further enhance the pleasure of drinking good wine every day.

Wine collecting can be expensive. It is tempting to buy by the dozen when you find a delicious wine at an affordable price. At the same time, every issue of both *Wine Spectator* and Robert Parker's *The Wine Advocate* contains a new list of wines that excite the professionals. You probably want to budget for these options as well as old favorites.

It is a worthwhile exercise to drink a new wine with a professional's tasting note in front of your glass. Although you may not share the critic's opinion, you will probably remember the wine if you thoughtfully read the critique as you sip.

An Auction Shopper's Wish List
of Classic Wines

There are many wonderfully delicious wines from all over the world. You may choose to focus on the bottles of a specific region, or you may find it more appealing to gather first-rate bottles from throughout the wine-growing world. Regardless of your particular style and goals, the following list will assist you in expanding and improving both your wine collection and wine knowledge. The wines included here are generally accepted as the top wines and vintages.

The list is divided by region. The recommended wines are followed by the most coveted vintages. Other wines and vintages have yielded comparably delicious wines, but the examples listed here tend to be the subject of particularly intense interest among collectors.

Bordeaux

For red Bordeaux:

☐ Recommended châteaux: Châteaux Ausone, Margaux, Mouton, Lafite, Latour, Haut Brion, Cheval Blanc, Petrus, Pichon Lalande, and Le Pin.

☐ Classic vintages: 1961, 1982, 1990, and 2000.

For Sauternes, an expensive, high-quality dessert wine from Bordeaux:

☐ Recommended château: Château d'Yquem.

☐ Classic vintages: 1967, 1983, 1989, and 2001.

Burgundy

☐ Recommended wine growers: Domaine de la Romanée Conti, Leroy, Jayer, Louis Latour, Dominique Lafon, and Coche-Dury.

☐ Classic vintages: 1988, 1989, and 1990.

The Rhône Valley

☐ Recommended producers: Château Rayas, Jaboulet, Guigal, and Chave.

☐ Classic vintages: 1990 and 1998.

☐ Additional information: Etienne Guigal owns three vineyards—La Mouline, La Landonne, and La Turque. All three vineyards produce extremely collectible bottles.

Champagne

☐ Recommended houses: Don Perignon, Krug, Taittenger, Bollinger, and Salon.

☐ Classic vintages: All years; a personal favorite is 1990.

California

For classic Napa Valley Cabernet Sauvignon:

❐ Recommended producers: Robert Mondavi, Beaulieu Vineyards Private Reserve, Stag's Leap Wine Cellars, Dunn Howell Mountain, Heitz Martha's Vineyard, and Diamond Creek.

❐ Classic vintages: All years; bottles from the 1980s and early 1990s are particularly delicious.

For California Cult Cabernet:

❐ Recommended producers: Araujo, Bryant Family, Colgin, Dalla Valle, Harlan Estate, Screaming Eagle, and Sine Qua Non.

❐ Classic vintages: 1994, 1997, and younger, particularly 2001 and 2002.

For California Chardonnay:

❐ Recommended producers: Marcassin and Kistler.

Italy

For the Super Tuscans:

❐ Recommended wines: Sassicaia, Ornellaia, and Tignanello.

For classic Barbaresco, a red wine of Piedmont:

❐ Recommended producers: Gaja and Giacosa.

For classic Barolo, a red wine of Piedmont:

❐ Recommended producers: Conterno, Giacosa, and Mascarello.

Spain

❐ Recommended wine: Vega Sicilia Único.

❐ Classic vintages: Not produced unless of truly exceptional quality. A personal favorite is 1968.

Australia

For traditional Australian wine:

❐ Recommended wine: Penfold's Grange Hermitage.

For Australian wine of the new generation:

❐ Recommended wine: Any bottle that has scored 96 to 100 points from Robert Parker, such as Clarendon Hills Astralis or Wild Duck Creek Estate Duck Muck Shiraz.

Portugal

❐ Recommended houses: Quinta do Noval Nacional, Fonseca, Graham's, Taylor's, and Warre's.

❐ Classic vintages: 1963, 1983, 1985, and 1994.

A bottle that is sold out at both the winery and the retailers can usually be found at auction. You can start by searching the online auctions that allow bidders to buy individual bottles out of a case. Since buying twelve bottles of each wine requires both space and money, online auctions are usually the most economical way to add bottles to a collection. It will also allow you to try a larger variety of wines. When you are bidding in an online auction, try purchasing enough wine so that your total number of bottles is close to twelve or a multiple of twelve. This will allow the shipping to be done in full-case or nearly full-case quantities, and keep the shipping costs reasonable. If you are attending a live auction and want to try different wines, you may want to concentrate on winning mixed lots. The advantages of these lots were discussed in Chapter 3.

Investing in Bottles

An old-fashioned English exercise is to buy and hold onto a case of each first growth Bordeaux every vintage. As a couple of years pass, the value of the case appreciates. The buyer eventually sells the wine at auction and applies the profit to his everyday drinking stock. This method has proven successful through each market cycle.

Lots of collectors have made lots of money by laying down bottles and then reselling them. Of course, reselling wine for a profit is not as easy as it may look. If your goal is to profit from your wine purchases, the following guidelines should prove helpful.

Buy What the Collectors Buy

Collectors tend to pursue certain wines, and as an investor, you should consider following the pack. After all, the wines that are desired by collectors will be the ones to increase in value. First growth Bordeaux, for example, represent a historical standard of desirability, and collectors will go to incredible lengths to find and buy these bottles. As a result, these wines of Bordeaux are the industry's safest investment vehicles.

You've read about the influence of Robert Parker and *The Wine Advocate*. Wines given perfect or nearly perfect scores become investment-grade wines, because collectors and drinkers alike are looking for these bottles. However, the value of these wines fluctuates along with the stock market and various other trends. Remember that nothing is guaranteed. Never invest—in wine or any other product—a sum of money you can't afford to lose.

Track Prices Over Time

Tracking a wine's hammer prices over a several-year period will allow you to see how the bottle's value has changed as well as judge where it may be going. You can use published records, such as past editions of the *Wine Price File*, to gather these figures on wines in which you find yourself interested.

Many great wines increase in value over a relatively short period of time. As an investor/collector, you want to buy these wines to sell them and make a profit. Yet the price of a great wine can also vary depending on larger economic forces or wine-drinking fashion, and the smart investor/collector must be aware of this as well.

Studying auction results should provide you with clues as to the wine's future at auction. For example, if the hammer prices for a certain wine have recently begun to steadily decrease, you may be able to determine that its value will continue to fall. This wine, then, would probably make for a bad investment. Of course, you would have to check the catalogue for the provenance and condition of the specific bottles whose results you are interpreting before drawing any conclusions.

At the same time, the value of a bottle of wine can prove unpredictable. Let's look at a example of a specific wine's value at auction. In April 1997, a case of 1945 Château Mouton set the record for the most expensive case of wine ever sold at auction. It was sold for a hammer price of $100,000. Given the rarity of this bottle and its reputation as one of the world's greatest wines, you might expect the price to continue to appreciate. Now take a look at Table 12.1 to see the actual auction results since that world record price was achieved. As you can see, the price fell at the very next auction—and continued to do so drastically each year until the price spiked far above the previous record high.

TABLE 12.1. RECENT AUCTION RESULTS FOR A TWELVE-BOTTLE CASE OF 1945 CHÂTEAU MOUTON			
Date	**Company**	**Winning Bid**	**Pre-Sale Estimate***
April 1997	Zachys-Christie's	$100,000 hammer	$35,000–$45,000
October 2002	Zachys	$75,000 hammer	$50,000–$75,000
December 2003	Christie's NY	Passed/unsold lot	$30,000–$40,000
February 2005	Zachys	$55,000 hammer	$40,000–$70,000
September 2006	Christie's LA	$290,000 hammer	$80,000–$120,000

* These pre-sale estimates are for a full case of wine.

Win at the Right Price

As in stocks, real estate, and other speculative markets, buying at the right price is the most important aspect of investing in wine. To make a good investment, you need to obtain the wine at its best possible price in relation to future resale, while also factoring the costs of shipping, storage, and taxes into the equation.

Often times, buying wine at the right price means buying it as soon as it is released. Look into buying Bordeaux on *future*—ordering wine and paying for it in full as soon as its price is established, but long before the wine is bottled and shipped from the château. For each vintage since 1982, the price of a case of Bordeaux was higher when it came to auction than the price of the wine purchased on future.

Another way to buy wine at its release—and for the best possible price—is to be on its producer's mailing list, and buy the wine as soon as you receive word of the offering. This works, for example, with the high-scoring California Cult Cabernet. While no winemaker likes to see his wine flipped for profit, the frenzy for these highly allocated bottles guarantees a large profit from resale. In fact, many collectors today do with their California Cult wines the same thing that the Englishmen of the early twentieth century used to do with their Claret: They buy some bottles for resale in order to support their habits of drinking good wine.

"Claret" is a purplish-red color. English wine drinkers in the past used the word to refer to all red wines of Bordeaux.

When buying investment wine at auction, first research the prices and then bid on full twelve-bottle lots in their original wood or cardboard cases. (To read about these cases, see the inset on page 83.) When dealing with oversized bottles, aim at a purchase of six magnums. Try to buy wines from a consignor who purchased them upon their release so that the cases have not been shipped in and out of various cellars. When buying older vintages, be sure to buy cases in their best possible conditions. These wines will provide you the greatest return on your investment.

If handled wisely, wine investment can be quite lucrative. A colleague of mine accumulated a wine collection over a dozen-year period. During this time, he bought the world's best wines as and when he could afford them. Recently, he sold his small collection at a single auction. With his earnings from the sale, he easily paid the 20-percent down payment on a million-dollar home. Likewise, there have been many special vacations, college tuitions, and pieces of art bought and paid for by cautious investor/collectors.

Remember, however, that investments should be carefully thought through. Most importantly, buy what the collectors are buying, track auction results over time, and buy at the right time. Having the foresight to follow these suggestions is your first step towards investment success.

EXPANDING YOUR COLLECTION

The average bidder will spend anywhere from several hundred to many thousands of dollars at a wine auction. There is no a minimum amount to spend at an event. It is perfectly acceptable to leave an auction having won just one lot, regardless of its price. However, you were cautioned in Chapter 6 to set a maximum price for each desired lot; similarly, you should always set a *global total*—a maximum dollar amount to spend at a single auction. When items appear to be selling below market price and there are bargains to be had, some bidders get carried away and buy too much wine. Setting a limit and sticking to it by keeping a running total of your winnings will help you avoid spending too much at the event. (The global total can be applied to an absentee ballot as well. Turn to page 113 for more details.)

Yes, there *is* such thing as too much wine!

Below are suggestions for obtaining up to ten cases of wine, or 120 bottles, at a single auction, while remaining within your global total. Keep in mind that the budgeted dollar amounts do not account for any buyers' premium, sales tax, or shipping expenses.

A $5,000 Budget

If you decide upon a total auction budget of $5,000, you have to first determine how you wish to spend this money. Naturally, if you must add a several-thousand-dollar lot to your collection, the single purchase will use most of your available funds. You would probably leave the auction with a small number of bottles, but this may be perfectly acceptable to you. The more expensive bottles, however, will be discussed later in this chapter.

Another option when spending $5,000 at an auction is to spend less per lot in order to purchase more bottles. If you want to buy ten cases (or 120 bottles), you can spend between $35 and $45 for each bottle. You would probably want to concentrate on mixed lots, which consist of a variety of different wines grouped and sold together. To figure out the price per bottle, divide the estimated price by the number of bottles in the lot. Then, use the estimate range as a guide for determining your maximum bid for the lot.

price per bottle = number of bottles in lot divided by median estimated price

Consignments from well-established, long-standing collectors often contain mixed lots that reveal great treasures upon close inspection. Look for one or two very desirable bottles mixed in with a group of less-known or less-collected bottles. These consignments provide great opportunities to buy a few desirable bottles for a price well below what the full-case quantity would cost. Mixed lots will be your best chance to find classified growth Bordeaux and *grand cru* (top-quality) Burgundy.

If you collect California wines, search for those vintages that are collected less frequently. For example, look for 1991 and 1992 instead of 1994, and 1995 and 1996 instead of 1997. You will have a much easier time obtaining these bottles. Again, carefully estimate the per-bottle price for these lots and determine your limits.

With the exception of certain expensive white Burgundy, most collectors do not buy white wine at auction. They are cautious of older white bottles, which are notorious for having problems related to storage and condition. On the other hand, bidders who collect great young Chablis and young dry Riesling for drinking may find themselves in luck. These bottles are usually passed over by collectors with larger budgets, so others can often pick them up at decent prices. Always bid with caution.

Are you a Port lover? Try to obtain some older vintages at auction. Again, mixed lots are the way to go, because most Port from the declared vintages of the 1990s have already surpassed $35 to $45 per bottle.

When you attend an auction with a budget of $5,000, you can also consider buying originally released six-bottle and three-bottle cases. For certain wines, you may have to pay more than the budgeted $35 to $45 per bottle, but the cost will be significantly less than that of a full twelve-bottle case. This way, you are able to add original winery releases to your collection while making a smaller investment. Unfortunately, these sized cases are only available for expensive wines from the Napa Valley.

A $10,000 Budget

Each increase in budget will provide you with more options. The possibilities increase with a budget of $10,000, but you still have to watch closely and buy wisely. The treasure hunt is similar as to when you had $5,000, but now you can also look at bottles in the $75-to-$80 price range. Also, with this larger budget, you can buy an expensive full case, perhaps one around $4,000, and still be well funded for other great wines.

With $10,000, red wine drinkers can start to watch Bordeaux and Burgundy from the most popular vintages, although the search is still better confined to mixed lots. For Bordeaux, look for single bottles of the 1961, 1982, 1990, and 2000 vintages. For Burgundy, you can try to win a bottle or two from a great producer and the coveted vintages of 1988, 1989, or 1990. White wine drinkers, on the other hand, can start searching the mixed lots for Montrachet or Marcassin with this increased budget.

A budget of $10,000 is not enough to obtain any of these wines in full-cases quantities and still hope to take home 120 bottles. If you want to buy ten cases, look at well-cellared full cases of less collected, but still delicious, vintages. Bordeaux from 1981, 1983, 1985, and 1986 are all drinking wonderfully now. You can also look at 1993, 1995, and 1996 red Burgundy from top producers.

Are you a California collector? Start looking at the heralded and collectible 1994 and 1997 vintages as well as the Cult Cabernets, particularly in small lots. With $10,000, you can occasionally bag a top cult, and still retain a healthy part of your budget. The trick is to be extremely disciplined when setting and sticking to your maximum bid. Don't be discouraged if the bidding surpasses your limit: these California Cult wines appear and reappear at every auction.

You can also start to collect other trophies, such as those from Australia, Rhône, Italy, and Spain. Any wines that have been elevated to frenzy status, usually as a result of a Robert Parker review, will be very expensive, but within the realm of possibility if you have a budget of this size. Look at these wines as the "sauce on the side" rather than the meat and potatoes of your $10,000 auction experience.

A $25,000 Budget

Unfortunately, even the $25,000 auction experience cannot buy many full case lots of the very best wines, as that would allow for an average of only $2,500 per case. However, there is obviously much more room to play with when you are spending $25,000. You can afford two or three $4,000-to-$6,000 cases and still have plenty of money left for bidding on excellent drinking stock. With this kind of money, you can head straight to the great labels. You will still need to find lots smaller than twelve-bottle cases, but these wines are often sold in smaller bottle quantities.

Bordeaux wines from 1982 are extremely desirable among collectors. If you are interested in these bottles, a $25,000 budget will allow you to look confidently and buy a case or two. Still, the individual lots will cost more money than the mixed lots, and you'll still have to be careful to remain within your budget. You can also bid aggresively for bottles from Burgundy behemoth producers: Domaine de la Romanée Conti, Leroy, Jayer, Dujac, Ponsot, Lignier, and Ramonet red wines, and Sauzet and Raveneau white wines.

Your other options include buying bottles from the best Rhône producers; purchasing desirable Italian wines, particularly older Barolo and Barbaresco; and winning some California trophy wines. With $25,000, you are like a kid in a candy store with a generous budget: You will be able to walk out satisfied, but you still need to do some careful planning if you are going to spend your money to its best advantage. When you are looking at the fine and rare wines of the world, $25,000 can be spent faster than you can say "Château Pichon Comtesse de Lalande."

The Sky's-the-Limit Budget

There are some lucky collectors who have no budget. They can buy whatever they fancy, whenever they want. Clearly, if you have no budget, you can buy as many expensive full-case lots as you desire. At the same time, this is not always the best avenue for a serious wine collector, unless simple mass accumulation is the goal. If you have limitless finances, you still need to plan for your purchases if your collection is to take shape and direction. You need to know what you have already added to your collection as well as what is the next necessary addition.

You don't want to end up with so many bottles that you can't keep straight their names or locations. "Oh yeah, I think I've got some 1961 Petrus around here somewhere ..." will do nothing but frustrate your guests.

Your California Cabernet Collection

You may want to begin—or add to—your California Cabernet collection by gathering some of the following bottles. Your best bet for finding them will be at auction.

From early (pre-1966) Napa Valley production:

☐ Producers: Inglenook, Beaulieu Vineyards, Simi, Heitz, Beringer.

☐ Vintage: 1940s and 1950s.

☐ Price: $150 to $2,000.

From the 1966 Robert Mondavi-created "first wave":

☐ Producers: Robert Mondavi Winery, Chappellet, Joseph Phelps, Silver Oak, Shafer, Stag's Leap Wine Cellars, Chateau Montelena, Caymus, Ridge.

☐ Vintage: 1970s.

☐ Price: $150 to $250.

☐ Note: The condition of these bottles is very important.

From the "next generation":

☐ Producers: Grace Family, Dominus, Opus One, Staglin Family, Dunn Vineyards.

☐ Vintage: 1980s and 1990s.

☐ Price: $100 to $250.

☐ Note: Most of these bottles are currently drinking very well.

California Cult Cabernet:

☐ Producers: Araujo, Bryant Family, Colgin, Dalle Valle, Harlan Estate, Screaming Eagle.

☐ Vintage: Starting in the 1990s.

☐ Price: $250 to $2,500.

From other areas of California:

☐ Region: Sonoma County, including Sonoma Coast, Central Coast, Temecula.

☐ Price: Prices vary.

FOCUSING YOUR WINE COLLECTION

So far, this chapter has dealt with the fundamentals of a broad, international wine collection. The principals you have read, however, can also be applied to a more focused collection. Continue to follow the budget guidelines with which you are now familiar, but now you will be purchasing bottles that are related to a particular topic that interests you.

Some collections are gathered according to year. A *birth-year collection* refers to a collection made up of wines from the year the collector was born. You can also choose a year that marks a different special occasion. For example, a couple may save some bottles from the year they were married to open at future anniversary celebrations. Regardless of the event, this type of collection is formed by picking a year and gathering the wines of that harvest.

Most collections, though, are focused on a specific region. The goal of these focused collections is to provide comprehensive views of the areas of interest. You can learn more about these wine regions through study and travel. (You will read about studying wine and traveling to related places in Chapter 15.)

Let's look closely at a regional collection. Perhaps you would like to accumulate various California Cabernet bottles. Some wines from this region are much more expensive than others. The California Cult wines—Colgin, Harlan Estate, and Screaming Eagle—are among the highest priced auction wines, as are very old bottles of California wine in good condition, such as 1941 Inglenook. If your collection is focusing on California Cabernet, you would want to include examples of both, and would have to budget a fair amount of money towards obtaining these bottles. See the inset "Your California Cabernet Collection" on page 182 for tips on specific bottles you may want to gather for your collection.

CONCLUSION

Forming a wine collection is a very personal endeavor. Every collection can go in many different directions. Regardless of your specific focus, wine auctions can augment your collection by supplying wines that either cannot be found anywhere else, or can be bought for the best price on this secondary market. The amount you have to spend on your wine will dictate your collection's size, but it is important to realize that you can certainly attend an auction and even buy wine with less that $1,000. While your choices may be limited, you will nonetheless find special bottles. With foresight, practice, and patience, you will be able to grow your collection to eventually include almost every wine you desire.

13

Charity Wine Auctions

Every year, over $35 million are raised at various charity wine auctions throughout the United States. This business is fueled in part by the generosity of the wine industry. In this chapter, we will discuss why those in the wine industry are eager to participate in these events as donors, as well as how those attending as bidders can also benefit. We will then explore the Napa Valley Wine Auction, the longest running charity wine auction in the United States, and see how these events can be advantageous not only to the represented charities but also to the surrounding region.

The second half of this chapter is devoted to the ins and outs of running a productive charity auction. From properly promoting the charity to forming the guest list, this chapter will help you with the initial preparations. Then we will look at the most important aspects to consider as the auction draws near, such as the importance of employing a competent auctioneer and how to raise as much money as possible. Whether you are looking to spice up your annual event or are considering the wine-auction option for the first time, the following pages will prepare you for and see you through the day of the event.

REASONS TO PARTICIPATE

Charity wine auctions differ from commercial wine auctions in several ways. For example, people who offer items for sale at commercial wine auctions receive all proceeds from the sale—less any expenses—and are usually referred to as consignors. At charity events, on the other hand, the seller no longer receives any of the proceeds for the sale of his property. Therefore, these contributors are referred to as *donors* rather than sellers or consignors.

Charity auction bidders retain many of the same qualities as bidders attending commercial wine auctions. They are still buyers, and the live auction bidding process is similar to that of commercial events. However, guests at most charity auctions have paid to attend the event. Keeping the crowd pleased through entertainment, food, and drink is important to the day's success because attendees have paid for an enjoyable experience. At the same time, these bidders will often bid amounts far and above the perceived value of an item if the promoters have convinced them of their cause.

So, charity auction donors aren't making any money, and bidders may spend a good deal more money than they would at commercial wine auctions. Why, then, are these events so successful?

A Good Time

It is important to every charity auction that the guests have a good time. The fun is centered on wine and food. Larger charities invite different wineries to come and pour their wines in person. The winery representatives love to visit with the guests and discuss the year's harvest. Guests love these talks as well, and it is not unusual for them to walk away with a personal invitation to visit a winery. Guests also relish this opportunity to discover new wines.

Usually there are wine-related events before the auction even begins. Larger events sometimes offer educational seminars. These seminars are great bonding experiences among the guests and visiting vintners—another good way to meet new like-minded wine friends—while also providing valuable and interesting information on the subject at hand.

Winemaker dinners hosted in local homes are among the most enjoyable pre-auction events. Couples who offer to host these dinners, which usually include between twelve and twenty-four guests, tend to be people who love to entertain. They often go out of their way to showcase the food, which is prepared by a celebrity chef, and the wine, which is poured by a visiting vintner, as well as their home. The chef and winemakers often speak before the event to work their magic around a special menu, created just for that evening. The chefs always have a blast working in these private homes, most of which have state-of-the-art kitchens. The winemakers love telling their stories in such relaxed and elegant surroundings. And once again, the guests are the winners, having to do nothing more than take it all in. Many of these dinners get a little raucous—everyone is in a good mood. By the time the auction rolls around, people are ready to continue the party with their paddles!

Much of the work done by the charity event's organizers is focused on showing the guests a good time. They know that the amount of fun the guests are having is directly related to how far their wallets will open.

Possible Tax Deductions

The success of charity wine auctions relies on the eager participation of both donors and buyers. Many attendees not attracted to the fun and excitement become involved with the event because of the possible resulting tax deductions, which apply to both donated and purchased lots.

When you win an item at a charity auction, the amount paid over the fair market value is a *charitable contribution deduction*. In other words, it is tax deductible. To receive this tax break when you file your taxes, you will need to show that you paid an amount greater than the item's fair market value. As a winning bidder, you will probably receive a receipt that states both the purchase price and the item's fair market value. This is sufficient proof for you to receive your deduction. Be aware that this statement may come weeks after the event. Without this receipt, you can declare the deduction by using the auction catalogue (to show fair market value) and your proof of payment (to show the amount you paid).

There are also tax advantages to contributing wine to a benefit auction. The donor receives a tax break in the amount of the donated item's fair market value— regardless of the sum for which it is sold. This amount becomes the donor's charitable contribution deduction.

These potential tax benefits provide many bidders with enough reason to buy at a charity wine auction, particularly when rationalizing the sometimes-astronomical prices. For donors, they add another incentive to give away treasured bottles.

Groups organized for religious, scientific, literary, or educational purposes are usually non-profit organizations, and are exempt from certain sales tax payments.

As a charity auction participant, you should contact your accountant to determine the amount of any prospective deduction.

Exclusive Bottles

A charity auction is a great place to find rare, collectible bottles of wine. Many wineries donate bottles that are not available through normal sales channels. (We will discuss how auction organizers request donations from wineries later in this chapter.) These bottles include large-format bottles and one-of-a-kind artist decorated bottles, and often have great value to many collectors.

Local prominent collectors can be sources of great donations. Many times they donate rare bottles from older, classic vintages. For these wines, it is of utmost importance to the bidders that there be careful review of the sources. Older bottles sometimes have low fills, and those that do should be avoided entirely. Yet a good-looking bottle from a notable private source is a joy to find, so keep your eyes open. It is particularly fortunate to find these bottles in silent auctions, which traditionally have less competition than their live counterparts. (See the inset "Silent Auctions" on page 188 for more information.)

Good Press Coverage

Wineries are solicited by charity organizations to make various donations. In return, the wineries receive exposure not only when their products are sold, but also from pouring their wines at the event. In the wine industry, outlets for advertising are both limited and expensive, and charity auctions can be used to familiarize customers with the wineries' products. Sometimes they are given access to the charities' mailing lists, which provide them with another avenue for marketing.

There are celebrity winemakers and there are celebrities among the chefs who attend. Where there is good wine, there should be good food, and the most successful charity wine-auction events combine the two.

The participation of winemakers in auction events also provides the wineries with an opportunity to hand-sell their wines to a regional market. It helps the charities, too, when winemakers attend the events because many of today's winemakers are celebrities who attract a good deal of attention.

PREPARING TO BID

Much of your preparation for bidding at a charity wine auction should be very similar to that for bidding at a commercial auction. It is important to set a global limit. Decide how much money you wish to donate to the particular charity running the auction before you arrive. This will be your total limit for the evening. You can prevent morning-after regrets by not exceeding this set amount.

Determining that the top price you are willing to pay for each lot is firmly in place is even more important at a charity wine auction than at a commercial auction. As mentioned earlier, prices at these events often far exceed the wines' actual values because of the charitable donation aspect of the auction. Expect this and plan accordingly. Fixing individual limits will prevent you from participating in the out-of-control bidding that is encouraged by many successful charity auction organizers and their auctioneers. Delicious food and an abundance of great wines are there to lubricate the bidder's paddle arm. Mistakes are often made when a bidder is enjoying the process too much.

If a catalogue is available, look through it before you get to the event. You should be aware of everything that will be included in both the silent and live auctions so

Silent Auctions

Silent auctions are typically used to sell the less expensive donations. Donations of single bottles of wine, for example, may not merit the time it would take to include them in the live auction. With twenty lots sold per hour, event planners prefer to have each lot make the most money possible, and will often decide that a twenty-dollar bottle of wine shouldn't take the place of a lot with greater potential value. Silent auctions allow the charities to accept almost every donated item, no matter how small, as well as offer guests an opportunity to support the cause and walk away with a less expensive treasure.

Silent auction may also include items donated out-side the theme of the live auction. It is not unusual to find a teeth-bleaching session or a spa package in the silent auction at an evening dedicated to a wine auction.

The items in the silent auction are arranged on tables and are available for bid right from the beginning of the evening. Bid sheets are placed before each item on offer and guests write down a bid in excess to the one previously written. It's fun to peruse the different items while enjoying the evening's first glass of wine. The silent auction helps prime the competitive spirit for later bidding at the live auction. Usually, bidding at the silent auction ends just prior to the start of the live auction.

you can pinpoint the most interesting items on which to concentrate. Often, an auction catalogue will index all the items included in its pages, and you may find this helpful as you organize your bidding plan. (For more information on reading an auction catalogue, turn back to Chapter 5. For more information on auction preparation, turn back to Chapter 6.) It will also help to view the bottles in the auction displays to observe their levels, and you may wish to participate in wine-tasting activities.

The best lots to secure at a charity wine auction are the ones that are the most unique. Chances are, though, that there will be several other bidders looking at the same lots you wish to win. Even though it is a charity event, competition is often stiff. But the more auctions you attend, the more likely you are to go home with the goods.

If you end up overpaying for any given lot, try to look at the situation philosophically. The money will go to a good cause—and as a winning bidder, you no doubt had a great time.

AUCTION NAPA VALLEY

The longest running, most successful charity wine auction in the United States is the Napa Valley Wine Auction, now called Auction Napa Valley. This annual four-day wine-and-food extravaganza was founded in 1981. Since then, proceeds have totaled over $60 million. The money raised at the auction benefits local charities including health care organizations, youth services, and low-income housing. People come from all over the world to join the fun, meet great people, and drink fabulous wines.

At the Beginning

Robert Mondavi and his wife Margrit Biever developed the idea for a charity auction in the Napa Valley during the course of a 1979 community fundraising program. Familiar with the great European wine auctions, Mondavi saw the possibility of promoting the Napa Valley as a world-class wine growing region. Mondavi proposed the idea to the Napa Valley Vintners Association, suggesting that special releases from their wineries be offered at the auction. Intrigued by the possibilities and charged by Mondavi's enthusiasm, the group agreed to create a steering committee to plan a charitable wine-auction event.

Headed by Louis Martini of the Martini Winery, the steering committee included representatives from the Robert Mondavi Winery, Beringer Vineyards, Freemark Abbey, and Sterling Vineyards. They worked for several months to put together a formal plan for the event before successfully presenting it to the Napa Valley Vintners Association.

Sponsors and patrons provided the initial funds to cover expenses and the Meadowood resort was elected as the event's venue. The auction was set for June 20 and 21, 1981. Attendance was by invitation only. At the vintners' request, Michael Broadbent agreed to fly in from Christie's in London. In addition to lending his tremendous credibility to the brand-new event, Broadbent would assist with administrative aspects and, of course, preside over the event as auctioneer. (Broadbent's additional contributions to the wine-auction market were discussed in Chapter 1.)

The day was blazing hot when bidders gathered at the Meadowood, but none of the eager attendees felt dampened by the midday heat. The first paddle was issued to Marvin Shanken, owner and publisher of *Wine Spectator*. Broadbent opened the bidding on the first lot, a bottle of 1937 Beringer Vineyards Cabernet Sauvignon, at ten dollars. Paddles waved in the air as the bidding climbed higher and higher. Shanken was the eventual victor with a bid of $400, a previously unheard of price for a California Cabernet. The bidding on subsequent lots continued with similar gusto.

A case of 1979 Napamedoc Cabernet, a new Napa Valley wine not yet familiar to the general public, was the day's top lot. The wine—which would eventually be renamed Opus One—was sold to a New York retailer for $24,000. The record price of $2,000 per bottle left the bidders in the tent stunned, but not speechless. Great cheers and hoopla broke out.

The wines continued to sell for huge prices that were many times in excess of their retail values. The vintners were shocked at the event's level of success. The day's take was $324,000 for the 596 lots offered. The Napa Valley Wine Auction was off to a great start.

An Annual Event

Guests are willing to pay the high price of attendance not only because the event is important to them, but also because the money benefits local health care, youth services, and low-income housing. In 2006, for example, Auction Napa Valley raised $8.4 million for these charities.

Amazed by the eager bidders who had traveled great distances to support the auction, the vintners realized that subsequent auction events would showcase not only their wines, but also the Napa Valley as a first-rate travel destination. The Vintners Association continued to sponsor the auction and it became an annual event, held in June of each year. The guest list soon increased to include more bidders, and the organization began encouraging different wineries to host the bidding guests at pre-auction wine tastings, lunches, and dinners.

The charity auction has proven to be a great event for the entire region. Only members of the Napa Valley Vintners Association are allowed to donate the wines offered in the auction, truly highlighting the wines of the region. Locals who wish to take part in the action can easily find a spot on the volunteer team—close to 1,000 people donate their time every year. Also, a different member of the Napa Valley Vintners Association chairs the event each year, keeping the energy fresh by bringing new ideas.

Each year, more bidders (over 1,000) scramble to secure the expensive tickets ($7,500 per couple). Auction Napa Valley is such a hot social ticket that the invitation mailing in March creates its own frenzy. Prospective guests peruse the year's invitation, which reads like fantasy camp for wine-drinking adults, with their checkbooks and FedEx envelopes in front of them. Each year, the event becomes oversold within a few weeks of mailing the invitations.

In addition to the auction, the annual event also includes activities at different wineries. Guests have to choose among the festivities because they overlap. But whether at a lavish black-tie party for a hundred guests or an intimate vineyard lunch for twenty people, each guest has the opportunity to share the Napa lifestyle with its creators. The Napa Valley becomes the star of four days of wining and dining—until the wines and the huge auction prices steal the show.

Auction Napa Valley set the precedent for a national charity wine-auction business. The first attendees came from all over the country, and returned to their cities with tales of great fun and astonishing prices. A winning formula for both the wineries and the charities, benefit wine auctions modeled after the great Auction Napa Valley have raised many millions of dollars for not-for-profit organizations. (See the inset on page 192 for a list of successful wine auctions.)

LAUNCHING AN AUCTION

Charity wine auctions are a very popular avenue for raising money. Unfortunately for many, gone are the days when wineries would gladly supply any requesting event with both wine for pouring and a top-notch donation. There are simply too many great causes calling out to the wine industry's generosity. Also, more and more wineries are developing charity-giving programs to focus their donations on those charities in which they have a special interest. As a result, it has become more difficult to put together a profitable fundraiser. The next section addresses issues of importance and provides tips for organizing a successful charity wine auction.

The Charity

It will add to the auction's credibility if the charity is well established, with a proven track record of directing nearly all of the proceeds to their cause, rather than to event-related costs. If the charity is a start-up organization, on the other hand, a compelling mission statement can convince people of its altruistic intentions. Donors and bidders like to be assured that their donations will turn into cash for those who need it, so charitable organizations that are able to define how funds raised will be directed are usually the most successful.

The Volunteers

If you are organizing a charity wine auction, you will need to assemble several committees comprised of dedicated, hard-working individuals, each of whom share the

Charity Wine Auctions in the United States

A great source of information on charity wine auctions is *Wine Spectator* magazine, which lists around 150 events each year. There are countless others of all shapes and sizes that take place throughout the country. The wine industry's contribution to the various charities is unprecedented and certainly adds to the fundraising efforts of each community that hosts a benefit wine-auction event. The following are among the country's top grossing wine auctions. (For more information on these events, turn to page 220 of the Resource section.)

- Auction Napa Valley (formally the Napa Valley Wine Auction) in Napa, California, founded in 1981.

- The Naples Winter Wine Festival in Naples, Florida, founded in 2001.

- The Auction of Washington Wines (formally the Auction of Northwest Wines) in Woodinville, Washington, founded in 1987.

- L'Ete du Vin in Nashville, Tennessee, founded in 1980.

- The High Museum Atlanta Wine Auction in Atlanta, Georgia, founded in 1993.

- The Sun Valley Wine Auction in Sun Valley, Idaho, founded in 1982.

- The Jackson Hole Wine Auction in Jackson Hole, Wyoming, founded in 1995.

same fundraising goals. Do not overlook members of the charitable organization for which you are raising money when you look for people to help out with your event. Consider asking local wine professionals, who have regular contact with those in the industry, to join your cause. People with existing contacts in the local wine trade will be able to reach out to their winemaking friends for donations and help in other areas.

Be sure to gather enough people to successfully complete the event. Some small charitable organizations underestimate the time and manpower needed. You must assess the available human resources and then estimate the number of outside volunteers and paid workers you will need to help run the auction. For any large-scale event, you will also need to appoint a strong volunteer leader at the outset of the planning.

The Guest List

Once the committees and volunteers are in place, it is time to develop the guest list. The guest list ultimately determines the financial outcome of the event and is therefore one of the most important aspects of any charity auction. Who attends may be even more important than the quality of the assembled wines. After all, guests who attend in the spirit of supporting the cause will buy even mediocre auction lots. But the greatest auction donations in the world will be lost on an audience that did not come to spend money.

For an example of the effect the guest list can have on the success of an event, let's take a look at a particularly well-known winery donor's donation. Harlan Estate produces some of the Napa Valley's most prized wines. Harlan Estate is also very selective in choosing charity events to support. A donation from this winery indicates that the charity's foundation has been well built: the mission statement is a compelling one, and the representatives soliciting donations have well conveyed to Harlan Estate the group's intentions. This winery typically donates one double-magnum (three-liter bottle) of wine, to each different event. The bottle has sold for between $3,000 and $135,000 at different charity auctions. This wildly varied difference in price from one auction to another is attributed to the guest list, which directly affects the amount of money spent.

The Sponsors

It can be extremely beneficial to find sponsors willing to donate money in exchange for publicity. The organizers of most successful charity wine auctions solicit a variety of sponsors to pre-fund their events. They appeal to both corporate and private businesses for this start-up money, and offer the company publicity in return, as well as complimentary tickets to the event. This should be taken care of before invitations are sent to the guests, because a major sponsor may wish to be mentioned in the invitation.

Hosting an annual wine auction is increasingly costly because prices for venues, goods, and services rise each year.

The Donations

It has become increasingly challenging to obtain winery donations because of the mass number of solicitation letters wineries receive. Your best chance to be given a really great donation is through personal contact with the company, whether by a committee member's pre-existing relationship with the winery or by having members of your organization go out of their way to get to know the targeted winery and its employees. A personal visit or telephone conversation will often result in a larger or more valuable donation than a simple letter of request.

The most successful solicitations are specific requests. Wineries get hundreds of letters of solicitation, and have to choose among them. The easier the winery finds it to satisfy your request, the more likely it is to do so—and it is far easier for a staff member to fulfill your specific request than for that staff member to come up with a donation idea and then get it approved. Try asking for a large-format bottle, a twelve-bottle case, or a tour and tasting at the winery. Nothing will stop the winery from adding to a specific request if it is enthusiastic about supporting the cause.

It is more efficient to suggest a specific donation that can be easily fulfilled than to ask the winery to donate something of its choice.

If the event you are hosting occurs annually, you will see familiar faces each year. With each passing year, you will become more aware of your patrons' desires, and therefore able to request specific lots that suit prospective bidders.

The Bidders

For many people, each week's mail offers several invitations to fundraising events. The children's school, local hospital, museum, symphony, and animal shelter all need extra funds to continue providing a high level of service. How do you distinguish your event from the rest and lure a bidder's dollar your way? The first way to guarantee attendance at any event is the *quid pro quo:* I'll-come-to-yours-if-you-come-to-mine. This is the way the fundraising world works, and is an important reason to comprise your committees of community-minded individuals.

Those attendees not motivated by the *quid pro quo* will probably be people who see some sort of value, over and above contributing to the cause, associated with the event. Celebrity chefs and celebrity winemakers are usually great draws, as are the meals to be served and the wines to be poured. A sophisticated wine collector will know the value of a great wine dinner, and the price of the event should take this into account. When the ticket price far exceeds the perceived value of the event, some guests will assume that their contribution to the charity was included in the ticket price and will not bid on anything at either the silent or live auction.

One way to assure attendance is to make your party distinctive from competing events. If every other wine auction in the area follows the same nighttime black-tie dinner, perhaps an informal barbeque will draw bidders to your event. Much of this strategy is dependent upon the local social scene.

Guests want to be entertained, and the most successful events never lose sight of this. A well-run, friendly, and fun event, regardless of whether it is elegant or low key, will bring the guests back the following year. When people have a great time, word of mouth travels fast, and there will be even more new faces at the next year's event. The auction portion of the event needs to be especially well organized and smoothly run so that bidders can easily pay for and receive their purchases, without any hitches.

The Pace and Length

For a charity wine auction to be successful, it must be well paced. Some event organizers feel that bids become higher once the crowd has enjoyed plenty of wine. Yet receptions tend to go on way too long when this is the goal. Also, there are so many events today that some couples attend two in one evening, and people who have budgeted an amount of time for the event will stay for the reception and leave early in the auction. Also, some guests may become too well lubricated to follow the action.

Another common mistake is having too many items in the live auction. Organizers may feel that offering more items will bring in more money, but this is not always true. When fewer items are offered, the price per lot tends to be higher. Guests usually want to make a donation while at the event. But if there are too many items, they will not compete intensely for any one item, since there are so many lots yet to come.

You also have to consider that guests may become bored if the auction runs too long. A good auctioneer will be able to keep a crowd's attention for about twenty minutes before the majority of guests return to their socializing. An hour-long auction is plenty, and consider two hours as the absolute maximum for an evening event.

As you plan the schedule for your event, keep in mind that most auctioneers sell between twenty and thirty lots in an hour.

For the same reason, event organizers must be careful not to carry on too long with introductions, awards, presentations, videos, or sponsor recognition. The crowd knows why they are there and will appreciate the sell if it is short and sweet. Always remember that the point of the evening is for everybody to have fun while the funds are raised. If the evening is a drag, few guests will want to return the following year.

The Auctioneer

The auctioneer can make or break an auction. The most spectacular events will fall flat with the gavel in the wrong person's hand. You may have suffered through an evening where the sale of each lot dragged on to the point of boredom. What a shame for the people who worked so hard to put together a wonderful fundraising event.

The choice of auctioneer is important even before the auction begins, because it may influence sponsors and their pre-auction donations. A big name can often draw big donations. During the event, the auctioneer's level of experience is crucial. His knowledge of the lots and, most importantly, of the assembled audience is essential for extracting the most money possible from the audience. The auctioneer must be able to engage the guests while keeping the auction moving at a nice pace. If the auctioneer is boring, boorish, or amateurish, the audience may simply lose interest in the auction—the worst possible scenario for any fundraising situation.

Hire a professional. There are plenty of professional auctioneers around. The big auction houses, Sotheby's and Christie's, have representation in most major metropolitan areas. There are also small regional auction houses in most large cities. Other enterprising individuals have created professions around charity auctioneering and advising. They can be found in the phonebook or on the Internet.

The main difference between a professional auctioneer and a once-a-year auctioneer is that the professional knows when to stop talking and when to end the bidding.

Some auctioneers charge a flat fee for their services, while others work on a commission basis. Others do not charge for their services, but expect their travel and accommodation expenses to be covered by the charity. The price of the professional auctioneer should be more than recouped in the price realized for each lot. Whatever the financial arrangement, the charity must secure the agreement in writing well before the event. In addition to the auctioneer's compensation, each party should discuss their responsibilities and expectations, and include the appropriate points in the letter of agreement.

Experienced charity auctioneers will enhance almost any auction. As the event coordinator, you should consult the auctioneer on lot-related issues, timing the event, and the number of volunteers needed to ensure a smooth auction. Some professional auctioneers become more involved in the planning than others, and how much time you expect from the auctioneer needs to be discussed at the very start of the relationship. A good auctioneer studies the catalogue before the event, has an understanding of the charity, and attends the pre-auction festivities to get a feel for the crowd.

When a professional auctioneer cannot be found or is outside the event's budget, the charity can pick an amateur. The amateur auctioneer should have a strong voice, time to practice with the microphone, a strong presence, and a connection to the crowd. Some amateurs do an excellent job and should be rewarded with a token of appreciation, such as a bottle of wine. Local personalities, either celebrities or individuals well known to those gathered, have the best chance of motivating the crowd.

The Catalogue and Lot Display

It is the auctioneer's job to get the most money for each lot in the live auction, but event organizers can take steps to support his efforts long before the start of the event. Producing an accurately written and organized catalogue, for example, is crucial to the auction's success. The attention span of an audience that has just finished eating and drinking is rather small. Bidders often need a catalogue to help them focus on the matter at hand, rather than on the socializing and activity in the room. Most bidders do not come to a charity auction knowing what will be offered or what they will buy. These potential bidders will flip through the catalogue either before or during the auction to see which lots look appealing. The best catalogues are illustrated, which can help the bidders keep pace with what is being sold.

The auctioneer has a split second to make a lot appealing enough so that several bidders will want and start competing for it. Some charity auctions use large slides of each lot so that bidders can see what is being sold. It helps, too, to have each successive lot number prominently displayed on stage. This will focus the crowd's attention on the lot being sold. Finally, the auction lots should be arranged prior to the auction in an attractive display, to get the guests excited to bid. Many of the best charity auctions use very elaborate lot displays in an attempt to add value through pre-auction visual appeal.

The Administration

When launching a charity auction, organizers must consider everything from the potential to raise a significant amount of money to the availability of great donations. Yet the successfulness of an event largely depends on its being well organized and orchestrated from an administrative point of view. The business end of the evening is ultimately the charity's greatest concern.

Guests must flow through the evening without ever seeing the incredible amount of logistics and back office preparation. For example, upon arrival, each guest must register and receive a catalogue, bidding paddle, and possibly a seat assignment. Payment and collection instructions should be available at registration, so bidders can plan for their success. Smooth administration of the check-in process ensures that the guests enter the party carefree and without frustrations—there is, after all, nothing worse than starting a party by standing on a line.

Equally important is a competent accounting team. This group will record the successful paddle numbers and prepare invoices for easy checkout. Guests are tired after the festive evening and the excitement of the auction, and will not appreciate waiting to pay for and collect their auction items.

The best charity auction organizers never forget to acknowledge and thank their sponsors, donors, and successful bidders. Supporters of a charity auction like to know that their efforts are noticed and appreciated. Gratefulness expressed throughout an event and at its end will encourage the guests to return to the next event.

CONCLUSION

Charity auctions are great events. They are a wonderful way to support your favorite cause, as long as you and the other event organizers plan carefully to offer a quality event and the beneficiary receives a fair portion of the proceeds. These events offer the opportunity to taste a large variety of wines, many times poured by the winemaker himself. The benefits make the ticket price almost incidental to the learning experience for the passionate wine enthusiast. Besides the food and wine, people are usually in great moods, and many new wine friends can be made at a charity wine auction.

14

Drink and Learn

Some collectors consider the hunt at the auction to be the fun part of the wine experience, and it is always satisfying to take home a coveted bottle. That, however, is not the end of the wine lover's road. The full potential of any prized bottle is only realized when its cork has been pulled, glasses have been poured, and the wine has been tasted.

A wine lover and collector is not just any wine drinker. You are probably compelled to know as much as you can about the vast world of wine. This brings you to the final chapter of wine collecting. You will learn how tasting, talking, and traveling can deepen your understanding of the magic, mystery, and majesty of wine.

YOUR WINE EDUCATION

There are many facets to collecting and drinking wine. You will find that as you learn more about the subject, your appreciation of each bottle will dramatically increase. Here are several ways to add to your wine education.

Books

There are many books that educate readers about wine. Each year, in fact, excellent books are published for every level of wine drinker. There are also those tried-and-true books that are found in every serious wine enthusiast's library, such as *The Oxford Companion to Wine*, edited by Jancis Robinson. The Resource section on page 216 includes a list of noteworthy wine books, with subjects ranging from general overviews of the world of wine to specific looks at individual wine-growing regions.

When trying to choose between several wine books, I usually prefer to choose one that includes detailed, easy-to-read maps. Better understanding of a wine region often comes from studying a map of the area. A confusing label or text, for example, may be more easily understood if accompanied by a map. You will read more about maps of wine regions later in this chapter.

The Internet

The Internet is a tremendously valuable research tool. A huge number of extremely useful websites are devoted to wine. Some pages are much more informative than others. For a list of the best websites, turn to the Resource section on page 218. These sites can be extremely useful for gathering information in short bursts of time. Yet they usually do not replace quality time spent with a particularly educational wine book.

Back to School

Some university extension programs end their courses by handing out certificates, which you may enjoy hanging near your cellar.

There are many different wine courses, available both in person and online. Nearly every large city offers some form of wine education, whether through a university extension program or at a local retailer's wine club. You can find these courses by looking online or asking around at wine shops. Most wine classes are set up as weekly sessions that are divided into lecture and tasting portions. Both parts can be extremely effective towards advancing your wine proficiency. Frequently, these courses also provide you with the opportunity to meet like-minded wine drinkers with whom you may be able to meet outside of the class for further, usually less formal, tasting and drinking.

Many larger retailers set up classroom-style tasting rooms in their stores. Sometimes stores will offer theme-based, single-session classes to accommodate wine drinkers with schedules that prevent them from committing to a longer course of study. Regardless of its frequency, a class will offer you the opportunity to discover and taste wines under the guidance of a wine expert, which will accelerate your learning process.

Online wine courses are very popular. The most effective ones are interactive and involve tastings. Prior to the course, a list of wines to be tasted and discussed will be posted on the website so you can prepare by buying the appropriate bottles. This type of learning environment tends to yield the best results when several people participate together and share the wines' costs. Online classes may administer quizzes and examinations, and require as serious a commitment as a class attended in person. *Wine Spectator* offers excellent courses, ranging in level from introductory to professional, at its online wine school. Visit www.winespectator.com/wineschool for details.

WINE TASTINGS

You will probably discover that it is much more valuable to taste wines and share opinions with a colleague than it is to sip on your own.

An art onto itself, wine tasting is the ultimate enjoyment of wine collecting. After all, for most wine lovers, the point of amassing a collection is to eventually open and share the bottles. You may attend a wine tasting organized by someone else, or you might decide to host one yourself. Both situations offer the opportunity to develop and hone your palate while discussing your favorite topic with like-minded friends. In the following pages, you will first read about styles of wine tastings in more detail, and then learn about hosting your own event.

The Organized Tasting

Interest in wine is constantly growing. As a result, there are more wine tastings than ever before. They are held at local retailers, charity events, wine schools, wine clubs, and commercial auctions. You can find advertisements for these tastings in both local newspapers and national wine publications.

Some events charge a fee while others welcome tasters at no charge. When faced with an admittance fee, you should request a list of wines to be tasted. Usually, the price of the tasting is far less than the amount you would spend buying a bottle of each wine. If the list reveals wines you already own, the tasting can provide you with the opportunity to chart the development of the wines as they age. If you have had no experience with the wines at a certain tasting, it may be a great opportunity to expand the boundaries of your knowledge. Any tasting of top-quality wines can be an important and valuable learning experience.

As a serious wine taster, seek professional guidance during your education. Consider reading one of the many excellent books that outline the process of wine tasting. Several are listed in the Resource section on page 216.

You should also ask about the tasting's format, particularly if you will be paying a large fee to attend. Tastings are conducted with guests either sitting down or standing and walking around, and you may develop a personal preference for one of the two styles. Find out how many other people will be tasting, as well as how many bottles of each wine will be opened. You are looking for assurance that there will be enough wine to go around, as well as that there will be enough space to comfortably taste the wines and write your notes. (See the inset on page 203 for more on writing tasting notes.)

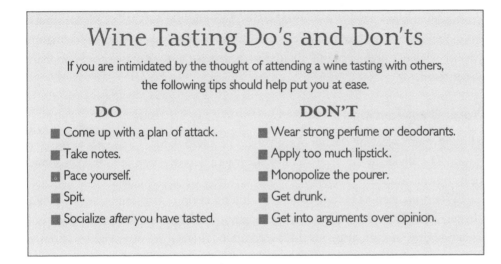

Wine Tasting Do's and Don'ts

If you are intimidated by the thought of attending a wine tasting with others, the following tips should help put you at ease.

DO	DON'T
◾ Come up with a plan of attack.	◾ Wear strong perfume or deodorants.
◾ Take notes.	◾ Apply too much lipstick.
◾ Pace yourself.	◾ Monopolize the pourer.
◾ Spit.	◾ Get drunk.
◾ Socialize *after* you have tasted.	◾ Get into arguments over opinion.

Attending a Seated Tasting

The flights may be poured in front of guests or they may be pre-poured. Tasters should feel free to start smelling right away.

Seated tastings offer the most constructive wine tasting experience as this arrangement allows for notes to be written comfortably. These events are usually led by a professional and are most often meticulously planned. The organizer knows how many participants will be attending, and should arrange to have enough of each wine so that every guest gets a taste. To a certain extent, even the order in which you will taste the wines will probably be determined beforehand. The wines are poured in *flights*—groups of several glasses, each with a different wine, that are served together and may share some commonality. You may be able to choose the tasting order within the flight. However, some organizers may arrange the order to be conducted with a specific goal in mind, in which case their intentions will most likely be clearly indicated to those gathered.

Preparing for the Walk-Around Tasting

At a stand- or walk-around tasting, the drink order is usually left up to the individual taster. If you know what wines will be offered at a tasting you will be attending, you can organize your plan of attack beforehand. This provides the event with structure, and may help you later recall what you tasted.

A $500 admission fee may seem astronomical—until the list reveals that the tasting includes each first growth Bordeaux from the 1982 vintage. A single bottle of any one of these wines costs well over $500!

When you arrive at a tasting without already knowing which wines will be on display, take a few moments to develop a tasting plan. Consider the wines being served and the atmosphere around you. At a crowded and informal stand-around tasting, start with the wines in which you are most interested, to assure that a pour will be available. Otherwise, develop a tasting plan that will highlight each wine's flavors. You may prefer to begin with the oldest wines and work your way to the youngest, or start with the lighter-style wines before moving to the heavier glasses.

Every person's tasting plan will be different. I often find a friend who has been setting up and has already tasted the wines, and ask him which wine is creating a buzz. You can always ask one of the pourers for a suggestion. After following my friend's advice, I usually head for wines with which I am unfamiliar, so I can learn about them.

Your Own Tasting

Hosting your own wine-tasting event should be exciting for you as well as for your guests. The advice in this section will help ensure that the wine on display is shown to its best advantage.

When planning a tasting of several different wines, it is important to pick a theme. The theme can even be "miscellaneous," which would refer to the lack of a commonality to each wine tasted. More often, themes are arranged by varietal,

Jotting Down Your Tasting Notes

To make the most of any tasting event, it is crucial to take notes. Very few wine drinkers—if any—are able to commit to memory the details of every wine they have ever tasted. As a result, all serious tasters take notes for future reference. Note taking enhances the pleasure of each glass of wine because it transfers the experience from the senses to the intellect. It also accelerates the process of learning the language of wine.

Properly recording and saving each note helps me remain organized. I find breast pocket-sized, hard-covered notebooks to be extremely efficient for my notes. These books are easy to carry around. They also allow the note taker to write with one hand and hold the book in the other, so that it is less of a struggle to record every taste. Some wine lovers record their notes electronically, into a Palm Pilot or some other organizational device. Regardless of where and how you choose to keep your notes, it is important to establish a consistent note-taking routine.

Even when working with a pocket-sized notebook, you will probably have to set your glass down, which is not always an easy thing to do at a stand-up tasting. If necessary, take your glass to a place where you can taste quietly and write a note immediately. Even if the entry is merely two or three words, the discipline of recording the note is vital for your greater appreciation of wine.

If you have never written a tasting note, it may help to start by reading and imitating one of the greats. The two most famous professional wine tasters of our time are Robert Parker and Michael Broadbent. Both of these men have their own style that they apply to every tasting note. This consistency is very important. Once you establish your own style, your notes will become brief and logical, and writing them will become second nature.

The object of each note is to record the wine's appearance, aroma, taste, finish, and other characteristics, as well as your overall observations—in that order. You can choose whether to assign a numerical score to each glass of wine. However, the number is significantly less important than your ability to describe what is in the glass. Here is a breakdown of the attributes to include.

Appearance

What does the wine look like? Move past the obvious distinction of red and white, and note the color's shade. Red wines range from light rose to deep, saturated purple. White wines can have a clear, greenish hue or may appear heavier, like a deep gold. Is the wine clear or cloudy? Begin your tasting note with these visual characteristics.

Aroma

The average person can recognize over 10,000 different smells, while tasting only four distinct tastes. A wine's smell may deliver its greatest pleasures. Identifying each individual scent will become easier with practice and study, as will articulating the aroma with the appropriate descriptive terms. (Read the section Wine Talk on page 207 for more on expanding your wine vocabulary.) Start by referring to other tasters' notes while sipping the wines about which the notes are written. Michael Broadbent gave excellent advice on smelling wines when he said, "If it smells nice, it will taste nice."

Taste

Our taste buds recognize sweet, sour, salty, and bitter flavors. As you have read, the flavors of wine often have more to do with our olfactory senses than our taste buds—but tasting the wine reveals characteristics apart from flavor. The impression the wine makes on the mouth is called its *mouth feel.* Measure the weight and texture of the wine. How the wine feels in your mouth provides clues to the type of grapes and the style of winemaking used to create that particular juice. Experience will polish your ability to articulate the taste sensations.

Finish

The *finish*—the sensation left in the taster's mouth after the wine has been swallowed—also reveals whether the wine has balance, complexity, and elegance. Every well-made wine should be *well balanced*—a seamless integration of aroma, flavor, and texture. There should also be a harmonious balance of fruit, acidity, and tannins. This will be determined by how the wine finishes. Weigh, measure, and note the finish, because the wine's final impression is as important as its first.

Overall Impression

After noting the appearance, aroma, taste, and finish, you can make a general statement regarding your overall impression of the wine. This summary of your experience with the wine is usually the most personal aspect

of the short note. It also tends to be the first thing one taster shares with another. Many people like to assign a number score to the wine. This is popular partly because it sums up the wine's impression with a single number instead of a sentence or two. Numerical scores are as personal as the note itself.

Putting It All Together

Every note should be dated. Wine continually evolves in the bottle, so it is important to record when each tasting occurs. Record the name of the wine, along with its vintage, producer, and region. Next, include the wine's appearance, aroma, taste, and finish, followed by your overall impression or score. Some tasters like to include the wine's price in their notes.

Still weary about writing your own note? Read more published tasting notes. Become familiar with the individual note-taking styles of several authors. Remember that notes are both intensely personal and invaluable reference points. They are the best way to share the experience of a wine with anyone not fortunate enough to be there when the cork was pulled. In time, you will develop your own flow.

such as a Cabernet Sauvignon tasting; by region, such as a Napa Valley tasting; or by vintage, such as a tasting of wines from the 2000 vintage. This enables guests to taste within the context of the theme, adding another level of consideration to each wine.

The amount of wine you will need to provide will be determined by the number of guests. In general, each bottle will yield up to fourteen tasting pours. However, you should expect to get only ten to twelve pours at a friendly, informal tasting at which tasters may expect to drink rather than swirl and spit from each glass. Always be prepared for the unfortunate possibility that a bottle will be corked (foul smelling and tasting because of bacteria) or otherwise unfit to drink. You can either have a backup bottle of the same wine, or simply forgo tasting that wine entirely. The inset "How Much Wine Will I Need at My Event?," found on page 206, further explores the number of necessary bottles.

As the host, you will have to determine how to run the event. You can supply all the wine, or you can ask your guests to each bring a bottle or two. If you choose the latter, give each wine-bringing attendee exact instructions for preparing the wine. For example, you may want to ask everyone to stand their bottles upright for one day before the tasting, or request that the bottles remain as stationary as possible before their transportation to the event. This will allow the different bottles to be on as equal footing as possible when the tasting begins. If at all feasible, have the contributing guests deliver their tasting bottles to you a week prior to the event, so that all the wines can be kept in identical storage situations.

You will need the following equipment for your wine tasting. Although you should have no trouble locating any of these items, gather them prior to the day of the event so you can spend that afternoon setting up for your guests. (For information on serving the wine to your guests, turn to page 43.)

Proper Glasses

Use the best stemware available to you. Ideally, you should provide a separate glass for each wine. Yet few people own the amount of glassware needed for a multi-guest, multi-wine tasting. One option is to rent glasses. Rental companies may not have the best brand names available, but it is more important that the stems be appropriately sized. Some of the larger wine retailers have glass-rental programs that are perfect for hosts who throw infrequent tasting parties. If you can't provide differently shaped glasses appropriate to each different varietal, use international standard tasting glasses (ISO) for each wine. These can be found everywhere fine wine glasses are sold, including many online stores.

As you read in Chapter 2, the 20/20 rule is the simplest way to prepare to serve wine at the correct temperature: Put red wines into the fridge twenty minutes before serving. Take white wine out of the fridge twenty minutes before serving.

You may want to number each glass so that the different wines can be readily identified. Glasses are traditionally numbered with small stickers. Don't use grease pens directly on the glass because the numbers will smudge. Test the stickers on a single glass to make sure they easily come off, particularly if you are renting or borrowing the glassware.

If you aren't able to provide every guest with a new glass for each different wine, make sure that the tasters can easily empty their glasses in a bucket without having to leave their places.

A Spit Bucket

Every guest should be near a spit bucket. These buckets are usually stainless steel. Two tasters can share a bucket—but if the buckets are to be shared, make sure the bowls are large and deep, and emptied well before they become too heavy to pass around. Buckets can be rented from rental companies or borrowed from some retailers. Some hosts put sawdust in the spit buckets to absorb the liquid and prevent the spit from splashing back.

How Much Wine Will I Need at My Event?

When you are gathering bottles in preparation for a wine-drinking event, it is important to consider both the type of event and the number of guests who will be attending. The following guidelines—all of which are based on 750-milliliter bottles—will help you determine how many bottles to have ready. Don't forget to prepare for bottles that may be bad!

■ Plan on 12–14 tasting pours per bottle for a formal wine-tasting event.

■ Plan on 10–12 tasting pours per bottle for an informal wine-tasting event.

■ Plan on 6–7 glasses per bottle for a multi-course dinner at which each course has its own wine.

■ Plan on 4 glasses per bottle for a dinner at which only one wine is being served.

■ Plan on $1/2$ bottle of champagne per person at a reception.

■ Plan on $1/2$ bottle of wine per person at a party serving only hors d'oeuvres.

Failing a stainless steel bucket, you can provide each taster with a large plastic cup. It is best to have the plastic cup be colored instead of clear, since several rounds of spitting wine into a clear cup can be quite off-putting.

Fresh Water

You may want to have water available for your guests, for either rinsing glasses or cleansing the palate between tastes. Set a separate glass at each place. The water should be fresh, cool (not iced), and still (not sparkling).

Plain Crackers or Bread

At each table, provide some plain bread product with which the tasters can recalibrate their tastebuds. There are many possible products you can offer. Carr's Table Water Crackers are particularly popular, and are usually found on a small plate or in a basket at the center of the table. There are no rules or restrictions as to what to offer as a palate cleanser. Roast beef, for example, is sometimes offered between flights of heavy Cabernet Sauvignon-based wines.

A White Table Cloth or Tasting Mat

Color is an important aspect of each wine's evaluation. The best way to note color is against a white background, so wines are traditionally tasted at tables draped with white cloths. If white tablecloths are not available or practical to the situation, set each place with a white paper placemat. These can be found in grocery stores near the paper plates. You can draw numbered circles on the mats to indicate where each wine glass should be placed. These circles help keep each wine separate and more readily identifiable.

A List of Wines

Every participant will appreciate receiving an official list of the wines tasted. It can help straighten out any confusing tasting notes the guest may have jotted down. The list also serves as a souvenir of the event.

Extra Pens and Paper

Every guest should be able to write tasting notes, so make sure you have extra pens and paper available for those who forget to bring their own. Keep them nearby to save yourself a time-wasting scramble after the wines have been poured and are ready to be tasted. (See the inset on page 203 for information on writing a tasting note.)

The Corkscrew

Don't forget that you will need a corkscrew to open the bottles! Believe it or not, it has happened before. There is no one corkscrew that is better than another, so find one with which you are comfortable.

Michael Broadbent has attended more wine tastings, and tasted more wines, than anyone in the world. To this day, he records a tasting note for every bottle, no matter how familiar he already is with the wine.

After all the preparation you will have done collecting the above materials, you will want the conversation to flow as easily as the wine. The next section will provide you with the basics for talking like a wine expert in time for your next tasting.

WINE TALK

Your mastery of wine vocabulary will lead to a higher level of wine appreciation. It will also add depth to your wine-tasting experiences. This is where a wine drinker becomes more serious, venturing beyond the vague, "I like this," or, "This one is my favorite." When you verbalize the taste of a wine or write a valuable tasting note, certain terms will most accurately convey your experience. Your use of these generally accepted phrases will help your fellow tasters fully comprehend your voiced opinions.

To expand your wine vocabulary, you may want to head back to the notes of a professional wine critic. The notes of both Robert Parker and *Wine Spectator* can be found online and at most libraries. You will see that many of the same wine descriptors—viscous, full-bodied, red currant, hot, balanced, big, thin, cherry, lychee—come up again and again. Your using these words will give the listener an accurate sense of what you are tasting. Becoming proficient in the language of wine is a matter of study and practice, and, of course, tasting and talking with others.

Many books and Internet sites include glossaries of wine-tasting terms. Having a glossary on hand while reading a professional critic's notes is immensely useful as you try to pinpoint the critic's remarks. It may be less practical to bring a glossary to a tasting, but you can write down your thoughts and what others are saying, and return to your notes later to look up the terms.

After registering this initial impression, you will narrow your focus to more specific attributes. Is the scent dominated by an earthy, fruity, spicy, herbal, sweet, or stinky smell? Once this has been determined, you can delve more deeply within the general category. Does your glass of wine smell fruity? If it is a red wine, perhaps it smells of cherries, plums, figs, or raspberries. If it is a white wine, determine if the smell reminds you of apples, pears, or melons. (Surprisingly, tasters hardly ever say that their wine smells like grapes.) Maybe your first impression is earthy. The next step is to describe the earthy characteristics more precisely. Is the wine reminiscent of dirt? Moss? Rock? Asphalt?

Enology is the science, study, and art of wine and winemaking. People who work in this field are called enologists, and widely referred to as vintners, winemakers, wine growers, or simply wine professionals.

One of the very best tools for learning about wine flavors and vocabulary is the Wine Aroma Wheel. Developed by University of California enology professor Ann Nobel, the wheel breaks down each general group of smells into more specific components. The middle of the chart lists general attributes, such as nutty, caramel, woody, and fruity. After you sip from your glass, choose the appropriate general smell. Perhaps your wine tastes nutty. You would then follow the nutty section of the pie towards the outer tier, where your choices are walnut, hazelnut, and almond. The chart helps narrow down specific tastes, while also adding to a common understanding between tasters of what each described taste actually means. (See Resources on page 221 for information on obtaining a Wine Aroma Wheel.)

Talking about wine should be practiced with the same enthusiasm as tasting wine. If you initially find it intimidating, don't give up. The language of wine will become increasingly more enjoyable as you become more and more competent at using it.

WINE TRAVEL

Traveling to and within any wine-growing region will add yet another educational and pleasurable level of appreciation to the wine lover's hobby. Whether you take a long weekend in the Napa Valley or a month-long exploration of Australia's wine regions, there is no substitute for standing among the vines of wine country.

Begin By Reading Up On the Wine-Growing Regions

The best place to start your trip is your armchair. There is no shortage of excellent travel books, and they cover each corner of every significant vineyard in the world. Before hitting the travelogues, you may want to begin by reading maps. Those featured in books such as Hugh Johnson's *The World Atlas of Wine* serve as a perfect point of departure for any wine-related trip. Wine maps illustrate where particular vineyards and wineries lie in relationship to other properties, and indicate the areas that are most interesting to explore. Once the locations of vinous interest are located, you can then explore other travel books for suggestions on various travel accommodations.

In addition to the many travel books written on these areas, there is a tremendous amount of research that can be done online. Almost every wine-growing region is represented by a marketing organization that can supply you with specific information, including more maps. The Napa Valley Vintners Association, for example, represents the Napa Valley area. This organization provides information on its website, www.napavintners.com. European wine-region marketing associations also have informative websites (that include information presented in English), such as www.bordeaux.com.

Go First to the Region that Makes the Wine You Like

Vacation time is often at a premium. Take your first wine-country trip to a region about which you are already somewhat knowledgeable. If you know about and enjoy drinking Napa Valley Cabernet Sauvignon, for example, you may enjoy traveling through Napa more than taking a week in Tuscany. (This is not to say that you should pass up a trip to Tuscany!) You probably have a favorite wine or region, about which you are already familiar. Put the knowledge you have to good use and target the properties of your choice. You will be able to cover more ground than you would see otherwise, while also being more confident about where to visit.

A visit to the wineries of Tuscany or Burgundy can be quite different from traveling through the California wine country. Once you have chosen a European destination, you will want to begin pinpointed research. Many American travelers, used to walk-in tours at the Napa Valley wineries, are surprised to learn that most European wineries will not receive visitors without appointments. Diligent research will cut down on disappointment.

Talk to Others Who Have Made the Trip

After reading up on a particular region, you should continue your research by discussing the trip with people who have already visited the area. They can provide

If you are really interested in visiting a particular winery, don't be discouraged by a tale of a poor reception on its property. Both people and places can have bad days now and again.

valuable snippets of information on hotels, restaurants, and tasting rooms. In particular, gather as much information as you can regarding the treatment they received at each property. These discussions will help you avoid making time-wasting moves. Of course, the opinions of others should always be weighed against your good judgment and gut instincts. Take every critique with a grain of salt.

Set Goals and a Reasonable Pace

Professionals on a tasting trip may visit four or five wineries before lunch, and another four or five after lunch. Unless this is a normal pace for you, do not attempt to power-taste your way through a wine vacation. You will miss out on many of the pleasures of a vacation in wine country. Your palate, unused to the assault of so much wine, will most likely give up.

Set a goal for your trip. Are you looking for rest and relaxation? Are you determined to taste through a new vintage? How much ground do you wish to cover? Do your travel companions share your goals? Outlining what you wish to accomplish will help you set the pace for your time away. A reasonable weekend at the Napa Valley includes two wineries before lunch and one more before dinner. If you are visiting tasting rooms without touring each winery, you may be able to visit three wineries in the morning and another three in the afternoon. This will largely depend on the distance between each property. As you plan your days, keep in mind that your palate will be at its freshest in the morning.

Most wine-growing regions are in gorgeous parts of the world where there are a number of other sights to see. Pre-trip research will help you decide how much time—if any—you wish to devote to non-wine activities. If you want culinary exploration to be part of your experience, leave yourself plenty of time to rest in between visiting a winery and sitting in a restaurant. Don't be so exhausted when you dine that you can't appreciate an excellent meal!

Travel to Regions You Would Like to Know More About

Once you have some wine-country travel experience under your belt, you may find that the easiest way to learn about new wines is by traveling to their regions of origin. There is no better way to discover wines of a particular region than standing in a vineyard or a winery.

When you are traveling to an area you don't know much about, your pre-travel research becomes even more vital to the experience. If at all possible, talk to others who have made the trip. You may even want to travel with someone who has been to the area, or hire a professional tour guide to show you around. Be sure to ask the guide for his recommendations.

Pack Your Bags with Common Sense and Courtesy

As a wine traveler, your most valuable assets will be common sense and common courtesy. Common sense should remind you to pack comfortable shoes and appropriate dress. Err on the side of too dressy—especially in Europe—and you will be treated respectfully. Flip flops, shorts, and ratty t-shirts are usually not acceptable even in the United States, and tasting rooms tend to be cool in temperature anyway. Common sense should help you remember your tasting notebooks, your camera, and your manners.

Common courtesy is just as important as common sense. Almost every wine trip includes the "story of the jerk," whether in a tasting room or a restaurant. Steer clear of these people—and never become one. This is important to remember if you find yourself or one of your travel mates indulging in too much alcohol. Never forget your goals, including your desire to calmly taste and critique wine. When you are planning to travel through a foreign country, it is well worth your time and effort to learn the country's basic greetings, including "please" and "thank you." These can often go a long way. A smile and a "Bonjour, Madame" may be able to get you through a previously closed door.

CONCLUSION

The fun of acquiring wine bottles at auction is a small part of this wonderful world. This is a hobby highlighted by a love of wine, food, conversation, and travel. You will become knowledgeable in all these areas as you journey through the world of wine, a world almost limitless with regard to providing pleasure. Once you are past the initial intimidation of talking about wine with others, you will find that wine tastings and wine travel offer wonderful opportunities to learn and share with other enthusiasts. Many great friendships are born from a love of the grape.

Conclusion

Whether you began reading this book as a wine novice or an experienced wine collector, you are now ready to confidently immerse yourself in the world of wine auctions. You are familiar with the history of wine auctions and the fundamentals of wine basics, as well as the details behind how modern day auctions are conducted. This background information, coupled with your extensive knowledge of each auction worker's responsibilities and potential to help you, is key to your auction success.

Your wine education doesn't end here. There is always more to learn on this subject. As you have read, opportunities for further learning include taking classes, attending wine tastings, reading books, and conversing with people in the industry. Keep building on what you already know and your appreciation will continue to grow. Your wine education will assist you at every auction you attend.

You now have the ability to participate in an auction as buyer or seller, and will probably find yourself experiencing both sides of the coin. You are up to the challenge, because *The Wine Lover's Guide to Auctions* has prepared you. From setting your bid limits to deciphering a proposal, you are ready for every stage of being both an auction buyer and an auction seller.

You can also expand your role beyond that of buyer and seller. You have all the necessary information and advice to organize a successful wine-related event. Arrange a charity auction, throw a wine tasting for your friends and family, vacation to a wine region, or plan a day trip to a local winery. There are endless possibilities for utilizing and expanding your knowledge of wine.

Between the rare bottles, the delicious food, and the investment potential, you will never be at a loss for a reason to participate in an auction event. I have found that the opportunity to interact with people who, like yourself, are fascinated with this marvelous beverage is usually the best incentive to attend. The most effective and interesting way to learn about any bottle of wine is in the company of other wine enthusiasts—and there is no better place to find these potential friends than at a wine auction.

I hope that you have enjoyed reading about this wonderful hobby as much as I have enjoyed sharing the knowledge I have gained from years of experience. Keep the tips I have imparted in mind when you expand or condense your wine collection, or attend an event as a spectator to see these rules and principles put into effect.

I look forward to seeing you at the next auction!

Resources

AUCTION HOUSES

Acker Merrall & Condit
160 West 72nd Street
New York, NY 10023
Phone: 877-225-3747
Website: www.ackerwines.com

Bonhams & Butterfields
220 San Bruno Avenue
San Francisco, CA 94103
Phone: 415-861-7500
Website: www.butterfields.com

The Chicago Wine Company
5663 West Howard Street
Niles, IL 60714
Phone: 847-647-8789
Website: www.tcwc.com

Christie's London
85 Old Brompton Road
London SW7 3LD
England
Phone: 44-020-7930-6074

Christie's Los Angeles
360 North Camden Drive
Beverly Hills, CA 90210
Phone: 310-385-2603

Christie's New York
20 Rockefeller Plaza
New York, NY 10020
Phone: 212-636-2270
Website: www.christies.com

Hart Davis Hart Wine Co.
363 West Erie Street
Chicago, IL 60610
Phone: 312-482-9996
Website: www.hdhwine.com

Langton's
52 Pitt Street
Redfern NSW 2016
Australia
Phone: 61-2-9310-4231
Website: www.langtons.com.au

Morrell & Company
729 7th Avenue, 15th Floor
New York, NY 10019
Phone: 212-307-4200
Website:
www.morrellwineauctions.com

Sotheby's London
34-35 New Bond Street
London W1A 2AA
England
Phone: 44-020-7293-5050

Sotheby's New York
1334 York Avenue
New York, New York 10021
Phone: 212-606-7865
Website: www.sothebys.com

Zachys Wine & Liquor, Inc.
39 Westmoreland Avenue
White Plains, New York 10606
Phone: 914-448-3026
Website: www.zachys.com

BOOKS

The Basics:
Best Choices for New Wine Lovers

Broadbent, Michael. *Wine Tasting*. London: Mitchell Beazley, 2003.
One of the best books on the principles of wine tasting since its original 1968 publication, *Wine Tasting* is a short and well-organized guide. Broadbent distills huge amounts of information into essential sips. *Wine Tasting* is a volume that readers will revisit often.

Goldberg, Howard. *All About Wine Cellars*. Philadelphia: Running Press, 2004.
Read this book before investing in storage for a new wine collection. Goldberg advises on all aspects of the various storage systems. He also touches on a wide range of other wine topics, ellaborating with his personal experiences in a way that is often charming and always insightful.

MacNeil, Karen. *The Wine Bible*. New York: Workman Publishing Company, 2001.
With over ten years worth of writing and a lifetime of passion, MacNeil organizes the world's wine-producing areas by region, including the largest producers and the smallest boutique wineries. *The Wine Bible* was awarded one of Amazon's best books of 2001.

McCarthy, Ed and Mary Ewing-Mulligan. *Wine For Dummies*. Indianapolis: Wiley Publishing, 2006.
This husband-and-wife team offers readable and unpretentious information as only true experts can. The basic knowledge in *Wine For Dummies* is best for the novice. It provides a great foundation on which new wine lovers can build an education.

Robinson, Jancis. *How to Taste: A Guide to Enjoying Wine*. New York: Simon & Schuster, 2000.
Robinson presents wine-tasting exercises that can be done alone or with a like-minded group of wine-loving friends. She provides the novice with the vocabulary necessary to describe the taste and smell of a glass of wine. A fabulous review for any collector interested in the constant development of his palette, this book is a hugely fun and informative key to wine tasting.

Zraly, Kevin. *Windows on the World Complete Wine Course*. New York: Sterling Publishing Company, updated annually.
The nation's bestselling wine book with over 2 million copies sold, this book is a fabulous gift choice. Zraly addresses everything newcomers need to know about wine in an informal yet comprehensive format. It is also a good review for the experienced oenophile.

Indispensable Reference:
Must Buys for Every Collector

Bellucci, Diana. *How to Pronounce French, German, and Italian Wine Names*. La Jolla: Luminosa Publishers, 2003.
A simple—yet extensive—list of wine names and their proper pronunciation, this is a wonderful reference for collectors of European wine. It is also a great confidence builder for anyone who enjoys talking about wine.

Broadbent, Michael. *Michael Broadbent's Vintage Wine*. New York: Harcourt, 2002.
This is *the* source for detailed tasting notes of the world's finest, rarest, and oldest wines. Broadbent's eloquent notes recreate the sensory experience of wines, many of which the average drinker will never have the opportunity to taste. *Michael Broadbent's Vintage Wine* is both an important reference work and an indulgent fantasy read.

Johnson, Hugh and Jancis Robinson. *The World Atlas of Wine*. London: Mitchell Beazley, 2001.
Now in its fifth edition, this invaluable reference book contains maps of major wine regions from around the world. It is the definitive source for up-to-date information including climate, production methods, and relevant laws for the different areas. *The World Atlas of Wine* is incomparable in the ever-changing world of wine.

***The Oxford Companion to Wine*. Edited by Jancis Robinson. Oxford: Oxford University Press, 2006.**
This book is an absolute must for anyone interested in the vast subject of wine. Over seventy of the world's greatest wine authorities have contributed to the entries, which number more than three thousand. Arranged alphabetically, *The Oxford Companion to Wine* covers nearly every aspect of wine.

Parker, Robert M., Jr with Pierre-Antoine Rovani. *Parker's Wine Buyer's Guide.* **New York: Fireside/Simon & Schuster, 2002.**
This is a compilation of the tasting notes of Robert Parker, one of the most respected and important wine critics. Parker utilizes the hundred-point system that he created and has become so popular among wine drinkers. Equally important, *Parker's Wine Buyer's Guide*, now in its sixth edition, includesParker's insight into the wineries, winemakers, regions, and vintages of an incredible amount of the world's finest wine.

Phillips, Rod. *A Short History of Wine.* **London: Harper Perennial, 2002.**
Rod Phillips is a historian as opposed to being a wine expert. As such, he offers a fascinating and unique look at wine's place in the world, from ancient times to the modern day. A glass of wine becomes an even more complex beverage after reading this scholarly and entertaining book.

Wine Price File. **Edited by William Edgerton. San Francisco: Wine Appreciation Guild, updated semi-annually.**
Auction results from the major auction houses are reported in the *Wine Price File*, which is updated semi-annually to incorporate the latest results. It includes over 70,000 listings and is a great source of information on any wine that has appeared at auction.

Research by Region: Starting with One Book on Each Region

Australia
Clarke, Oz. *Oz Clarke's Wine Companion.* London: Harvest Books, 2004.

Bordeaux
Parker, Robert M., Jr. *A Consumer's Guide of the World's Finest Wines.* New York: Simon & Schuster, 2003.

Burgundy
Coates, Clive, M.W. *Côte D'Or: A Celebration of the Great Wines of Burgundy.* Berkeley: University of California Press, 1997.

California
Kramer, Matt. *Matt Kramer's New California Wine: Making Sense of Napa Valley, Sonoma, Mendocino, and Beyond.* Philadelphia: Running Press Book Publishers, 2004.

Champagne
Stevenson, Tom. *World Encyclopedia of Champagne and Sparkling Wine.* San Francisco: Wine Appreciation Guild, 2003.

Germany
Pigott, Stuart. *The Wine Atlas of Germany: And Traveller's Guide to the Vineyards.* Suffolk: Antique Collectors Club Ltd., 1996.

Italy
Bastianich, Joe and David Lynch. *Vino Italiano: The Regional Wines of Italy.* New York: Clarkson Potter, 2002.

The Rhône Valley
Parker, Robert M., Jr. *Wines of the Rhône Valley: Revised and Expanded Edition.* New York: Simon & Schuster, 1997.

Spain
Radford, John. *The New Spain: A Complete Guide to Contemporary Spanish Wine.* London: Mitchell Beazley, 2004.

ONLINE STORES FOR WINE BOOKS

The following websites are excellent sources for purchasing the above books.

www.amazon.com

www.wineappreciation.com

www.wineloverspage.com/winebook.shtml

PERIODICALS

The Wine Advocate
Website: **erobertparker.com**
The infamous tasting notes of the world's most influential palate, that of Robert M. Parker Jr., are available in newsletter form. Email wineadvocate@erobertparker.com to subscribe.

The following is a list of free wine publications. They are wonderful, informative sources for all wine lovers, from beginners to experts. To arrange for a subscription, visit the indicated website. Sign up using your email address. Also, the websites themselves offer quality news items and features, and are updated daily.

Decanter Magazine
www.decanter.com

Food & Wine
www.foodandwine.com

Wine & Spirits Magazine
www.wineandspiritsmagazine.com

Wine Enthusiast
www.wineenthusiast.com

Wine Spectator
www.winespectator.com

WEBSITES

General Wine Information
www.burghound.com
Allen Meadows, a Burgundy-wine devotee, created this site to offer advice for buying his favorite beverage. Every serious Burgundy lover visits this site often for the latest news from the region. It also includes weekly top wines and lists events that feature Burgundy. You can also subscribe to Meadows' newsletter, the self-proclaimed "Ultimate Burgundy Reference."

www.internetwineguide.com
A guide to many wine-related websites from all over the world, InternetWineGuide.com can direct you to sites dedicated to wine auctions, wine accessories, and wine tours. My favorite category is "Wine News."

www.erobertparker.com
Robert Parker's online presence, this website is entry into Parker's database of over 80,000 tasting notes. Much of the website is a pay service, but features such as vintage charts and summaries of Executive Wine Seminars public tastings are invaluable research tools.

www.wineaccess.com
On the internet, WineAccess has exclusive rights to Stephen Tanzer's International Wine Cellar. Browse through Tanzer's expert tasting notes and buy any of wines reviewed with just a click of your mouse. Or, if you are shopping and browsing through various wines, you will find that each bottle's description includes a helpful tasting score from Tanzer or another reputable source. There are also discussion forums and a very interesting Market Monitor that is available by subscription.

www.wineloverspage.com
Robin Garr's Wine Lovers Page contains just about everything a wine lover needs and wants: great news snippets, articles, links, and forums. One worthwhile featured link is to Wine Library TV, which consists of daily videos of its wine-expert host tasting wines and answering viewers' questions. The goal of the Wine Lovers Page is to make wine accessible and affordable to anyone interested in the hobby.

www.winespectator.com
This is the website for *Wine Spectator* magazine. Although more in-depth access is available on a subscription basis, you can visit the site for free features such as Daily Wine Picks, which includes options for several price ranges; blogs from respected wine aficionados; and highlights from recent auctions.

Wine Prices & Auction Results

Check these websites for the current market values of different wine bottles. This information is also available from individual auction houses, each of which archives its own results and makes them available online. The website addresses for the major auction houses can be found with their contact information, beginning on page 215.

www.wineappraise.com

On this website, you will find a group of independent wine appraisers. For a reasonable price, they will review your inventory list and estimate the worth of your collection. Another, more expensive option is to pay for an appraiser to visit your collection in person before making his estimation.

www.wineprices.com

Here, purchase the official *Wine Price File* book, the ultimate auction pricing database. This book offers a complete list of auction results from each major auction house, and is updated twice a year. The cost is $49.95 with a discount offered for buying two volumes.

www.wine-searcher.com

Wine-searcher.com, *"the* resource for locating and pricing wines," is an excellent search engine for anyone looking to buy wine. The entries include the inventory and prices of many retail stores and several auction houses. Search for specific bottles or browse through general categories. A paid membership offers price comparisons between stores so that you can always buy your bottles for the best possible prices.

CELLAR MANAGEMENT

Inventory Software

The following programs are incredibly useful to anyone with a wine collection. They help collectors stay organized and aware of every bottle they own. Each has its own features but most keep track of important information such as purchase price, personal tasting notes, and more.

CellarTracker!

Website: www.CellarTracker.com

CellarTracker! is a great way to keep track of your wine collection. The program is easy to use and includes community tasting notes, illustrated labels, and access to barcode labels. (Barcode labels allow bottles to be added to and removed from the virtual cellar with ease.) There is no charge for general access to many of this website's features, although certain areas are restricted to paying members.

My Wine Collection

Website: www.my-winecollection.com

With My Wine Collection, collectors can create a simple, easy-to-read inventory list. The program specifies the location of each bottle, tracks wine maturity dates, and offers suggestions on pairing wine with food, while using an auto-entry feature to track down additional information about each bottle.

Vintage Manager

Website: www.vintagemanager.com

This time-saving program has a particularly useful "Auto-Fill" feature that enables users to retrieve all necessary inventory information about their bottles after entering only names and vintages. Vintage Manager also provides barcode label services, shopping list management, and alphabetized shared tasting notes.

Management Programs

Much more than inventory software, these are online areas for managing a wine collection. Each site combines technology and expertise to offer a single resource for all of your collecting needs, and can be accessed from any computer with an internet connection.

VinCellar

Website: www.vinfolio.com

A segment of the online wine store Vinfolio is VinCellar, a free and easy-to-use cellar management program. It provides barcoding, graphic analyzation of the collection, and access to professional tasting scores and drink dates. It also provides an estimation of the cellar's value by supplying up-to-date market values of each bottle. All wine bought from Vinfolio is entered into the program automatically and free of charge.

Vintrust

Website: www.vintrust.com

Vintrust, known for its accuracy and efficiency, has a storage facility where it expertly keeps track of each of your bottles. It offers features such as digital images of each bottle, small barcode labels, and the option to include your own tasting notes. Customers also have the ability to ship any number of bottles to anywhere of their choosing. Vintrust can even provide gift wrap so that the bottles' presentation is as impressive as the wine they contain.

ONLINE WINE AUCTIONS

You can participate in an online auction as either buyer or seller. The advantages and details of an online auction were discussed in Chapter 1.

Brentwood Wine Company
Website: www.brentwoodwine.com
This Pacific Northwest retailer has a successful online auction branch. Brentwoodwine.com takes wine on consignment, but will also buy a seller's inventory directly. Also available from this website are stemware, wine racks, and storage systems.

Cellar Exchange
Website: www.cellarexchange.com
This peer-to-peer wine auction website is free to both buyers and sellers. It also offers helpful suggestions for appraising your own collection (or one you are interested in purchasing) to make sure you are aware of its appropriate cost.

WineBid.com
Website: www.winebid.com
Founded in 1996, this is the largest and most successful online wine-auction site. WineBid.com's temperature-controlled warehouse is located in Napa Valley, California, and every bottle is inspected there by its team of experts. WineBid.com was selected by *Forbes* magazine for its "Best of the Web" list.

WineCommune
Website: www.winecommune.com
In partnership with erobertparker.com, this peer-to-peer wine auction site is the most popular of its type. Sellers describe their wine and send it directly to the successful bidder. The bidders send their payment directly to the seller. This procedure reduces both time and the bottles' burden of traveling.

CHARITY AUCTION WEBSITES

Auction Napa Valley
Website: www.napavintners.com
Location: St. Helena, CA
Month: June
Benefiting: local health care, youth and housing organizations, and other special projects

The Auction of Northwest Wines
Website: www.auctionofwashingtonwines.org
Location: Seattle, WA
Month: August
Benefiting: Seattle Children's Hospital

The Central Coast Wine Classic
Website: www.centralcoastwineclassic.org
Location: San Luis Obispo, CA
Month: July
Benefiting: a variety of Central Coast community outreach programs and charities

The High Museum Atlanta Wine Auction
Website: www.atlanta-wineauction.org
Location: Atlanta, GA
Month: April
Benefiting: The High Museum of Art

The Jackson Hole Wine Auction
Website: www.gtmf.org/wineauction/wine.html
Location: Jackson Hole, WY
Month: June
Benefiting: The Grand Teton Music Festival

Naples Winter Wine Festival
Website: www.napleswinefestival.com
Location: Naples, FL
Month: February
Benefiting: local children's charities

The Sun Valley Wine Auction
Website: www.sunvalleycenter.org
Location: Sun Valley, ID
Month: July
Benefiting: The Sun Valley Center for the Arts educational programming

CHARITY AUCTION CONSULTANTS

Reynolds & Buckley Fundraising Auctioneers
David Reynolds, Auctioneer
PO Box 460430
San Francisco, CA 94146
Phone: 415-648-0386
Website: www.Reynolds-Buckley.com

WAREHOUSING/ TRANSPORTATION SERVICES

Western Carriers
2220 91st Street
North Bergen, NJ 07047
Phone: 800-631-7776
Website: www.westerncarriers.com

STEMWARE AND DECANTERS

BestWineGlass.com
Website: www.BestWineGlass.com
Visit this site for a list of glassware retailers and an informative explanation of different glass shapes. It features the glassware and other products of high-end retailers Riedel, Schott Zwiesel, and Ravenscroft.

Riedel Glassware
Website: www.riedel.com
Riedel Crystal is the number-one brand in wine glassware. It was Claus Riedel who discovered that the shape and size of a glass had an effect on wine properties and characteristics. Riedel Crystal makes glassware of excellent quality, and serving good wine out of good stemware enhances the enjoyment of wine drinking. Riedel glasses and decanters are sold at many fine retailers and websites. Shop around for the best prices as Riedel vendors have occasional sales.

AROMA IDENTIFICATION TOOLS

The ability to name any scent found in a particular wine is key to writing good notes and having profes-sional-level wine conversations. The following items will train you to pinpoint these smells.

Le Nez du Vin Wine Aroma Kit
Le Nez du Vin Wine Aroma Kit is the quickest way to sharpen your sense of smell. Each glass vial contains a different chemically composed scent found in wine. Scents are available for both red and white wines. Find this kit at a number of websites, including www.wineenthusiast.com.

Wine Aroma Wheel
Developed in1984 by sensory chemist and educator Ann Noble, the Wine Aroma Wheel is considered the definitive mapping of wine's many possible olfactory characteristics, as well as an attractive and handy educational tool that can be kept on hand during a tasting. It also helps develop wine vocabulary.

HOME STORAGE

EuroCave
Website: www.eurocave.co.uk
EuroCave was the first company to develop self-contained temperature- and humidity-controlled wine storage. Ideal for home or office, these containers come in various sizes that can hold as few as one dozen bottles to as many as several hundred. Shop the internet for best prices, although your first stop should be the Wine Enthusiast catalogue (see page 218).

Vinotheque
Website: www.vinotheque.com
Another leading manufacturer of high quality wine-storage cabinets, Vinotheque is also a great resource for finding cellar doors and cooling systems.

Vintage Cellars
Website: www.vintagecellars.com
Through Vintage Cellars, many beautiful cellaring systems as well as racking equipment from a variety of brands can be ordered. The website also includes important information on constructing your cellar when it arrives.

Glossary

Words that appear in italic type are defined within this glossary.

absentee bid. Placed in advance by a *bidder* who cannot attend the auction. There are several different kinds of absentee bids: *written-order bids, telephone bids*, and *representative bids*.

addenda notes. Information handed out or announced to the auction's audience regarding corrections to the *catalogue*.

after-sale notification. After the auction, this list is sent to each seller. It includes the *hammer price* for each *lot* of his that sold.

American-style auction. Auction sale at which the bidders raise their paddles to meet the call of the *auctioneer*. This is unlike the *English-style auction*.

appellation. Defines and names an area where specific grapes are grown.

appraisal. The *inventory* list complete with pre-sale *estimates*, returned to the *consignor* by the auction house.

ascending-bid auction. Sale in which each bid is higher than the one previous to it. The last bid establishes the *hammer price* and wins the wine.

auction. A sale to the highest bidder.

auction catalogue. See *catalogue*.

auction house. A company where an auction sale is held.

auctioneer. Conductor of the auction sale. At each auction, it is the goal of the auctioneer to extract the highest possible price for each *lot*.

auctioneer's discretion. The auctioneer's ultimate authority to make in-the-moment decisions regarding the sale of any given *lot*.

balance. The harmonious integration of a wine's sweetness, acidity, alcohol, and *tannins*.

berry. Each individual grape in a cluster.

"Bought In." Also called a BI. This is an auction item that remains unsold after having failed to reach its *reserve price*. The lot may have failed to receive any bids at all.

bid. A dollar amount offered by an individual to an *auctioneer* in hopes of purchasing an auction item.

bidder. An individual indicating to an *auctioneer* his intent to purchase an auction item.

bidder pre-registration form. This form, found in the auction *catalogue*, allows anyone interested in the auction to fill out their paperwork prior to the sale day so they can save time at the actual event.

bids clerk. A member of the auction staff who stands near the *auctioneer*. The bids clerk deals with all bidding issues, such as recording the final bidding price and looking for any *bidders* the auctioneer may have overlooked.

bin soiled. A stained or dirty bottle label due to dirty or dusty cellar conditions or careless handling. A bin-soiled label is oftentimes not an indication of compromised quality of the wine.

Bordeaux bottle. Tall and cylindrical with strong, squarish shoulders. Traditionally, this bottle contains wine from the Bordeaux region of France, as well as wine made in other parts of the world from Bordeaux *varietals*.

Botrytis cinerea. See *noble rot*.

bottle shock. The temporary alteration of a wine's components. Bottle shock is caused by movement, predominately from traveling. To get the wine to regain its flavors, allow the bottle to rest and settle down for several days.

Burgundy bottle. Has gentle, sloping shoulders and usually contains wine from the Burgundy region of France, as well as wines from other parts of the world that are made from Burgundy and Rhône *varietals*.

buyer. The successful bidder of an auction item. The buyer is the individual recognized by the auctioneer as having offered the highest price for a lot.

buyer's premium. The commission paid by the buyer to the auction house for his purchase. This commission is added to the *hammer price* of each lot.

capsule. The lead, tin, or plastic seal, usually red, protecting the top, rim, and neck of a wine bottle. See *corroded capsule*.

case lot. A lot for sale that consists of a full case of wine. The total liquid volume of a case of wine is 9 liters. If the bottles are 750 milliliters, a full case has twelve bottles. If the bottles are *magnums*, there are six bottles in a case.

catalogue. The printed list, in book-form, of the auction items. Catalogues are written and illustrated to various levels of expense and sophistication.

cellar book. A handwritten volume, remaining in or near the cellar, in which wines were logged in and out of the collection. These are used much less frequently today, because most collectors keep their inventories on computer.

Champagne. *Sparkling wine* from the French province of the same name.

Champagne bottle. Contains *sparkling wine*. These bottles have gentle, sloping shoulders and are made of very thick glass in order to accommodate the pressure from the bubbles.

charitable contribution deduction. The amount paid by a winning bidder over the fair market value of an item. The charity contribution deduction is an incentive for bidders to participate in charity auctions, because the winning bidder may receive a tax break in this amount.

château. An estate in Bordeaux at which wine grapes are grown and wine is made. There are over 7,000 châteaux in Bordeaux.

château bottled. Wine made from the grapes of a *château* and bottled on location. This is strictly controlled by French law, and indicated on the label by "mise en bouteille" or "mis au château."

Classification of 1855. The ranking of Bordeaux wines relative to prices achieved by the marketplace in 1855. The goal of the classification was to equate quality to marketplace value, and it is still recognized today. The *first growth* wines are among the world's most expensive and highly prized wines.

commission. See *buyer's premium* and *vender's commission*.

conditions of sale. Regulatory guidelines under which one company conducts its auction sales.

consignment. All the items that a seller is offering for sale at auction.

consignor. The owner of property being offered for sale at auction.

corked bottle. A bottle that has been affected by *cork taint*.

cork shrinkage. When the cork stopper becomes smaller over time, usually a result of being in an environment that is not temperature controlled. Wine may begin to evaporate or leak, and the cork can even drop into the bottle. The auction company is not responsible for and insurance does not cover problems related to the cork.

cork taint. A bottle infection of the chemical compound TCA. Although not dangerous to ingest, the presence of this compound can ruin the wine's natural aromas and flavors. The presence of cork taint is often accompanied by an off-putting, wet-cardboard smell.

corks. Wine bottle stoppers inserted into the bottle's neck and made of natural cork harvested from trees. Some *wineries* today experiment with bottle closures made of synthetic material instead of the increasingly expensive and less reliable natural cork.

corroded capsule. Damage to a lead *capsule*, usually the result of excessive moisture or cellar humidity. Heavy corrosion may indicate some compromise to a bottle's condition.

crown cap. Fastening found on beer bottles.

cru. A French term which refers to a vineyard and the resulting quality of its wine.

Currency Conversion Board. An electronic board at the front of the auction room that shows the prices being bid in different currencies. It also displays the hammer price for several seconds after each lot is won.

cuvee. A French term for a particular blend of wine.

damp-stained label. A *label* compromised by water damage from excessive moisture in a cellar. No damage to the juice is indicated by a damp-stained label.

descending bid auction. Auction sale at which the *auctioneer* starts at a price well above the perceived value of the *lot* and moves down to progressively lower sums. The first *bidder* to accept an announced price wins the item.

dessert wine. Any type of very sweet wine, usually served at the end of a meal. Sauternes is the world's most coveted sweet wine.

domaine. An estate in Burgundy where grapes are grown and wine is made.

donors. People who offer items for sale at a charity auction.

Dutch auction. See *descending bid auction*.

en primeur. French term for the first sale offering of a wine, sold prior to its release. See also *futures*.

either/or bid. *Absentee bid* option that enables the *bidder* to win either one lot or the other of two or more choices.

English-style auction. Auction sale at which the *auctioneer* calls a dollar amount in response to a paddle raise. This is unlike the *American-style auction*.

estate bottled. Term used on California labels to indicate that the wine was bottled at the winery, with the property's own grapes.

estimate. A guide to a lot's value based upon past auction results. The estimate is usually reported as a range and is included in the catalogue's *lot entry*.

fermentation. Sugar from the grape's juice reacts with yeast and turns into alcohol and carbon dioxide. The fermentation process is completed under the careful eye of the winemaker.

finish. The lingering aftertaste of a sip of wine.

first growths. Wines of Bordeaux that are labeled as being of outstanding quality according to the *Classification of 1855*. The first growth wines, from Châteaux Mouton, Margaux, Lafite, Latour and Haut Brion, are among the world's most expensive and highly prized wines.

flights. Groups of several glasses, each containing a different wine, that are served together.

fill level. The amount of wine in a bottle, as indicated through the neck of the bottle. The lower the fill level, the more the wine may have aged. Given two bottles of the same wine, the more desirable of the two will be the one with the higher level. See also *ullage*.

futures. Ordering wine prior to its release and appearance in the marketplace. Wine obtained on futures is paid for in full at the time of purchase.

German bottle. A tall, slender shape that bottles high-quality German white wines such as Riesling.

global total. A total dollar limit set by a bidder for the entire sale's purchases. A seller may set a global total for the expectation of an entire *consignment's* proceeds.

glue stained. A *label* which exhibits evidence of the glue, which adheres the label to the bottle, seeping through the front. A glue-stained label in no way affects the quality or condition of wine in the bottle

group lot. Different wines being sold together as a *lot*. Although the bottles are often unrelated, they may share commonalities such as the same producer, *appellation*, or *vintage*.

guarantee. A promise made by the auction house to pay the *consignor* a certain amount of money for each *lot*, or entire collection, regardless of actual auction results.

hammer price. The amount of the final, winning *bid* at the fall of the *auctioneer's* gavel.

horizontal collection. A *lot* consisting of different wines from the same *vintage*.

humidity control. The attempt to regulate the humidity in a wine-storage situation. Ideal humidity for red wine storage is around 70 percent.

ideal storage. The attempt to control a wine-storage environment at 50° to 59° Fahrenheit and 70- to 75-percent humidity.

imperial. An oversized Bordeaux-shaped bottle that holds six liters of wine.

in bond. Wines held at a *winery* or a commercial storage facility that have not yet been subject to taxation.

insurance. A charge for the protection of wine against damage or loss. The auction house charges a small percentage of the wine's estimated value to cover the bottles while in transit or while waiting for transfer to buyer.

inventory. A list submitted by a potential *consignor* to the auction house that includes all the items he wishes

to sell. An inventory can also be a collector's list of all the wines in his cellar.

invoice. Itemized bill that lists the lots won by the bidder along with their costs. An invoice can be requested when the bidder leaves the auction, or it will be mailed to the bidder at the address given on the registration form. Once the invoice is received, the bidder should verify the invoice's information as soon as possible.

jeroboam. An oversized bottle. If it is from Champagne or Burgundy, it holds three liters of wine. If it is from Bordeaux, it holds four-and-a-half liters of wine.

label. The primary means to identify the wine in the bottle. Today most labels are paper, printed with information that is both regulated by the government and chosen by the producers.

large format. Any bottle larger in size than the standard 750 milliliters.

lead capsule. See *capsule*.

level. See *fill level*.

limited warranty. Terms of sale that state that an auction house sells all wine "as is" and does not guarantee a lot's quality, condition, fitness for a particular use, provenance, rarity, or importance.

lot. Item or items sold at auction as a unit.

magnum. An oversized bottle that holds one-and-a-half liters of wine.

minimum price. See *reserve price*.

mixed lot. See *group lot*.

noble rot. A fungus (called Botrytis cinerea) that causes grapes to dry out. In the best of circumstances, the resulting shriveled grapes become very concentrated and are used to make some sweet wines.

oc. See *original cardboard carton*.

online auction. A computerized auction sale. *Bidders* look at *lots* and place *bids* on a website. Each transaction is executed electronically. In online auctions, a software program replaces the *auctioneer*.

order bid. See *written-order bid*.

original cardboard carton. Indicated in the auction *catalogue* by *"oc,"* this refers to the box in which the bottles were originally packaged. *Case lots* are more desirable when sold in its original cardboard carton or *original wooden case*.

original wooden case. Indicated in the auction catalogue by *"owc,"* this refers to the box in which the bottles were originally packaged. The value of a *case lot* is often greater if it is being offered with its original wooden case or *original cardboard carton*.

owc. See *original wooden case*.

paddle. Often numbered cards, these are raised by *bidders* to indicate *bids*.

parcel lot. Identical cases of wine that are offered as separate *lots*. The winner of the first lot is offered the remaining lots at the same price before they are separately auctioned off to the other *bidders*.

passive storage. Storing wine bottles someplace in which the temperature and humidity levels are not controlled. Although this type of storage can be satisfactory if done where the temperature and humidity remain fairly constantly at levels that are perfect for wine storage (such as in San Francisco), there are many more areas where passive storage can ruin a wine's quality.

per doz. Some catalogues give *estimates* for twelve bottles of wine, regardless of the quantity offered in each lot. It is the *bidder's* responsibility to determine what price to pay for the number of bottles in the *lot*. The per doz price is a guideline of the wine's value.

plus-one bidding. Choosing this *absentee bid* strategy gives the representative handling your *written-order bid* permission to make a bid that is one increment over your limit.

pre-registration. Prior to the day of the auction, potential buyers, after identifying themselves to the auction house, can fill out the paperwork and obtain *paddle* numbers prior to the day of the auction. Pre-registering saves time at the auction.

prices realized list. Record of the final price, including *buyer's premium*, for each *lot* sold at an auction. These lists, which are public record, are usually available on the auction house's website and by request.

professional storage. A commercial, temperature-controlled wine storage facility. A collector is charged either by the case or size of the area, ranging from a ten-case area called a locker, or a walk-in area for hundreds of cases.

provenance. The traceable history of a wine's ownership, including where the wines came from and how they were stored.

quinta. A Portuguese wine estate that has a winery and vineyards.

reconditioned bottle. A bottle returned to the winery to be opened, tasted, and if sound, topped up into the neck with wine (from the same *vintage* if possible), and recorked. A strip label will then be applied indicating that the bottle has been reconditioned.

red wine. Wine made from red grapes. The color comes from the grapes' skins, which remain with the juice during the *fermentation* process.

repacking charge. Additional cost added by the auction house to cover the extra materials used if the bottles need to be repacked into cartons.

reserve price. The confidential minimum price agreed upon by the seller and the auctioneer, below which the lot cannot be sold (unless the seller has granted *auctioneer's discretion*).

residential storage. Temperature-controlled storage area in a private home, ranging from an electric stand-alone refrigerated case to a sophisticated and expensive cellar room.

right bank châteaux. French winemaking estates located on the right side of the Dordogne River. The two most famous *appellations* are St. Emilion and Pomerol.

rosé wine. Wine with a pinkish color. Rosé wine is either made with red grapes, removing the skins from the *fermentation* process once the wine has reached the desired color, or by blending a small amount of red grape juice with a larger amount of white grape juice.

rostrum. The podium behind which the *auctioneer* stands and upon which he places his paperwork and bangs his gavel.

sale-by-candle auction. Auction sale at which bidders shout out increasingly higher bids as a candle burns nearby. The last bidder heard by the auctioneer before the candle goes out wins the *lot*.

sales tax. Regulated on the state level and levied by the auction house as mandated. In the United States, wine is taxed at the same rate as other goods in each individual state.

salesroom. The room in which the auction is held.

salesroom announcements. Any announcement made prior to or during the auction. *Addenda notes* are read as salesroom announcements.

seepage. Wine leaking through the cork and evidenced on the bottle, sometimes pooling up around the edge of the *capsule*. Seepage is usually an indication of change in storage temperature.

settlement statement. The *consignor's* second *after-sale notification*. This statement shows the final payment amount—the *hammer price* less the negotiated commission charges.

silent auction. Auction sale at which the bidding does not involve an *auctioneer*. Bid are usually recorded by each *bidder* writing on a sheet of paper, entering a dollar amount higher than the one already present. Silent auctions can also be executed electronically. See *online auctions*.

single-bottle lot. A bottle being offered at auction on its own. Only valuable or rare bottles are sold as single-bottle lots.

sommelier. Restaurant manager in charge of wine service.

sparkling wine. Wine that has undergone a second *fermentation* while under pressure in the bottle, resulting in captured bubbles.

spit buckets. Bowls placed around the table during wine-tasting events, into which guests can spit out wine after tasting it.

star lot. Items sold at auction that are very rare or very expensive. Star lots are often used to advertise an auction.

stock lot. An auction *lot* that has become property owned by the auction company. Many returned lots become stock lots and are resold in future auctions.

strip label. A regulated paper *label* indicating exporter and/or importer information of foreign wine sold in the United States.

super lot. A very large and expensive grouping of wine that the auction team chooses to sell together rather than dividing into separate, smaller lots. Super lots often generate excitement at the auction.

table grapes. Grapes that are grown to be eaten as opposed to being made into wine.

tannins. Components from the seeds and skins of grapes that give wine an astringent character and aid in a wine's ability to age.

telephone bid. An *absentee bid* placed by a bidder who is the phone with an auction representative. The phone line is booked prior to the day of the sale.

temperature-controlled storage. A storage environment consistently regulated to accommodate the proper aging of wine.

terms of sale. Commission charges and other associated costs paid to the auction house that puts the consignment up for sale. These costs will be outlined in the proposal, and may be negotiable.

terroir. The somewhat mystical combination of soil, sun, water, wind, and vineyard location and the effect they together have on the final wine product. *Terroir* roughly translates from French as "earth" or "soil."

title for sale. Part of the auction catalogue's *lot entries*. A title for sale marks the beginning of each new *consignment*, and is descriptive of the consignment.

trophy wine. Wine that is either produced in very small quantities or is very expensive, so that the acquisition and ownership of the wine is particularly enviable.

ullage. The *fill level* of wine in a bottle.

Ullage Chart. Explanation of abbreviations within catalogue that describe the level of wine in each bottle. The Ullage Chart was created in 1967 by Michael Broadbent.

under-bidder. Any bidder competing for a *lot* until it is sold to the winner.

unsold lot. An auction lot which fails to sell because either the bidding did not reach the *reserve price*, or the lot did not received any bids at all.

unsold lot fee. A small charge on any lots that fail to sell at auction. This charge is usually negotiated out of every deal.

varietal. The dominant grape used in a particular wine. Wines from New World regions are referred to by their *varietal*, while wines from Old World regions are named after their place of origin.

VAT. Value Added Tax. A sales tax levied in London auctions. The VAT may be refundable by American buyers upon completion of certain documentation.

vendor. The seller of goods at an auction. See also *consignor*.

vendor's commission. A percentage of each lot's *hammer price* that is paid to the auction house by the *consignor* in exchange for its selling the items. This rate is often negotiable.

venue. A place where an auction is held.

vertical collection. A lot consisting of wines from the same producer but different *vintages*.

vineyard. A place where grapes are grown.

vinification. The entire process of turning grapes into wine.

vintage. The year of a single harvest season.

Vitis vinifera. Species of grape that accounts for over 90 percent of the world's wine production.

white wine. Wine made from white grapes.

winery. A place where wine is produced.

written-order bid. An *absentee bid* placed using the absentee bid form found in the *catalogue*. At the auction, the bid is executed by either the *auctioneer* or a representative from the auction team.

young wine. Wine that is not yet at its full maturity and would benefit from further bottle aging.

About the Author

Ursula Hermacinski was named "goddess of the gavel" by *Food & Wine Magazine* when she captured its prestigious Golden Grape Award for "perfecting the art of auctioneering." Her career began in 1984 at Christie's in New York. In 1992, Ms. Hermacinski became the first woman auctioneer at the world-famous Napa Valley Wine Auction, and has since headed many charity auctions across the country. She also helped established Christie's New York wine department along with the fine wine retailer Zachys before going out on her own in 1998 to begin pioneering interest in online wine auctions. Currently, Ms. Hermacinski takes the rostrum at numerous national and international wine auctions.

Ms. Hermacinski is a highly sought-after lecturer. She has been profiled on *CNN Marketplace* and is a frequent guest on radio shows dealing with wine and its investment potential. In addition to her auction responsibilites, she directs the sales and marketing efforts for two prestigious California wineries: Screaming Eagle, Napa Valley, and Jonata, Santa Ynez Valley. Ms. Hermacinski lives in St. Helena, California.

Index